Profit, Prudence and Virtue

ST ANDREWS STUDIES
IN PHILOSOPHY AND PUBLIC AFFAIRS
Founding and General Editor:
John Haldane, University of St Andrews

Values, Education & the Human World
edited by John Haldane

Philosophy & its Public Role
edited by William Aiken and John Haldane

Relativism & the Foundations of Liberalism
by Graham Long

Human Life, Action & Ethics: Essays by G.E.M. Anscombe
edited by Mary Geach and Luke Gormally

*The Institution of Intellectual Values:
Realism & Idealism in Higher Education*
by Gordon Graham

*Sensibility & Sense:
The Aesthetic Transformation of the Human World*
by Arnold Berleant

Life, Liberty & the Pursuit of Utility
by Anthony Kenny and Charles Kenny

Distributing Healthcare: Principles, Practices & Politics
edited by Niall Maclean

Liberalism, Education & Schooling: Essays by T.M. Mclaughlin
edited by David Carr, Mark Halstead and Richard Pring

The Landscape of Humanity: Art, Culture & Society
by Anthony O'Hear

*Faith in a Hard Ground:
Essays on Religion, Philosophy & Ethics by G.E.M. Anscombe*
edited by Mary Geach and Luke Gormally

Subjectivity & Being Somebody
by Grant Gillett

Understanding Faith: Religious Belief & Its Place in Society
by Stephen R.L. Clark

Profit, Prudence & Virtue: Essays in Ethics, Business & Management
edited by Samuel Gregg and James Stoner

Practical Philosophy: Ethics, Society & Culture
by John Haldane

Profit, Prudence and Virtue

Essays in Ethics, Business and Management

Edited by Samuel Gregg and James Stoner

St Andrews Studies in Philosophy and Public Affairs

imprint-academic.com

Copyright © This collection Imprint Academic, 2009

The moral rights of the authors have been asserted.
No part of this publication may be reproduced in any form
without permission, except for the quotation of brief passages
in criticism and discussion.

Published in the UK by Imprint Academic
PO Box 200, Exeter EX5 5YX, UK

Published in the USA by Imprint Academic
Philosophy Documentation Center
PO Box 7147, Charlottesville, VA 22906-7147, USA

ISBN 9781845401597 (pbk)
ISBN 9781845401580 (cloth)

A CIP catalogue record for this book is available from the
British Library and US Library of Congress

Cover Photograph:
St Salvator's Quadrangle, St Andrews by Peter Adamson
from the University of St Andrews collection

Contents

Contributors vii
John Haldane, Preface xii
Samuel Gregg & James R. Stoner, Jr., Introduction 1

FOUNDATIONS

Harold James, The Ethics of Business Life:
Some Historical Reflections 9

Roger Scruton, Virtue and Profit:
A Critique of Managerial Reasoning 24

David Novak, Natural Law, Human Dignity, and the
Protection of Human Property 42

Robert P. George, Business and Family in a Decent and
Dynamic Society 57

PRACTICAL CHALLENGES FOR ETHICAL MANAGEMENT

Anthony Daniels, Management and the Corporate State:
Private Enterprise Without Enterprise, and Public Service
Without Service? 67

Wilfred M. McClay, A Strategic Humanist: George Keller,
Academic Strategy, and the Management Revolution in
American Higher Education 79

Sean Kelsey & Thomas R. Krause, Leading with Ethics 93

TEACHING ETHICS IN BUSINESS SCHOOL

R. Edward Freeman & David Newkirk, Business as a
 Human Enterprise: Implications for Education 106

Kevin T. Jackson, Cultivating the Ethics-Economics Interface. . . 128

Edwin M. Hartman, Teaching Business Ethics with Aristotle . . . 155

James O'Toole, Aristotle and the MBA: The Odd Couple 174

AFTER THE CREDIT COLLAPSE

Christopher Megone, Integrity, Virtue and the Financial Crisis . . 195

Samuel Gregg, Failure and Reform: Business Schools and the
 2008 Financial Crisis 211

Philip Booth, Learning from the Crash, and Teaching after it . . . 225

Edward Skidelsky, Capitalism and the Good Life. 242

Index 254

Contributors

Philip Booth is Editorial and Programme Director at the Institute of Economic Affairs and Professor of Insurance and Risk Management at Cass Business School, City University. He was formerly Associate Dean of Cass Business School and Programme Director of the Specialist Masters Programme. He has published widely in the fields of actuarial science, social insurance, pensions and regulation.

Anthony (A.M.) Daniels is an English writer and retired physician, who frequently uses the pen name 'Theodore Dalrymple.' He has written extensively on culture, art, politics, education, and medicine, both in Britain and overseas. Before retiring from medicine, Dr. Daniels worked as a physician and psychiatrist in Zimbabwe, South Africa, Tanzania, and more recently at a prison and a public hospital in Birmingham, in central England. He has written columns appearing in *The New Criterion*, *The Spectator*, and in *City Journal*, a magazine of the Manhattan Institute. He is the author of such books as *Coups and Cocaine* (John Murray, 1986), *Zanzibar to Timbuktu* (John Murray, 1988), and most recently, *In Praise of Prejudice: The Necessity of Preconceived Ideas* (Encounter Books, 2007). He is the Dietrich Weismann fellow at the Manhattan Institute.

R. Edward Freeman is a philosopher and Professor of Business Administration at the Darden School of Business at the University of Virginia. He also has taught at the University of Minnesota and the Wharton School. Professor Freeman is particularly known for his work on stakeholder theory and business ethics. His latest book is *Managing for Stakeholders* (Yale University Press, 2007, with Jeffrey Harrison and Andrew Wicks). He is currently working on a book called *Stakeholder Theory: The State of the Art*. Professor Freeman received a BA from Duke University in 1973 and a PhD from Washington University in 1978.

Robert P. George is McCormick Professor of Jurisprudence, founding director of the James Madison Program in American Ideals and Institutions at Princeton University, and the Herbert W. Vaughan Senior Fellow of the Witherspoon Institute. He is a member of the President's Council on Bioethics and formerly served as a presidential appointee to the United States Commission on Civil Rights and was a Judicial Fellow at the Supreme Court of the United States. His books include *Making Men Moral: Civil Liberties and Public Morality* (Oxford University Press, 1993), *The Clash of Orthodoxies: Law, Religion and Morality in Crisis* (ISI Books, 2001), *In Defense of Natural Law* (Oxford University Press, 1999), and *Embryo: A Defense of Human Life* (Doubleday, 2008, with Christopher Tollefsen). Professor George has won numerous Prizes and Awards. A graduate of Swarthmore College and Harvard Law School, he holds a doctorate in legal philosophy from Oxford University.

Samuel Gregg writes and speaks on questions of political economy, ethics in finance, and economic history. He is Director of Research at the Acton Institute and a consultant for Oxford Analytica Ltd. He holds an MA in political philosophy from the University of Melbourne, and a DPhil in moral philosophy and political economy from the University of Oxford. Dr. Gregg is the author of several books, including *Morality, Law, and Public Policy* (St. Thomas More Society, 2000), *Economic Thinking for the Theologically Minded* (University Press of America, 2001), *On Ordered Liberty* (Lexington Books, 2003), and *The Commercial Society* (Lexington Books, 2007). The latter was awarded a 2007 Templeton Enterprise Award for being one of the best books published on the culture of enterprise. His forthcoming book, *Wilhelm Röpke's Political Economy*, will be published in 2010.

Edwin Hartman is Visiting Professor of Business Ethics and the Peter and Charlotte Schoenfeld Visiting Faculty Fellow at the Stern School of Business at New York University. He was previously director of the Prudential Business Ethics Center at Rutgers Business School. Professor Hartman is the author of *Substance, Body, and Soul: Aristotelian Investigations* (Princeton University Press, 1977), *Conceptual Foundations of Organization Theory* (Ballinger Publishing, 1988), and *Organizational Ethics and the Good Life* (Oxford University Press, 1996), along with many articles.

Kevin T. Jackson is Professor of Legal and Ethical Studies at Fordham University in New York City and Visiting Professor of Politics at Princeton University. Formerly on the faculty of Georgetown University and Peking University, he has published numerous journal articles as well as books, such as *Building Reputational Capital* (Oxford University Press, 2004) and *Charting Global Responsibilities: Legal Philosophy and Human Rights* (East-West Press, 1997). Professor Jackson frequently gives analysis of legal and moral issues for the media and has presented seminars on business integrity and leadership. His advice on mutual-fund industry-regulation reform has been published in *The New York Law Journal*.

Harold James, who holds a joint appointment as Professor of International Affairs in the Woodrow Wilson School of Princeton University, and as Marie Curie Professor at the European University Institute in Florence, studies economic and financial history and modern German history. He was educated at Cambridge University (PhD, 1982) and was a Fellow of Peterhouse for eight years before coming to Princeton University in 1986. Professor James's books include a study of the interwar depression in Germany, *The German Slump* (OUP, 1986); an analysis of the changing character of national identity in Germany, *A German Identity 1770–1990* (Routledge, 1989); and *International Monetary Cooperation Since Bretton Woods* (OUP, 1996). He was coauthor of a history of Deutsche Bank (Weidenfeld and Nicholson, 1995), which won the Financial Times Global Business Book Award in 1996, and he also wrote *The Deutsche Bank and the Nazi Economic War Against the Jews* (CUP, 2001). Professor James's most recent works are *The End of Globalization: Lessons from the Great Depression* (Harvard, 2001); *Europe Reborn: A History 1914–2000* (Pearson Longman, 2003); *The Roman Predicament: How the Rules of International Order Create the Politics of Empire* (Princeton, 2006); and *Family Capitalism: Wendels, Haniels, Falcks, and the Continental European Model* (Harvard, 2006). In 2004 he was awarded the Helmut Schmidt Prize for Economic History, and in 2005 the Ludwig Erhard Prize for writing about economics.

Sean Kelsey has been Associate Professor of Philosophy at the University of California, Los Angeles since 1998. He received his BA from Thomas Aquinas College (1992) and his PhD in philosophy from Princeton (1997) within the Program in Classical Philosophy. Professor Kelsey specializes in ancient Greek philosophy, especially Plato and Aristotle.

Thomas Krause is Chairman of the Board for BST, a consulting firm specializing in comprehensive safety solutions. Since he founded BST in 1979, he has helped thousands of companies worldwide to prepare and implement successful change systems. Dr. Krause is actively involved in leadership coaching. He has spoken widely on a multitude of topics at national and international conferences and is regularly quoted by the media. Dr. Krause has authored several books and articles on safety and leadership, including *Leading With Safety* (Wiley, 2005). His latest book, *Taking the Lead in Patient Safety: How Leaders Influence Behavior and Create Culture*, was published in 2008. Dr. Krause received his MA in liberal arts from St. John's College in Santa Fe, New Mexico, and his PhD from the University of California, Irvine. Dr. Krause is a licensed psychologist.

Wilfred M. McClay has been the SunTrust Bank Chair of Excellence in Humanities at the University of Tennessee, Chattanooga, where he has also been a professor of history since 1999. Professor McClay also has taught at Georgetown University, Tulane University, Johns Hopkins University, and the University of Dallas, is senior scholar at the Woodrow Wilson International Center for Scholars in Washington, D.C., and is senior fellow at the Ethics and Public Policy Center in Washington, D.C. He is author of *The Masterless: Self and Society in Modern America* (University of North Carolina Press, 1994) and *Figures in the Carpet: Finding the Human Person in the American Past* (William B. Eerdmans Publishing, 2007). Professor McClay was educated at St. John's College (Annapolis) and the Johns Hopkins University, where he received a PhD in history (1987).

Chris Megone is Professor of Applied Inter-Disciplinary Ethics at the University of Leeds where he is Director of Inter-Disciplinary Ethics Applied (IDEA CETL). He teaches on subjects ranging from Medical Ethics and Business Ethics to Ethics in Engineering, Dentistry, and Media. He also teaches Ancient Philosophy at Leeds and has research interests in moral psychology as well as ethics, applied ethics, and political philosophy.

David L. Newkirk is CEO of Executive Education at the University of Virginia's Darden School of Business. He is responsible for the development and delivery of a range of open enrollment and custom programs for senior executives. Mr. Newkirk has spoken and written widely on issues of strategy and marketing. He holds degrees in mathematics and philosophy from Carleton College in the United States and from Oxford University, where he was a Marshall Scholar.

David Novak has held the J. Richard and Dorothy Shiff Chair of Jewish Studies as Professor of the Study of Religion and Professor of Philosophy at the University of Toronto since 1997. He is a member of the University of Toronto's University College, Centre for Ethics, and Joint Centre for Bioethics. Previously, Professor Novak taught at the University of Virginia. He is the author of fourteen books, most recently *The Sanctity of Human Life* (Georgetown University Press, 2007). Professor Novak received his AB from the University of Chicago in 1961, his MHL (Master of Hebrew Literature) in 1964, and his rabbinical diploma in 1966 from the Jewish Theological Seminary of America. He received his PhD in philosophy from Georgetown University in 1971.

James O'Toole is The Daniels Distinguished Professor of Business Ethics at the University of Denver's Daniels College of Business. He received his DPhil in social anthropology from Oxford University, where he was a Rhodes Scholar. Professor O'Toole is the author of fifteen books, including *Creating the Good Life: Applying Aristotle's Wisdom to Find Meaning and Happiness* (Rodale, 2005), on which his article in this volume is based.

Roger Scruton was until 1990 Professor of Aesthetics at Birkbeck College, London, and subsequently Professor of Philosophy and University Professor at Boston University, Massachusetts. He is now Research Professor at the Institute for the Psychological Sciences in Arlington, Virginia. Professor Scruton has published over thirty books, including works of philosophy, literature, and fiction, and his writings have been translated into most major languages. His most recent books are a study of Wagner's Tristan und Isolde, titled *Death-Devoted Heart* (Oxford University Press, 2004), *Gentle Regrets (an intellectual autobiography)* (Continuum, 2005), and *Culture Counts: Faith and Feeling in a World Besieged* (Encounter Books, 2007).

Edward Skidelsky is a lecturer in philosophy at Exeter University. His first book, *Ernst Cassirer: the Last Philosopher of Culture*, was published by Princeton University Press in 2009. His next book, a collection of essays on ethics, is forthcoming with PUP in 2012.

James R. Stoner, Jr. is Professor of Political Science at Louisiana State University, where he has taught since 1988 and where he now chairs the Department of Political Science. He is the author of *Common-Law Liberty: Rethinking American Constitutionalism* (University Press of Kansas, 2003) and *Common Law and Liberal Theory: Coke, Hobbes, and the Origins of American Constitutionalism* (University Press of Kansas, 1992), as well as a number of articles and essays. He received his AB from Middlebury College in Vermont and his MA and PhD degrees from Harvard. In 2002–03 he was a visiting fellow of the James Madison Program in American Ideals and Institutions at Princeton University, and he served from 2002 to 2006 on the National Council on the Humanities.

John Haldane

Preface

The present volume derives from another entitled *Rethinking Business Management: Examining the Foundations of Business Education* edited by Samuel Gregg and James Stoner which was published in 2008 by the Witherspoon Institute at Princeton. That original work was the outcome of a project developed by the Social Trends Institute based in New York, in collaboration with Witherspoon.

Writing in the foreword to *Rethinking Business Management*, Carlos Cavallé, President of STI, explained the background to the initiative:

> So much is happening in our modern world that has a bearing on business management. Certain aspects of business are changing much faster than ever before, while business management has a tough time keeping up, let alone leading the way. Still, amidst all of this change, some values, principles, and practices remain the same, or at least should remain the same, no matter what innovations come along tomorrow or the day after. We could refer to them as business management principles, or even business management foundations. ... It is therefore pertinent to ask whether modern business education has successfully tied together the discoveries of the present with the wisdom of the past, the ephemeral with the permanent.

In order to address this and related questions a conference was convened at Princeton in May 2007. While this explored the state of business education it also reached out to identify core issues regarding the ethics of business, ownership and markets. The papers from that conference, together with some additional commissioned essays, were edited to produce *Rethinking Business Management* and most of that material reappears now in the present volume.

In the interval since Carlos Cavallé conceived the need to address business management and education, and Luis Tellez, Director of the Witherspoon Institute, helped assemble the scholars for the conference, and the team who turned its proceedings into the original book, the world has had compelling reasons to consider the ethical foundations of business and banking.

Having peaked in the year prior to the conference, the US housing bubble then began to deflate, at first slowly, then more rapidly and dramtically as it became apparent that it rested on an extensive base of unsecured borrowing. Between summer 2006 and early autumn/fall of 2008, US housing prices declined by over 20% and the process of foreclosing was growing rapidly. As property values collapsed investors shifted money into commodities such as oil and gas, but in driving up the price of these that put further pressure on households which then fell further into debt, or curtailed their other expenditure. What began as a US (and European) banking crisis quickly developed into a worldwide economic recession and the process is still continuing.

Against this background it seemed well worth bringing the fruits of Cavallé's and Tellez's project to a wider readership. The result is the present volume which differs from the original first in the omission of some chapters, and second and more significantly in the addition of a new final section containing four essays commissioned specially for it in light of the banking, business and economic crises of current times. The result is a valuable and timely collection of essays by philosophers, political theorists, economists, historians, social scientists, and social commentators, business practitioners and academics: a set of studies of theory and practice; an exploration in the field to which this book-series is devoted, namely that of philosophy and public affairs.

The original volume acknowledged the role of a number of people who helped organize the Princeton conference, and edit and produce *Rethinking Business Management*. As regards this immediate descendent it is appropriate to acknowledge again Carlos Cavallé and Luis Tellez, and to add thanks to the editors, in particular Samuel Gregg, and to Anthony Freeman who oversaw the setting and production of the present volume.

Samuel Gregg & James R. Stoner, Jr.

Introduction

To say that business management is in the midst of an ethical crisis or that the schools of business are leading it there would certainly overstate our current situation, but there is a palpable sense among observers that renewed attention is due to the place of ethics and ethics education in the modern global economy. Perhaps this is the result of major scandals in the United States and in Europe. Perhaps it follows from intellectual developments in fields such as philosophical anthropology and psychology that call into question the assumptions about the human person on which post-classical economics has been based. Perhaps it is simply that, after a generation of experience with the revived prestige of free market economics, the collapse of communism, and the subsequent expansion of free trade and the development of an unprecedented global market, it is simply time to pause and take stock of the state of business in world affairs. No doubt the financial crisis that gripped the global economy from late 2008 onwards has raised significant questions about what was hitherto being taught in business schools.

They and business education are very much a phenomenon of the second half of the twentieth century. While professional schools for those involved in trade and commerce date back to the middle-ages, the contemporary business school with its emphasis on producing managers who can literally be employed in any private- (and increasingly public-) sector company or organization is something that first emerged in force after the Second World War. The modern business school continues to shape the management and dynamism of 21st century capitalism in a globalized environment, and the number of people studying in such schools continues to rise. In many instances, it is a business person's only post-undergraduate point of contact with universities, or at least only contact with graduate education.

This book contains a collection of essays that reflect upon the state of business schools at the beginning of the twenty-first century. For the most part, they are based upon papers delivered at a public conference entitled 'Rethinking Business Management', held under the aegis of the Witherspoon Institute and under the direction of Professor Harold James at Princeton University in May 2007. The conference sought to examine experiences of business school education in light of social and ethical responsibilities. The thesis presented for the discussion at the conference was that effective management is grounded both on good business science *and* on robust ethical and anthropological conceptions of human flourishing.

A number of considerations helped to frame the conference, many of which manifest themselves in the essays that appear in this volume. A single approach, it was suggested, seems to dominate management education in most of the world's business schools. While this approach invariably speaks about 'values' as a driving force behind business decisions, this raises a number of uneasy questions. Which values are identified as central to business? Why are these given priority and not others? The current moral-cultural atmosphere of 'neutral morality' — better understood as moral relativism — that marks so much of the educational environment of many Western European and North American universities makes it difficult for a considerable number of people to identify objective moral principles that ought to guide business decision-making. This is complicated by the fact that many business schools educate managers to focus almost exclusively on profits and to base their professional careers largely on monetary achievements (Mitroff, 2004). While some business schools have established new departments of social sciences to get beyond an exclusive focus on profit, these seem to impart mostly *pragmatic* values. To be pragmatic, as many of the authors of the following essays insist, is not necessarily the path to virtue and moral flourishing.

In this light, it is little wonder that there is also a growing concern for exploring the anthropological, ethical and sociological foundations of management in the context of business. Some attention is now being paid to the importance of grounding these foundations upon an accurate philosophical anthropology of the human person, especially the notions that (a) humans are at the same time body and spirit, making a substantial unity, and (b) humans are social and develop within society, of which business is an integral part. There is also growing appreciation of the fact that ethics is not simply prohibitive, but also—at least in its classical form—speaks about the possibility of human fulfillment. This has led some to suggest that the typical business school approach of treating ethics as a compartmentalized subject such as 'business ethics' ought to be replaced by a holistic approach to the moral life that should permeate all areas of life in business.

There is also considerable discussion of the nature and goals of business in the wider community. Business is, of course, an essentially social exercise at serving society through the production and distribution of goods and services, thereby creating jobs, creating and accumulating wealth, and contributing to human progress. Some argue that businesses contribute to the common good when they carry out their mission in a sustainable and conscientious relationship with those who are immediately touched by the activity, such as shareholders, employees, clients, and consumers. Others, however, suggest that the social responsibility of business goes beyond these confines, and ought to consider the interests of what some describe as stakeholders. Yet others hold that 'stakeholderism' is simply an agenda for foisting politically-correct objectives onto the operations of business. These questions do and should occupy the attention of business schools, their professors, and their students.

Readers of these essays will observe that most of the authors generally agree that a free enterprise economy is a basically sound system for organizing economic life, or at least the best available system under contemporary conditions and in light of the fact of human fallibility. The modern return of the free market is accepted—and in some instances celebrated—by the authors, which distinguishes these papers from many other similar collections, even in the wake of the 2008 financial crisis. It is a mistake to think that all people working in business or teaching in business schools are invariably in favor of free markets. Many are not.

Likewise, although some of these essays raise questions about the issue of the size of business, and a number indicate a preference for smaller-scale enterprises, the authors generally accept that the modern market has global reach. This means that the issues confronting business schools and the executives and managers they train cannot be addressed by isolating oneself or one's culture from the larger world. The global economy is here to stay, and business schools need to take this into account when thinking through reform of their curricula and teaching methods.

Lastly, while these essays affirm that the development of a global economy has not been matched by anything like a corresponding growth in adequate moral formation, few suggest that this situation can be primarily resolved by legislation. Increased regulation, some authors observe, would have done relatively little to address some of the major forces driving the 2008 economic meltdown and recession. Many of the markets in question are often already highly regulated —and in some instances, positively over-regulated—and it seems generally to have been agreed that mandating an extra set of additional 'ethics rules' would not only increase the costs of compliance, but would fail to address the substantive ethical questions facing business executives, managers, and the schools in which many of them are trained. Instead, the authors appear focused on developing an understanding of the moral life as more than a set of rules, but rather as a matter of developing virtuous human character and to ensure that the prohibitions of morality protect and promote certain virtues rather than simply existing for the sake of making business life more predictable. After all, ethics is in a sense necessarily prior to legislated rules, for one's attitude toward the obligation of rules and towards the incentives they entail is already a question of ethics. A number of essays suggest that the reform of ethics education in business schools should not be focused so much on the development of new techniques, but rather address more closely questions of moral formation. In this sense, some of the authors show a distinct preference for the type of reflection about the meaning of morality associated with figures such as Aristotle and Thomas Aquinas, rather than more contemporary scholars such as John Rawls.

We have clustered the essays in four groups. The first group is concerned with the historical and theoretical foundations of business in relation to the human person and to social life as a whole. Historian Harold James addresses the origins of modern business and business education, finding them as a counterpart to the rise of the state and its ability to guarantee by law an extended marketplace that does not rely alone on personal relationships of kinship or friendship; the challenge to business today is to recognize that the establishment of legal personhood in the corporation does not dispense with the need for moral persons in its ranks. Roger Scruton develops a similar theme, applying to modern business Aristotle's distinction between the ends that are sought by means of action and the happiness that comes from acting well; in a healthy corporation, profit comes, like happiness or friendship, not because it is a calculated goal, but as a consequence of doing one's business well, and justice emerges not from a government's seizing and redistributing profits, but from a society permeated by attention to justice as a virtue, as a characteristic of action throughout. Philosopher David Novak examines the contribution that natural-law thinking can make toward understanding the predicament of life in the modern economy; instead of accepting that self-interest is the only guiding principle of social life, natural law points to universal rights and duties that are in fact widely known and widely shared. McCormick Professor of Jurisprudence at Princeton, Robert George, concludes our study of foundations with reflections on the dynamic character of the modern world economy and the pillars on which any decent and dynamic society rests. These include not only respect for the human person, the rule of law, and institutions of research and learning, but also families and businesses; George draws attention to how good firms and sound business practices strengthen personhood, law, education, and family, and are in turn sustained by these.

The second group of essays concerns questions of ethics in the management of various social institutions, public as well as private; as a group they are meant to be suggestive, certainly not exhaustive, and they vary markedly in attitude and approach. Anthony Daniels writes from experience as a physician in the British health care system about the incentives, often perverse, that result from modern attempts at bureaucratic management; he casts an eye back to an earlier ethic of public service, a tradition of administration from within the learned professions (e.g., of hospitals by doctors), and an era of institutional pride. Historian Wilfred McClay, writing about the American university, takes a seemingly opposite tack, praising the work of Columbia-educated George Keller in bringing the principles of modern management to a recalcitrant setting; according to McClay, Keller at once helped to lay the groundwork for the remarkable success of modern institutions of higher learning and, thanks to his humanist's eye, fostered an appreciation of the diversity of academic institutions and their role in contemporary civil society and our complex economy. Philosophy Professor Sean Kelsey and business executive and consultant Thomas R. Krause suggest that the successful revolution in managing workplace safety over the past generation gives reason for optimism if the same outlook can be applied to workplace ethics, a project that begins, they argue, with a clear understanding of the cooperative character of economic life.

In the third group of essays, several professors at major business schools reflect on the study of ethics in the modern business curriculum and propose different ways to think about ethics and to impart a habit of ethical reflection among their students. University of Virginia Professor of Business Administration R. Edward Freeman and his colleague, business executive David Newkirk, argue that reform of business education requires rethinking the character of business itself, understanding the corporation in relation to its stakeholders, not only its shareholders, and adopting, instead of the 'separation fallacy' that isolates business activity from other spheres of human activity, an 'integration thesis' that connects business seamlessly to ethics and the full range of human affairs. Kevin Jackson, who teaches business at Fordham University, refines stakeholder theory by proposing its connection to the traditional attention paid by business managers to shareholders through the concept of 'reputational capital'. Both essays develop their theoretical perspective before thinking through how business courses could be altered in their light. In separate but congruent essays, Edwin Hartman of New York University and James O'Toole of the University of Southern California argue that the key to the reform of business education lies in the study of Aristotle. Both elaborate how Aristotle's account of the human things weaves together economic goods and ethical good in a pattern that makes analytical sense and offers practical counsel even today. Hartman sees in Aristotle a way of addressing the questions that business students ask themselves as they plan their careers. As character depends on virtue and as virtues are formed by habits and choices, according to Aristotle, so students effectively choose the kind of people they will be by where they choose to work, and companies in turn establish their character by the people they employ and the activities they promote. O'Toole looks at the relation of work and leisure, an Aristotelian theme, in the context of individual job choice and company policy. He suggests that Aristotle's account of justice as involving both inequality and equality can prove helpful in considering the distribution of goods within organizations, even or especially on the matter of executive compensation. His conclusion, attributed to Aristotle, that 'a strong ethical foundation was a requirement for an open society' captures, we think, the spirit of the essays in this volume as a whole.

The fourth and last group of essays was commissioned after the 2008 economic crisis and addresses a number of questions that business schools must inevitably consider as a result of the problems experienced by the financial industry throughout the world. Christopher Megone examines post-crisis business from the standpoint of the idea of integrity. Having suggested that modernity tends to encourage a high degree of compartmentalization of the various aspects of a person's life, he argues that this may account for some of the questionable behavior exhibited by some business leaders and politicians during the 2008 financial meltdown. Presenting a philosophically-robust account of the idea of integrity, he applies it to the idea of business and argues that it indicates that business could have a broader conception of its responsibilities than is often supposed. It also, he argues, may act as a corrective to compartmentalizing tendencies in practical business life. Samuel Gregg underscores the inadequacies that have been highlighted in the ethical formation of business leaders as a result of the crisis, but also the need for business schools to give their students a more solid grounding in a number of subjects that have hitherto been relegated to the 'optional-extras' part of business school curriculum, such as entrepreneurship. He also argues for a more solid integration of basic moral reflection into subjects that appear relatively 'technical' (such as credit and finance), but which in fact rely upon a range of basic moral assumptions about human beings and human action for their economic efficacy and moral legitimacy. Philip Booth argues that perhaps the most important thing that post-crisis business schools could do in terms of adjusting their curriculum would be to provide their students with a philosophically-defensible and empirically-grounded account of what went wrong in 2008, instead of simply echoing mythologies that have already established a grip on the popular imagination. He underscores the importance of accuracy in these areas, not least because false or misleading accounts will be of no service to future business leaders. Finally Edward Skidelsky asks some searching questions about capitalism and the good life, many of which are likely to figure on the intellectual and moral horizons of most business school students and graduates at some point of their lives. Economist-philosophers such as John Maynard Keynes, he notes, have always wrestled with the issue of how one aligns economic activity with the moral life. Skidelsky suggests that part of the problem with modern secular liberalism is that it 'lost the conception of a way of life as good in itself and of wealth as a means thereto'. When means and ends are confused, the result is economic and moral disharmony. It is an open question whether business schools are necessarily the best institutions to address such matters in detail (though these are surely not beyond the purview of business school professors), but what they cannot do is pretend that these matters and questions are peripheral to the thoughts and activities of those involved in business.

Bibliography

Mitroff, Ian (November 2004), 'An Open Letter to the Deans and Faculties of American Business Schools', *Journal of Business Ethics* 54, pp. 185–189.

Harold James

The Ethics of Business Life
Some Historical Reflections

There exists a long tradition of demonstrating the importance of ethics in the conduct of a business life that is both efficient and just. This tradition did not supply simply utilitarian reasons for behaving ethically, but it did emphasize that ethical behavior brings many benefits, and that an unethical society is dissatisfied and destructive.

Its most elaborate exposition (which is celebrated in other contributions to this volume) occurred in Thomist elaborations of Aristotelian ethics. Enlightenment thinkers also made ethical conduct a central feature of their political economy. David Hume explained why: 'The same age, which produces great philosophers and politicians, renowned generals and poets, usually abounds with skilful weavers, and ship-carpenters. We cannot reasonably expect, that a piece of woollen cloth will be wrought to perfection in a nation, which is ignorant of astronomy, or where ethics are neglected' (Hume, 1987).

By the beginning of the twenty-first century, however, these older approaches appeared to have become largely extinct. New sorts of institutional answers—legal and corporate—had evolved to the questions once addressed by the ethical tradition. It is possible that the institutionalization of business education through the establishment of business schools played some part in this erosion. Today, business schools are widely blamed for the ethical failures of business, and anniversaries such as the 2008 centenary of the Harvard Business School are seen as much as occasions for self-examination and self-criticism as for unencumbered and unreflective celebration. Why is it that according to many ratings Harvard seems to have lost its way? According to the *Economist* Intelligence Unit's latest (2006) ranking of world business schools, Harvard was only at seventh place, while the top spot was occupied by the much younger IESE, which celebrated its fiftieth anniversary in 2008.

The current criticism should lead to a sustained reflection on the purpose of a business education. Many observers, including some within the business school community, think that the unstated purpose was simply to make their students and alumni feel good about themselves and about their school. But in fact the problem lay in the explicit purpose of many business schools: as they had evolved in the twentieth century, the schools tried primarily to find ways of helping business leaders understand how the legal and managerial world of what might be termed the 'modern economy' functioned. The new answers reflected the shift toward a managerial economy. In this world of functionally integrated and interdependent agents, the task lay in solving logistical problems. Solutions were exclusively technical. Much of Hume's formulation in consequence became for a modern audience quite unintelligible, perhaps even wholly absurd.

In particular, a strong ethical framework had once answered a critical and quite practical question that is central to the operation of a market economy: how can I trust the person with whom I am conducting business? Markets depend on promises about future conduct, but promises can be broken when circumstances are not conducive to keeping them. If the contract is one that is often repeated, between partners who know each other, the partners have an obvious self-interest involved in not reneging on it. They do not have such immediate self-interest in the case of once-only transactions, especially if they are separated by a long distance. Then there is a multiplication of the incentives to cheat.

On these grounds, Aristotle was skeptical about the possibilities of long-distance trade, which he thought provided temptations for immorality and abuse. In the Aristotelian tradition, businesses developed simply as an extension of the household, the *oikos*, and the kind of trust that was required for business dealings developed simply as an extension of personal honesty and reputation. There was no distinction between personal and business behavior.

Later, in the Enlightenment, a highly influential school of thought developed according to which commerce was the originator of a civilizing impulse. This tradition also tended to celebrate local commerce, which brought people into regular contact and thus educated them, and to disparage commercial contacts with very different types of people a long way away which were necessarily much more occasional. For both Aristotle and this Enlightenment school, the market was far from an abstraction, but rather a daily education in civics.

In the course of modern economic development, the traditional approaches were overtaken by two developments that appeared to hold out the possibility of faster economic growth: the regulation of business conduct through legislation emanating from states which had a new kind of legitimacy founded on popular sovereignty, and the growth of the modern notion of a business corporation which could internalize its ethical problems and could appear to be fully rational. These provided the foundation of the modern managerial economy. But this managerial economy was constantly evolving, and in the course of the evolution major flaws and weaknesses were exposed.

I

Let us take up first the state regulation of business conduct. Modern economic development brought an answer to the problem of trust that did not depend on personal honesty. It was institutional innovation (rather than personal behavior) that allowed the establishment of relations, based on confidence over a long distance. In consequence, business conduct became quite separated from personal conduct. It was correspondingly judged by different measures. Different spheres of human activity carried expectations of different behavior, or even multiple personalities. A business man would be calculating and aggressive in his firm, and then come home to be warm and emotional in his family. (This was a contrast to the Old World, in which there was often no physical separation between home and work, and in which—incidentally—in consequence women would play a much more prominent role.)

The primary cause of a new confidence about business dealings came from changes in the legal environment. It was the law rather than an advanced ethical sensitivity that made for a newly enhanced sense of security in commercial transactions, and allowed for an explosion of economic activity. An influential interpretation ('law and economics') of British and American developments sees in the common law a legal form that made these societies uniquely and unprecedentedly successful. According to Morton Horwitz, the crucial breakthrough came in the eighteenth century, when contracts were no longer annulled by courts when they might be held to violate some rather vague concept of natural justice. Business figures no longer needed to fear that some objection might make their business calculation obsolete. Unfettered property rights made it possible to expand almost infinitely the areas of life that were subject to contracting. As a result, the factors of production could be combined much more efficiently, and a colossal wave of increasingly shared and universal prosperity followed (North and Weingast, 1989).

Almost every modern interpretation of the preconditions for successful economic development emphasizes the importance of the effective enforcement of property rights. For this reason, states should refrain from destroying expectations of stability by simple expropriation or by monetary experimentation. Where there is no legal security, or the legitimacy and dependability of the political system is eroded by widespread corruption, potential entrepreneurs will have no faith that their property rights will be respected, and in consequence will hold off from entrepreneurial activity.

The rise in government and legal regulation was in the first instance the great facilitator of market transactions. Early modern European states in general were quite weak, and found mercantile ventures quite threatening, especially when they crossed state borders. Some companies or corporations behaved like states without actually being territorial states. The Teutonic Knights and the Knights of Malta organized defense systems, fostered commerce, provided social networks and services (such as hospitals or schools), and of course did a great deal of fighting. These proto-NGOs were dedicated to a cause that was overwhelmingly important to their adherents (a religious crusade). But larger companies had to act in an analogous way.

The great merchant companies of early modern Europe indeed had their own armies: the most notorious examples are the French and the English East India Companies. The British East India Company indeed had an important army at a time when the crown (i.e., the state) did not have a standing army at all. The companies took on regulatory and quasi-state powers with which they could exclude any competition: they were conceived as monopoly corporations. Political pressure flowed from protests against such privileged private corporations, and erupted in the American and French revolutions.

The debate produced a new type of state: a state that, because it derived its legitimacy from popular will ('We the people'), would deal with companies and non-state actors in a very different way. The state after the French Revolution would claim moral superiority in dealing with business corporations, instead of seeing itself as simply a party to a transaction that could be more or less cynically calculated (as Jakob Fugger had dealt in his lending operations with the Emperor Charles V).

It is a crude fallacy to think that the development and growth of the state necessarily brings disadvantages for enterprise or business culture. On the contrary, to the extent that the strengthening of the state made business life much more predictable, wealth-generation became easier. If the competition between European states made for more dynamic business life, the constitutional ordering of the popular will made life more certain. Previous monarchical borrowers had been prone to sudden bankruptcy, and the Habsburg and Valois dynasts had regularly turned on their creditors and used force (the threat of execution for usury) to renegotiate on better terms (see Reinhart and Rogoff, 2004).

The business response to this was one of grateful relief. As long as conditions were stable, it made sense to respect the will of the people as expressed in a systematically and constitutionally ordered way in whatever state a company did business. By the early nineteenth century, some large-scale lenders such as the Rothschilds began to insist that their customer states introduce constitutions or representative assemblies, because this made the repayment of credit more secure (see Ferguson, 1998). This was a foreign policy driven entirely by self-interest, but it was of course also a highly enlightened one. This point that businesses should be 'good citizens' in response to the institutional environment in which they function has actually become something of a modern platitude.

This leads us to the second development that appeared to hold out the possibility of faster economic growth: the growth of the idea of a business that could internalize its ethical problems. The introduction of the modern limited-liability joint-stock corporation made possible a much broader range of contracts: with the providers of finance (thus solving a finance issue that had previously restrained economic development); with suppliers and customers; and with workers. Corporations in medieval and early modern Europe were highly restricted in what they might do. Especially after the big, speculative bubbles of the second decade of the eighteenth century, associated in England with the South Sea Company and in France with John Law's Mississippi scheme, joint stock companies were treated as abuses, in which privileged insiders could exploit the ignorance and greed of gullible outsiders. Such a theme characterizes not only much of the literature of classical political economy, it appears with remarkable force in Adam Smith's *Wealth of Nations*. It is also echoed in a great part of the imaginative literature of the eighteenth and nineteenth century dealing with business, such as Anthony Trollope's *The Way We Live Now* and Theodore Dreiser's *The Financier and The Titan*, a lightly fictionalized account of the rise and fall of the Chicago and London municipal transport pioneer.

British legislation of 1844 and 1855 allowed the creation of joint stock companies with limited liability. Belgium also had a liberal company law, and the rest of continental Europe followed in the 1860s and 1870s. Large corporations were now capable of raising the large amounts of capital required in the Industrial Revolution. Legal changes also made it possible to substitute power (in the hierarchical organization of a company) for the market, with its problematical dependence on ethical behavior by others and the still partly uncertain and constantly costly legal enforcement of contracts. A company is a way of providing a substitute for the market where the market is too costly and uncertain: it allows, for instance, much easier enforcement of standardized measures and the maintenance of quality.[1]

Companies acquired a legal personality, and this was to have unexpected ethical implications for its employees. They could clearly be held to be legally accountable for their actions. When a company does something wrong, it—rather than the individuals who made the error—is responsible for the consequences of the decision. At the same time, new techniques of branding helped to give the impression that there also existed a corporate personality, a corporate culture, and a corporate social role. Companies began to think that they needed corporate biographies that told the story of how their structure and image molded the personalities of their employees. A strong corporate culture was widely thought to be important in motivating employees as well as customers.

In the twentieth century, the corporate image played a central role in the creation of consumer culture. Particularl companies that dealt with large numbers of customers needed to cultivate a personal image: either by the adoption of an animal or a human emblem, such as the Esso/Exxon tiger, or by naming the firm after a real or ficti-

---

[1] This is the way that Ronald Coase formulated the modern view of the function of the firm in Coase, 1937.

tious person, such as Martha Stewart or the fictitious Ann Taylor and Thomas Pink. In the last quarter of the twentieth century, especially in the United States, the celebrated CEO became an easy path to establishing a corporate identity. The path was pioneered by Lee Iacocca's charismatic use of his own personality to rebrand the staid image of Chrysler. By the 1990s, CEOs such as General Electric's Jack Welch or Hewlett Packard's Carla Fiorina became a standard part of the new American way of doing business. They found imitators elsewhere, such as Vivendi's Jean-Marie Messier, whose extravagant megalomania led him to style himself J6M (Jean-Marie Messier, *moi-même maître du monde*).

Out of the belief in a corporate personality developed the concept of Corporate Social Responsibility. In many cases, at least in the initial phases, it arose out of a desire to rectify an unfortunate or unpleasant image, as a simple marketing ploy. The United Fruit Company, notorious for its exploitative behavior in central America, started to use the term 'corporate responsibility' in the 1970s, in the aftermath of the Nicaraguan earthquake, which its chief executive Eli Black saw as an opportunity for the company to make some favorable publicity. Large petroleum companies, notably the British Royal Dutch Shell and British Petroleum, found an emphasis on corporate good deeds a way of compensating for the petroleum giants' bad reputation.

In consequence, in part as a response to legal and regulatory issues of corporate responsibility and in part as an extension of a motivational and marketing device, the analysis of behavior and personality moved from the individual level to that of the corporation. The analysts of this development often used medical and psychological language: companies could be healthy or sick, complacent or neurotic or even psychotic. The result was that, if the company was a real personality, the individuals working in it did not need to behave like real or ethical people.

II

The personalization of the corporation and the notion that it had a moral as well as a legal status went hand in hand with the rise of the managerial economy. But it was paralleled by the way in which by the last decades of the twentieth century academics—especially business school academics—came to view the role of individuals within a corporation. A remarkable movement took place away from thinking of business behavior in terms of character, toward a notion of a 'profession' detached from everyday life and everyday concerns.

In the early stages, many business school leaders, and especially many of the business owners and executives who helped establish the new institutions, saw the task of a modern higher-level business school primarily in terms of building character. Owen D. Young, the founding chairman of Radio Corporation of America and then chairman of General Electric—the businessman of the 1920s who made the greatest contribution to American foreign policy, in attempting to devise a solution to the politically fraught question of German war reparations—was acutely conscious of a sense of moral obligation. He made this the point of his address in 1927 at the dedication of the new campus of the Harvard Business School: it is vital, he said,

> that the ministers of our business, like the ministers of our churches, should appreciate their responsibility. ... We need today more than ever before men to administer this trust, who are not only highly skilled in the technique of business—men who have not only a broad outlook in history, politics, and economics—but men who have also that moral and religious training which tends to develop character (quoted in Khurana, 2007, p. 118).

This sounded deliberately old-fashioned: it echoed the arguments given for setting up colleges in general; and in particular it fitted perfectly with the Puritan tradition of the business calling or vocation. In other words, the founders of the business school reverted easily, when they thought of the mission of their institutions, to the older language of ethical and moral responsibility that went back to Aristotle and Aquinas, as well as to the Enlightenment. There needed to be a calling that did not emanate from a perception of individual self-interest.

But as they developed in the course of the twentieth century, graduate business schools aimed at professionalizing management. Especially in the United States, they were designed to give modern managers a new status that would be commensurate with a changed and enhanced role in an evolving and improving economy. The new institutions were sharply distinguished from the older commercial schools, which had emphasized practical and vocational training. Their founders wanted a higher prestige and a more abstract and academic education for managers who would form an elite.

For much of the twentieth century, business schools instructed their pupils in how to deal with government and regulation. Indeed, many business school leaders saw the idea of creating a modern management as inseparable from the development of a modern planned society, in which government would play a vital role and in which the critical development was that of a scientific managerial elite. Business would simply fit into a policymaking group whose task was to resolve problems. As the second dean of the Harvard Business School, Wallace Bonham, explained: 'Our objective ... should be the multiplication of men who will handle current business problems in socially constructive ways' (Khurana, 2007, p. 116).

The experience of the Great Depression strengthened this view, according to which economic catastrophe had been the consequence of short-sighted greed and individualism. Conversely, planned collective action, involving an association of business and government looked to be the only way of overcoming the Depression. The program on business and international government (or 'BIGI') remained a critical component of the HBS approach in the second half of the twentieth century. Big government and big corporations went hand in hand together.

In the world of mundane practice, however, business schools found it impossible to devise a curriculum that adequately reflected the founders' ideals. A widening gulf opened between a language of vocation that looked increasingly outdated and irrelevant and a practice aimed simply at producing new higher-status managers. Indeed, as Rakesh Khurana has pointed out in a new book, *From Higher Aims to Hired Hands,* the need to professionalize was intimately associated — as in medicine or engineering — with the need to transmit a particular and specialized knowledge that would serve as a boundary to the profession and exclude the amateurs. Unlike in medicine or engineering, it was never quite clear what the basis of that specialized knowledge was, since accounting, finance, and marketing might just as well be taught by the older commercial schools. That problem was not solved until the 1950s, when the Ford and Carnegie foundations used their resources to mold 'New Look' business schools, modeled on the Carnegie Institute of Technology's Graduate School of Industrial Administration. In this new approach, mathematized social science would make business schools academically respectable. Faculty would be recruited and tenured on the basis of published scientific work.

Khurana points out the irony that from the 1970s on this scientific turn pushed innovative business schools to adopt a particular version of neo-classical economics, which emphasized 'agency theory.'

The widespread adoption of its powerfully attractive language—it is an appealing model for understanding a world in which corporations are in flux, and ownership, markets, technologies are constantly changing—led to a disintegration and erosion of traditional notions of responsibility. This development brought the business school community even further from the original vision of the founder generation. According to the new academic approach, pioneered by Michael Jensen, William Meckling, and Eugene Fama, managers were agents whose interests were not necessarily aligned with those of the principals, the owners of a corporation, or the shareholders. The company was nothing more than a legal fiction, a network of contracts, as Oliver Williamson put it. In this network, there was no place for a corporate ethos or corporate responsibility. Managers sought primarily their own advantage, which was not that of the company, let alone the community. For instance, managers had incentives to increase their remuneration by expanding the size of the enterprise and increased their responsibility, even when there was no profit to be found in such an expansion.

Agency theory focused on the identification of methods for monitoring managerial performance and for providing incentives for managers to improve business performance. The financial innovations of the 1970s and 1980s, in particular the use of leveraging and debt to restructure corporations, had a powerful justification in terms of increased efficiency.

Business schools and their modernized curriculum were thus in at least some measure responsible for the corporate scandals that reached a dramatic height with the collapse of Enron and WorldCom. As Khurana sums up the discussion:

> That business schools might have actively fostered misconduct by instilling in their students, over the course of a generation, the idea that markets provide an adequate mechanism for motivating, monitoring, and disciplining managers and boards of directors who are not susceptible, in any case, to appeals to anything beyond self-interest was a distinctly minority view, but one that appears compelling in the context of the abandonment of the professionalization project in business education. ... By demoting managers from professional stewards of the corporation's resources to hired hands bound only by contractual requirements and relationships, business schools thus helped create the conditions and standards of behavior through which the market-based mechanism of stock options was turned into an instrument for defrauding investors, jeopardizing the livelihoods of

employees, and undermining public trust in managers and corporations (Khurana, 2007, p. 375).

The business school thus literally de-moralized its students. But the idea of the rational managed corporation was also being eroded at the same time, for technological and organizational reasons.

III

It is helpful to place the transformation of the business school curriculum in a broader context of the rise and then, in the last decades of the twentieth century, the fall of managerial capitalism and the changing answers to the problem of trust with which we began.

Since the Industrial Revolution, three developments have made the classical modern institutional answer to the problem of trust in economic transactions—namely the corporation as regulated by a sovereign state—more and more problematical. First, business increasingly is not confined to national frontiers. Second, innovative businesses are often good at anticipating and circumventing attempts at regulation: especially in financial services, there is a constant race between regulatory responses to perceived problems and innovation that makes the regulation obsolete or inappropriate. Third, the character and structure of a company is constantly changing with new technologies (especially information technology) and is as a consequence less subject to hierarchical control. Taken together, these developments make more and more problematical the idea that a particular sort of institutionalized corporate culture can by itself produce good behavior.

I will take the developments in order. First, the question of the citizenship of business corporations became deeply problematical in the course of the twentieth century, because they were increasingly operating across national boundaries. Anxious executives express over and over the idea that a responsible multinational or transnational corporation should be a good citizen not just in its country of origin but also in the host countries in which it operates. Here are quotations from two twentieth-century business leaders that may strike the reader as utterly unremarkable.

The first quote is:

> It is evident that a company which operates in a country where it is accepted and whose laws guarantee its protection has to be [unconditionally] loyal to that country and has to conscientiously comply with its wishes.[2]

The second is:

> Now I believe that if an international business, such as General Motors, engages in the commercial activity of any country with the idea of making a profit ... it has an obligation to that country, both in an economic sense as well as in a social sense. It should attempt to attune itself to the general business of the community; make itself a part of the same; conduct its operations in relation to the customs, and design its products so as to meet the needs and viewpoint of each community, so far as it can. I believe further, that that should be its position, even if, as is likely to happen and particularly as was the case during the past few years, the management of the Corporation might not wholly agree with many things that are done in certain of these countries (quoted in Turner, 2006).

The first comes from Max Huber, the chairman of the Supervisory Board of a Swiss company, the Rheinfelden aluminum works (AIAG), with substantial production facilities in Germany, writing in the introduction to an official company history in 1942. The second comes from a letter of Alfred Sloan, the chief executive of General Motors, to an angry shareholder worried about the company's German subsidiary in the Nazi era. Perhaps these are both exceptional circumstances, but if so, they are extreme versions of a more common dilemma: that states cannot be relied upon to be 'good'. The greatest problem of today is how and by what standards companies, or indeed NGOs, can criticize and intervene in the affairs of states, which when under attack like to remind critics of the international law notion of 'sovereignty.' Is there a broader or more universal law (of humanity) that businesses should have to obey? If so, who is in the position to explain or codify that law?

The second development—that each new regulation soon produces as a response a technology that makes it obsolete—means that

---

[2] Huber, 2002. I have added the word 'unconditonally' from the German original (German original: 'selbstver- ständlich, dass das Unternehmen seine volkswirtschaftliche Aufgabe in jedem Lande, desses Staat ihm Aufnahme und dessen recht ihm Schutz gewährt, in unbedingter Loyalität und mit dem Willen zu verständnisvoller Einordnung erfülle.')

businesses often cannot have any significant or effective guidance from governments in their day-to-day decisions because the subject matter is too complex. Governments are forced to rely on self-enforced and even self-formulated standards. This problem is quite well understood in some technical areas, such as the regulation and supervision of financial sector risk, where a modern international consensus has left large parts of regulation to the banks' own risk models. But it applies equally to areas where businesses need to make judgments about the kind of government they are dealing with when they extend their operations globally: should companies ignore poor human rights records that may be responsible for some of the attractions (reduced labor costs, for example) of a particular production location?

The third development—that new technologies make companies less subject to hierarchical control—provides greater possibilities for entrepreneurial action, but also frequently makes it impossible for top management to understand what is going on throughout the corporation. The complex hierarchical structures of classical companies as they developed in the nineteenth century, with layers of management controlling and transmitting instructions to inferior layers, while information was passed up the other way, have become much flatter. Improved information technology (IT) has made the control function of the classical company easier to implement, supplying up-to-date sales information, to which the central executives can respond immediately: they no longer need the buffer of an enormous management hierarchy. But it also provides much more room for autonomous action at all levels of the business. The emphasis is on flexibility rather than action in accordance with predetermined guidelines. A considerable role in the flattening of the corporate hierarchy is also played by changing philosophies, especially the popularization of agency theory, which has led individual business people to internalize a mode of analysis as a norm for behavior.

The remodeling of the corporation and a new self-understanding of behavior within the enterprise make their reputations vulnerable. In the absence of very clear hierarchies, and with much more initiative and responsibility delegated to distant and junior employees, it is much easier for the action of a single employee to damage a company's reputation or even to cripple it. It may be a question of inappropriate financial risk, combined with unauthorized and dishonest behavior to alleviate the consequences of that risk, as in the case of the old London banking house of Barings brought down by the actions of a Singapore manager Nick Leeson. It may be an issue of catastrophic negligence, as in the oil spill of the Exxon Valdez or the Texas oil refinery explosions of British Petroleum. In these cases, apparently isolated examples of bad behavior have profound impacts on corporations which have a global reach.

Cases such as these demonstrate the need for an ethic of personal responsibility that cannot simply be subsumed in some vague sense of corporate culture. Ethical questions become again absolutely central to a firm's reputation, and to its ability to do business. We are back in a world in which trust is a virtue that is required as a logical precondition of being an effective participant in markets.

IV

In a flattened business structure, where the corporation cannot be effectively controlled hierarchically, the individual personality matters much more. The individual is a whole person, whose activities cannot easily be broken up between business and private. In addition, where national regulation is increasingly ineffective or impotent as a result of the pace of technical change and of globalization, differences between systems of values and cultural norms become much more apparent. In consequence, there is more and more of a search for ways of guiding individual behavior so that it is trustworthy and constructive.

Some forms of enterprise that were largely ignored or discredited in the twentieth century have helped to fill the demand for true business personalities. Family firms have often been seen as relics of a pre-corporate age. But in fact, they play a vital part in the dynamism of many of the fastest growing regions of the world, in Asia and in Latin America. Family values can provide a basis of trust, of a long-term commitment of owners to their employees, their suppliers, and their customers. They make for an expectation of a particular kind of (trustworthy) behavior. They are one attractive answer—but not the only answer—to the question of reinserting commitment and values into business life.

There is a general malaise about what business schools teach, but it would be a mistake to treat this as simply a phenomenon of U.S. business life and the aftermath of the corporate scandals of the millennium and the attempted remedy in the form of the Sarbanes-Oxley Act of 2002. The problem cannot simply be unloaded onto governments and regulatory agencies, which are in no position to grasp the complexities of the problems they are required to solve. It is in these circumstances that a much older tradition, the tradition that demonstrates the necessity of ethics to efficient and just business, has a crucial part to play in a quickly changing and very modern world.

Bibliography

Coase, Ronald (1937), "The Nature of the Firm", *Economica*, Vol. 4/16, pp. 386–405.

Ferguson, Niall (1998), *The House of Rothschild: Money's Prophets 1798–1848* (New York: Penguin, Viking Press), pp. 231–56.

Huber, Max (2002), quoted in Independent Commission of Experts Switzerland—Second World War, *Switzerland, National Socialism, and the Second World War: Final Report* (Zurich: Pendo), p. 299.

Hume, David (1987), "Of Refinement in the Arts", in *Essays, Moral, Political, and Literary*, ed. Eugene F. Miller (Indianapolis, IN.: Liberty Fund).

Khurana, Rakesh (2007), *From Higher Aims to Hired Hands: The Social Transformation of American Business Schools and the Unfulfilled Promise of Management as a Profession* (Princeton, NJ: Princeton University Press), p. 118.

North, Douglass C., and Weingast, Barry (December 1989), "Constitutions and Commitment: Evolution of the Institutions Governing Public Choice in Seventeenth-Century England", *Journal of Economic History* 49, pp. 803–32.

Reinhart, Carmen, and Rogoff, Kenneth (May 2004), "Serial Default and the 'Paradox' of Rich-to-Poor Capital Flows", *American Economic Review* 94, pp. 53–8.

Turner, Henry A. (2005), *General Motors and the Nazis: The Struggle for Control of Opel, Europe's Biggest Carmaker* (New Haven, CT: Yale University Press).

Roger Scruton

Virtue and Profit
A Critique of Managerial Reasoning

In a free economy people give freely of their energies, talents, and knowledge. They do this because they wish the best for themselves and their families. And at the same time, 'by an invisible hand' as Adam Smith famously put it, they do the best for the economy as a whole, freely generating a productivity that dwindles just as soon as people are coerced into maintaining it.

The reasons for this have been much rehearsed, and perhaps by no one so thoroughly as F.A. Hayek, who drew on the work of Eugen von Böhm-Bawerk, Ludwig von Mises, and other members of the Austrian school in showing to a world corrupted by socialism and Keynesian mumbo-jumbo that there is a crucial flaw in all policies that propose state edicts in the place of the solutions spontaneously hit upon by our social instincts.

As the Austrian economists showed, a free economy sustains itself by generating the signals that enable individuals to make rational use of their powers (von Mises, 1951). In a free market price is a reliable guide to the utility and scarcity of goods, wages a reliable guide to the utility of a skill, and profit a reliable sign that a product is socially useful. In a free economy, therefore, individuals can plan to make the best use of their talents and skills, and to make money and spend it in the way that will bring the most reward. In short, individuals will be motivated to do what is best for themselves, and best for the strangers to whom they are bound in a network of mutual competition and support.

This does not mean that the motives that animate markets are merely self-interested, or that the invisible hand is nothing more than an impersonal corrective to personal greed. It was clear to Adam Smith that economic activity arises only among people who are guided by the moral sentiments, and therefore by conceptions of justice, responsibility, and obligation. And more recently, following Max Weber's celebrated work, *The Protestant Ethic and the Spirit of Capitalism,* published in 1921, it has been commonplace to connect the free economy with the Protestant, and specifically Calvinist, ethic. The Protestant posture of accountability toward God inculcates a spirit of honest dealing and accountability toward mortals too, and from this spirit there emerges a market economy and a habit of saving.

Weber's thesis is no longer credible—not because there is no connection between capitalism and the Protestant ethic, but because the connection is both wider and deeper, between the free economy and the religious frame of mind. Thus Peter Berger in a series of books, beginning with *Pyramids of Sacrifice,* has shown how religious beliefs promote the trust and entrepreneurship required by a free economy, and how wealth creation, far from being always an expression of 'materialist' values may sometimes be a spiritual exercise, with a deeply theological meaning (Berger, 1974 & 1990).

Berger writes from a Protestant perspective, but his thoughts are echoed by the Catholic theologian and philosopher, Michael Novak, who in *Business as a Calling* showed how the Catholic theological tradition, rightly understood, not only condones business, but sees it as a calling in which we can fulfil our duty to God and to our fellow human beings (Novak, 1996). For Novak, the capitalist economy is one part of a comprehensive social enterprise, the other parts of which are democracy and the rule of law. Between them these create the conditions in which individual initiative can be released and the creative potential of all members of society be given the opportunity to express itself and find fulfilment.

There is certainly an element of exaggeration in Berger and Novak, though this exaggeration is understandable, given the widespread contemporary view that businesspeople are somehow outside the fold of redemption, and that the 'profit motive' is both the engine of business and its disgrace. In this paper, however, I shall argue that the 'profit motive' is not the simple thing that appears either in the popular criticisms of business enterprise or in the micro-economic analysis that purports to show how business works.

Profit as By-Product

The old view of markets as driven by self-interest, and self-interest as the pursuit of profit (whether maximum, optimal, or satisfying), arises from *a priori* assumptions that are known to be empirically false. As Jim Collins and Jerry Porras showed in their celebrated study, *Built to Last*, the 'visionary' company — the one that succeeds in circumstances where its rivals falter or go the wall — is not the kind of 'profit machine' envisaged by the opponents of corporate capitalism (Collins and Porras, 2004). On the contrary, although it aims to be profitable, the visionary company understands profit in the way that a biologist understands oxygen — not the goal of life, but the thing without which there is no life. A corporation may be motivated by an ideology of group membership and consumer satisfaction, like Wal-Mart, or it may be fired by a desire to make a real contribution to society, like Hewlett-Packard. It may even impress upon the world and its workforce that its primary purpose is to honour God (Chick fil-A, for instance, or Dacor).

The point is that, however the company describes its motivating principles, profit does not usually appear among the goals, but is more often construed as a side-effect of pursuing them. In this connection it is worth quoting the words of John Young, CEO of Hewlett-Packard from 1976 to 1992:

> Maximizing shareholder wealth has always been way down the list. Yes, profit is a cornerstone of what we do — it is a measure of our contribution and a means of self-financed growth — but it has never been the *point* in and of itself. The point, in fact, is to *win*, and winning is judged in the eyes of the customer and by doing something you can be proud of. There is symmetry of logic in this. If we provide real satisfaction to real customers — we will be profitable (Collins & Porras, 2004, p. 57).

What Young is saying is clear: by aiming exclusively at profit you risk losing your sense of purpose; by pursuing your sense of purpose, profit comes to you as a by-product. The very same 'invisible hand' that, according to Mandeville and Smith, produces public good from the pursuit of private profit, produces private profit from the pursuit of public good. Moral and economic values are not in competition but, in the right context, to pursue the one is to obtain the other: and the dependency goes both ways. Moreover, as Collins and Porras show through the telling contrast between HP and Texas Instruments, the firm that puts profit at the top of its agenda, and regards all else as subservient to that goal, very soon begins to lose its competitive edge.

A team of researchers under the direction of William Damon, Howard Gardner, and Mihaly Csikszentmihalyi has shown the close connection, in particular cases, between moral conviction and business success. Through the exercise of 'moral imagination', Damon argues, a firm can further the moral goals of its members, providing them with the personal satisfaction that comes from doing good, without sacrificing profitability (Damon, 2004). Csikszentmihalyi goes further, in suggesting a kind of secular basis for the moral dimension of business, as people enter through business into moral relations with their fellows and work comes to function as the foundation of social harmony—performing the role that religion once performed, in imbuing life with purpose (Csikszentmihalyi, 2003). These studies take us far along the road to understanding the moral basis of capitalism, and the resources on which it draws. But they also point to interesting features of practical reasoning that get noticed by economists, as a rule, only as part of the amorphous idea of 'social capital.'

Social Capital

Social capital denotes the resources that are used in managing the day-to-day affairs of social existence, including customs, language, manners, and morals—in short, all the practices that are taught to us by our parents in order to make us fit members of society.[1] These things cannot be invented anew by each generation, since they are the distillation of a long process of accommodation. As Hayek and others have shown, the rules, customs, and traditions that enable people to live together in a great society are also products of 'the invisible hand' (Hayek, 1982). They are the beneficial results of cooperation and competition between neighbours, and the spontaneous by-products of our attempts to live in peace. The very same freedom that produces the capitalist economy also produces the social capital that is needed if it is to run successfully.

Like economic capital, social capital can be accumulated and invested. It is built through creating networks of trust and good will, which enable people spontaneously to pool their intellectual and physical resources in a common enterprise. As Francis Fukuyama has shown, communities in which there prevails a culture of trust and accountability are able to prosper in adverse circumstances and to create wealth seemingly *ex nihilo* (Fukuyama, 1996). Western societies have accumulated a great stock of social capital in the form of culture, networks, institutions, and laws. In each area of human endeavour

---

[1] The idea has been applied in the context of modern business by Cohen & Prusak, 2001.

they have added to this stock, accumulating works of art and music, games and sports, festivals and competitions, through which individuals rehearse their social feelings and refresh their commitments.

Social capital can be wisely invested, as when we found a school or a university and endow it with good teachers, good books, and good facilities, so helping the fund of knowledge and skills to grow. It can dwindle, as Robert Putnam shows, through the gradual retreat from social contacts (Putman, 2000) It can also be wasted, and the conspicuous waste of social capital is one of the most unhappy features of our societies today. This waste has been documented by several authors, notably by Charles Murray and James Q. Wilson, who have shown the way in which, by throwing economic resources into the welfare system, we do not merely waste those resources, we also waste social capital, producing the welfare-dependency that prevents people from learning how to be on equal and responsible terms with others, subsidising indolence and exhausting our teachers, social workers, and doctors with the thankless task of caring for people who are often unwilling to care for themselves (Wilson, 1993; Murray, 1984).

The social capital on which a business draws is in part its own creation. Among the 'savings' of a business we should count the activities devoted to building trust, commitment, and mutual respect among its employees, and to creating the social networks and good will that incorporate the firm into the feelings and plans of its members. And the theory of social capital goes some way to accounting for the fact that the 'profit motive' does not mean the single-minded pursuit of profit. Many of the things necessary for the reliable generation of profit can be achieved only by pursuing something else—something which cannot be conceptualized in balance-sheet terms, even if it is valued, in part, as a means to improving the balance-sheet.

Intrinsic Goods

Traditional econometric analysis can make the same place for social capital as it makes for any other kind of capital. However, there is a form of practical reasoning, every bit as important in business as in everyday life, which escapes the net of econometrics, and that is the rational deployment of intrinsic goods.

Consider friendship. The person with friends has help in his time of need, consolation in despair, and fellowship in rejoicing. In everything he attempts he is better off than the friendless person, and all his burdens are more lightly borne. But this does not mean that he values his friend merely as a means to achieving his own selfish goals. On the contrary, he values his friend for the particular person he is, and without thought for the benefit. The benefit is real, but it arises 'by an invisible hand', from actions with another intention.

Moreover, the person who treats another as a means to his own goals, however gently, with whatever compunction, is not treating the other as a friend. And if you do not treat someone as a friend, he ceases to be one. From this we can derive a striking conclusion. Friends are useful, so long as you do not make use of them! Treat someone as a friend, value him for what he is, and he will repay your friendship a thousand fold. Treat him as useful, however, and he will soon cease to be so.

On the other hand, although the true friend does not aim at the benefit of friendship, he has that benefit *in view*. He must be sensible of the good that has come his way, and show it through gratitude, affection, and a measure of dependency. If he should ever lose sight of the benefit entirely then the result will be comparable to that of pursuing the benefit too purposefully: he will become careless of the friendship and so lose it. He must maintain in view an instrumental value that will vanish, just as soon as he explicitly pursues it. La Rochefoucauld wrote that 'interest has many faces, including that of disinterest'; that is not what I have in mind. Rather the opposite: that disinterest has many faces, and one of them is the interest that we have in the benefits that flow from disinterest — an interest that must never be rewritten as a goal.

There is a simple model of practical reasoning, typical of the empiricist tradition in philosophy, but also recurring in sophisticated forms in modern decision theory and its offshoots, according to which practical reasoning consists in working out the means to satisfy our desires. In its modern form the theory goes as follows: we have certain preferences, and these are the data from which our practical reasoning begins. Preferences can be ordered — you prefer A over B and B over C — and also indifferent, as when everything preferred to A is preferred to B and A is preferred to everything to which B is preferred. Preferences for goods are also sensitive to time (how far they lie in the future), to probability (how probable is it that they will be obtained), and to risk (how probable are negative side effects and how negative will they be). And so on.

Enormous intellectual problems lie in the way of building a complete theory for the rational ordering of preferences, not least the problems of transitivity pointed out two centuries ago by Condorcet (it being relatively easy to construct cases in which an agent prefers A to B, B to C, and C to A). Nevertheless, the assumption in economics is that preferences are the raw material of rational choice, and that the rational person is the one who pursues as many of his preferences as possible to the point of fulfilment.

Against that picture I would put another, more consonant with the treatment of practical reasoning in Aristotle and Aquinas, and more consonant too with what we observe. People distinguish things they merely want from things they also value, and things they value instrumentally (either as a means to satisfy a want or as means to achieve some value) from things they value intrinsically. Wants can be weighed against each other and ordered in the manner of econometrics. Intrinsic values are more difficult to order, and sometimes impossible to weigh against each other. Yet things valued are also wanted, and usually have an instrumental value too. At the same time the condition toward which they are instrumental is something that we keep in view but do not pursue as a goal.

This condition, usually called happiness, self-fulfilment, or flourishing, comes, when it comes, as a by-product of other goals, and those goals can be pursued only by putting the benefit of obtaining them out of one's calculations. The example of friendship shows what it is, to keep in view the good things that follow from one's purpose, while not making them *part* of the purpose. It is plausible to suggest that this double intentionality is natural to self-conscious beings, and is also one of the roots—maybe even *the* root—of the moral life.

In friendship, therefore, people built up a capital asset, by aiming at something quite different from a capital asset, even while keeping that asset in view. The same is true of the motive of virtue—and this lies at the heart of an ancient insight, that virtue and friendship are connected, and that only the virtuous have true friends (as opposed to companions and accomplices).

Courage, for example, is supremely useful. It is the characteristic that puts your goals within reach, and so helps you to attain them. But that is not the motive of courage. The courageous person is not simply motivated by what he wants: the coward too has that motive. The courageous person is motivated in another way. He sees his action from outside, as another would see it. And he is proud to act as he does; he feels that duty, honour, and his standing in the world require him to take the risk. And it is precisely because he sees his action in this way, as the right thing to do, regardless of consequences, that he obtains the reward.

Planning for Success

It is a failure to grasp this feature of practical reasoning that lies at the root of the suspicion of capitalism and the market economy. Neo-classical economics proceeds on the assumption that firms aim to make a profit, and that the market is a system in which individual firms, each acting to achieve its profit (either maximally, optimally, or sufficiently), coordinate their actions and achieve equilibrium. But neo-classical economics does not examine, because it cannot, the actual motives of the people who compose those firms, and the precise way in which the profit motive arises within them. To the critics of capitalism, therefore, it has seemed as if the whole system were built on ruthless self-interest, and that if anybody paused, for a moment, to consider the sufferings of others, it was only to study how to make efficient use of them.

If we look back at the founder of classical economics, however, we find quite another picture. Adam Smith's picture of competition in the marketplace was intended as an adjunct to his detailed description, offered in *The Theory of the Moral Sentiments*, of human motivation, in which the pursuit of profit is tempered at every juncture by sympathy, benevolence, and the posture of the 'impartial spectator' forced on us by our moral nature. Human motives are never simple, Smith recognized. And what is, from one perspective, the pursuit of profit might be, from another and equally valid perspective, a gesture of benevolence. Often we achieve our goals by ignoring them, and the most profitable of our actions might be those in which we turn our backs on profit and act for the sake of honor, kindness, or compassion.

This is the kind of consideration that ought to lead us entirely to reject the caricature of capitalism that its critics love to reiterate. Private property, private initiative, private risk, and private profit are indeed all essential attributes of the capitalist system. But these things are economically effective only against a background of norms and values, in which profit may be kept in view, but seldom presented as the goal.

The Aristotelian position seems to be that happiness comes through virtue, but that the virtuous person does not aim at it, since his motive in all that he does is righteousness or honour (*to kalon*). Happiness, Aristotle makes clear, is not composed of fleeting sensations available equally to selfless and selfish people. It involves a settled contentment with one's lot, with oneself, and with others. It is not an experience but a condition, in which we flourish according to our nature, as a tree flourishes in healthy soil, or a fish in pure water. We teach our children to be courageous, wise, just, and temperate because we know that this will make them respected by their fellows, secure in their decisions, and able to take full control of their lives. That is the way to happiness. It is also the way in which the individual serves the community: the happiness of the individual and the prosperity of the community are both achieved through virtue.

Success in business is similar. It may come from a lucky accident. But lucky accidents cannot be planned. We prepare for success by acquiring virtues—dispositions that help us to take risks, to make decisions, to take responsibility for our actions, and to accept wise advice. These are the most important part of our human capital. But we do not invent them for ourselves. They form part of our collective inheritance. And through moral discipline we adopt them into ourselves.

The Pursuit of Virtue

Philosophers and moralists have tended to agree with Aristotle's list of the cardinal virtues—temperance, courage, justice, and prudence or practical wisdom (*phronesis*). By calling these virtues cardinal (from Latin *cardo,* a hinge), we emphasize that all else turns on them: that without them no other virtues can be reliably acquired or exercised.

But what is meant by calling them virtues? When I say that it is a virtue in a horse that it is steady in traffic, or a virtue in a chair that it is comfortable to sit in, I am relating the horse or the chair to the world of human interests. Being steady in traffic is an equine feature in which we, as riders, have an interest. From our point of view, the steadier the better. When I speak of the virtues of a human being, however, I mean something more far-reaching. I do not mean that he is useful to others. I mean that he has habits that contribute to human fulfilment and his own fulfilment first of all. We all have an interest in each other's character; but we also have a commanding interest in our own character, and what we do with it.

That is why we distinguish virtues from vices, recognizing that our most intimate self-conception will be affected by our habits, and that good habits bring not just success in our endeavours, but inner tranquillity and peace of mind. Moral judgements are universalizable, and the qualities we love or hate in others we will also love or hate in ourselves. It follows that virtue is a necessary condition of happiness, since it is the foundation of the self-approval without which no one can be truly at peace with himself.

Aristotle also was of that opinion. The context in which he developed his argument — the context of the Greek city-state, existing in fierce commercial and military competition with its neighbours — was very far from the context enjoyed by a modern corporation. Nevertheless, his argument was aimed at what is permanent in human nature, with a view to identifying the qualities that people need in all the circumstances of life, if they are to achieve the fulfillment of which they are capable.

He saw virtues as dispositions, which we learn by imitation and habit, but which are something more than knee-jerk reactions. The virtuous person does not merely acquire new and more disciplined behaviour; he acquires new and more fulfilling *motives*. To be genuinely courageous it is not sufficient to imitate the actions of a courageous person: in advance of the circumstances it is in any case impossible to know what those actions will be. To be courageous is to be moved as the courageous person is moved. It is to desire what is honourable and good, despite the cost in terms of personal discomfort and danger. The point about virtue is that it is reliable; and people become reliable when they are motivated in the right way. In a time of danger we look to the courageous person because we know that he will put the common good above his own personal safety, and therefore, through his leadership and example, create the best chance that the present danger will be overcome.

The Problem of Justice

The Greeks saw virtue as a unity. Each of the four cardinal virtues depends upon and amplifies the others. A courageous person must be temperate if he is not to over-step the mark. Intemperate courage is not courage but rashness, and temperance in turn needs courage if it is to face up to temptation and to the pressure of one's peers and still to say no. Prudence is involved in every virtue, and needs all other virtues if it is to be something better than a mean-minded refusal to take risks.

But one of the great difficulties that the Greek philosophers faced was that of integrating justice into their moral scheme. We can justify courage, temperance, and prudence as benefits to the person who possesses them — traits of character that bring success, and which make it maximally probable that the person who possesses them will overcome the difficulties that beset us in the trials of life. But justice is a much more 'other-regarding' virtue, and the question 'why be just?' troubled the Greek philosophers as it has troubled every thinking person since. It is the question that launches the argument of Plato's *Republic*. And it is the question dealt with by the Greek poets and tragedians in their most memorable bequests to us. It is also a question that bears directly on the conduct of business, since in so many contexts justice and profit seem to be at war. Indeed for the Marxists, with their zero-sum vision of all market transactions, the war can be ended only when private profit is abolished.

Aristotle defined the virtue of justice as the disposition to give to each person his due: and this is the definition taken up centuries later by Ulpian in his digest of the Roman Law. All rational beings need justice, Aristotle argued, since all need the cooperation of their fellows, and the trust upon which this depends. Moreover, without justice there is no friendship, since the friend is the one who both gives what is due and receives it. The most interesting feature of Aristotle's discussion of justice is his recognition that it is a quality of the individual agent and of the individual action. Justice is something that we do, and which we are blamed for not doing. And it has its root and motive in the virtue of justice: the virtue displayed by the person who sees others as his equals and who responds instinctively to their rightful demands.

That ancient conception of justice has been overlaid in modern times by a rival idea, which sees justice as a feature of 'society', rather than of individual actions. True, Aristotle already made a distinction between commutative and distributive justice, and this is often cited as authority by those who believe that social distributions can be assessed as just or unjust, regardless of their history. However, it is clear from his exposition that Aristotle believed that justice is a property of actions and agents, and that a distribution can be assessed as just or unjust only where people have collectively contributed to the production of a good, and thereby each established a title to some share in it. The idea — fashionable today, and indeed fundamental to the socialist-egalitarian world view — that distributions can be just or unjust simply as *states of affairs,* and without reference to the actions that brought them about, has no place in the Greek view of justice.

However, the socialist conception is not entirely new. The concept of 'social or public justice' gained a hold during the nineteenth century, under the influence of Christian social thought. It has a large part to play in the Calvinist theories of Abraham Kuyper, the theologian who was briefly Prime Minister of the Netherlands at the turn of the twentieth century. And there is a powerful tradition within Catholic theology which also sees 'social justice' as a primary obligation of the Church. The modern critics of the free economy make much of the 'social injustices' it supposedly creates and sustains. And they often frame their demands in terms of a distributive conception of justice, as in the celebrated work of John Rawls, *A Theory of Justice*. It seems that the conception of a *purely* distributive justice has been gaining ground, and sidelining the kind of reasoning about the virtue that Aristotle thought gave sense to the concept.

Social Justice

According to the Christian tradition, 'social or public justice' means a proper regulation of society, so that people can deal justly with each other in the *several* communities to which they belong. Social justice requires that we maintain the separate spheres of social interaction, so that each can be guided by its own spontaneous form of order: the order of the family, the club, the firm, the regiment, the school. That was what Kuyper understood by social justice: not the control of society by the state, but the retreat of the state from the self-governing spheres where it is not needed. A similar doctrine has been upheld by the Catholic Church under the name of 'subsidiarity', meaning the freedom of social institutions to govern themselves. The Catholic doctrine was taken over by Wilhelm Röpke in order to show how a capitalist economy can be reconciled with social justice, by supporting the institutions of civil society, through which people help each other and relieve the stresses of competition (Röpke, 1998).

In the modern context, however, 'social justice' has typically been held to require redistribution of goods by the state. In other words, it has come to mean the confiscation of property by bureaucrats who have no personal responsibility either in acquiring it or in giving it away. This use of the concept involves severing the idea of justice from that of individual accountability. And it condones the compulsory seizure of assets irrespective of whether they were justly or unjustly acquired. It is precisely this conception of social justice that authorized the great crimes committed in our day in the name of socialism and communism. And it is 'social justice', understood in the socialist way, that has crippled the capitalist economies of

Europe, to the great disadvantage of everyone, included those whom 'social justice' is supposed to benefit.

Back to Aristotle

By seeing justice as a virtue of individuals, however, we help to reintegrate the demand for justice into a healthy and creative economy. Justice regulates and upholds contracts; it encourages respect in the workplace and accountability both to customers and to shareholders. It distinguishes the phony demands of interlopers from the rightful demands of those to whom something is owed. And it furthers the long-term relationships of trust on which a successful business, and the larger community, both depend.

By emphasising the classical virtue as the core of justice, we once again put justice within our reach, and enable it to exert its benign influence over our actions. This does not mean that we can ignore the social conditions that surround us: evidently, where there is large-scale discrimination against minorities or blatant disregard of civil rights, justice demands that we take a stand on behalf of those who are being thus mistreated. But the important point is contained in that last word: for there to be injustice, there must be mistreatment. Someone must be *in the wrong*, and justice demands that the wrong be righted.

If we see justice in that way, however, we remove it from the frame of consequentialist reasoning that appeals to economists, and return it to the place where it belongs: among the motives and responsibilities of the individual agent. The just business is the one that treats others and its employees with respect, that takes responsibility for its faults, honours its agreements, and does not cheat on its rivals. And a business with such a disposition puts honour above profit in any conflict. Studies of virtuous companies have again brought home to us the empirical evidence for the view that justice, seen in this way, is not the enemy of profit, and that honesty remains the best policy — provided that it is not chosen as a policy.[2] At least this is so in the conditions of a free market, where profit is not arbitrarily confiscated and can therefore be openly declared, and where agreements are transparent and enforceable.

---

[2] See the examples in Damon, 2004, and Csikszentmihalyi, 2003.

Virtuous Business and its Enemies

However, there are two things that stand in the way of virtuous business: the state and the consultants. Both of them take a consequentialist view of justice, the state pursuing 'social justice', in the form of a distributive pattern, the consultants advancing an agenda of 'corporate social responsibility', which relegates justice to a side-line. State interference in the free economy, in order to secure some distributive pattern judged to conform to social justice, inevitably distorts the reasoning of private businesses. In a condition of enforced redistribution the virtue of justice begins to lose its appeal. Hence, in the state-monitored economies of France and Germany the black market accounts for nearly 20% of Gross Domestic Product, as the desperate attempt to maintain profits takes precedence over honest accounting. And, while doing their best to escape the grip of oppressive employment laws, businesses try to present a principled countenance to the world, by engaging in 'social responsibility' projects of a kind that will coincide with the state's egalitarian agenda.

However, virtue is not 'window dressing', and virtuous business is a long way from the kind of 'grafted on' public relations exercise the consultants favour. Enron was quite good at Corporate Social Responsibility (CSR), giving money to fashionable causes, making the right noises about diversity, equal opportunities, care for the environment, and whatever else the activists were concerned to investigate. But CSR, conceived in this way, is simply a kind of protection racket, whereby a corporation buys off the busybodies among the Non-Governmental Organizations, wraps itself in a veil of political correctness, and gets on with the business of profit-taking.

It is only superficially related to the ethical heart of a business, and may indeed be nothing more than a systematic deception—like the advertisements for oil companies which present them as engaged almost exclusively in environmental programs, and which never mention fossil fuels, still less green-house gas emissions. This is not to say that oil companies should not be involved in environmental projects—of course they should. It is rather to emphasize that a virtuous company is an honest citizen, and its virtue is not a public relations façade.

The considerations that might make us suspicious of CSR ought also to weigh against the current orthodoxies of 'business ethics', as this is now taught in business studies courses and MBA programs, and as it intrudes into the political sphere. 'Business ethics' as normally conceived too often consists in a set of rules—do's and don'ts—calculated to secure the approval of 'stakeholders,' and therefore of the activists who claim to represent them. It is all too often animated by a kind of political correctness which stems from the same suspicion of the 'profit motive' as the socialist resentments that poisoned the heart of Europe in the twentieth century. Diversity, multiculturalism, environmental rectitude, and other agenda-driven prescriptions are made into absolute values, to be enforced without regard to the nature of the business or the conditions under which it can flourish. And business ethics, so conceived, prompts governments to devise ever-more-detailed regulations, and to appoint ever-more-meddlesome committees of people, often ignorant of or hostile to business, to enforce them.

Of course, there is such a thing as business ethics; but it is no different from any other kind of ethics. It consists in one simple injunction, namely: strive to do good—the first principle of natural law, according to Aquinas. We obey this injunction through the exercise of virtue, and not through public relations exercises designed to appease politically motivated activists. Ethics is not about conformity to a political agenda; it is about the internal character, the moral stature, in short the soul of the firm. The virtuous company does not need to be told how to treat its employees, its customers, or the environment: it knows from the outset that it is a steward of all that it touches, just as virtuous people are. If it enters the political realm at all it is not as a craven follower of some political ideology, but as a corporate statesman, taking its place on behalf of its shareholders and workforce in the shaping of our common future.

The Soul of the Firm

That view of the corporation conflicts, however, with the emerging 'stakeholder' model. The stakeholder is to be sharply distinguished from the shareholder. The latter has risked his money in the firm, which is therefore bound to him by a fiduciary obligation not to waste or squander it. The former simply has a passing interest in the firm, whose obligation toward him is only that laid down by the general principles of morality and law.

Emphasis on the stakeholder should not be allowed to obscure the fundamental nature of the corporation, as an association of individuals, bound together by a shared risk and rewarded by a shared profit. The sharing of risk and profit creates relations of responsibility between management and workforce, owners and executives, and these endow the corporation with a soul of its own. Whatever the truth in the 'stakeholder model', it must not be allowed to obscure this fundamental point: that corporations come into the world as distinct individuals, with souls that are shaped by the social capital which has been invested in them.

Readers might baulk at the word 'soul'. Surely, they will say, corporations don't have souls in the sense that we have souls. There is no immortal essence to a corporation, nor does a corporation die and proceed to judgement. This talk of the corporate soul, they will say, is at best a metaphor. I would respond by saying that it is not a metaphor but a simile, and a simile grounded in real properties that are shared. For example, companies do things, they are blamed and praised for things, and they deliberate, take responsibility, and create bonds of loyalty and disaffection just as we do. And when you belong to a company you are acutely aware that it has its own way of proceeding, its own values, its own corporate culture, and its own ambient consciousness of how to conduct itself in business. The soul of the company is simply a special case of *l'esprit de corps*: the shared sense of belonging, following, leading, and obeying which unites the members around their common interests. Hence a company can be virtuous or vicious, just as an individual can be.

A virtuous company will be accepted in the economy not as a rapacious marauder but as a partner whose presence promises help, and which will conduct itself, wherever it might be, as a fellow citizen. Nothing is more valuable to a firm than its reputation for virtue. It is not enough to be 'visionary' in the sense made familiar by Jim Collins: a visionary company can easily offend through its messages or its aggressive presence, as Exxon offended the Czechs after the fall of communism, by erecting gas stations surmounted by eye-catching and landscape-disfiguring tigers, or as Exxon offended just about everyone by attempting to evade responsibility for the 1989 Valdez oil spill.

The need for virtuous conduct, rather than CSR, is nowhere more apparent than in the global marketplace. A company like UPS, which is perceived as a responsible citizen wherever it goes, has a clear trading advantage. But it cannot secure this advantage by window dressing. It must be led by a genuine ethos of concern and service: something that we see in UPS's involvement, for example, in educational projects in Poland — projects which have radically enhanced its local standing precisely because they are seen to be an expression of concern for the Polish people, rather than a shallow exercise in CSR.

The Root of All Evil

There is a skeptical approach to business and its denizens which is as old as the Old Testament, and which is echoed by Aristotle, Jesus, St. Paul, the Koran, and a thousand other moralists and sages. According to this approach we must distinguish businesses that produce what people need — agriculture, industry, construction, and so on — from businesses that deal only in money. The idea that one can make money simply by dealing in money has been looked at askance by moralists from the beginning of recorded history. Such a way of making money seems too much like trickery to earn our respect, and it excites all those 'zero-sum illusions' that inspired the nineteenth-century socialists. If someone is making money but selling nothing, someone else must be losing exactly that amount — and why isn't that theft?

This is not the place to mount a defence of the money market, of banking, of lending at interest, and so on. What is important is to recognize that banks too have souls, and that, in the normal case, it is by honourable conduct that they earn their place in the economy, and their opportunities for profit. To lend money at a market rate is to offer a service, and a firm can be entirely dependent on this form of business without sacrificing those other and higher goals which earn the trust of its customers and its own place in society. Think of the calamity that befell Baring's bank, in which the old and upright customs of the City of London were exploited from within by one of the new breed of self-centred nihilists. Or think of Lloyd's and its collapse, an episode that eloquently illustrates the distinction between honourable and dishonourable ways of using other people's money. Such examples remind us that it is as true of money as of any other business, that profit must come second to virtue, if it is to keep coming for long.

Of course, businesses have been radically changed by globalisation, by out-sourcing, by asset-stripping, and other practices that affect their accountability to others and to their own employees. New opportunities for misconduct and vandalism arise every day, and there is no way of extracting from my argument some neat formula that will apply to all of them.

Nevertheless, I remain persuaded that the model of economic activity I am proposing, which sees profit as the by-product of morally admirable goals, is the only one that will deliver a coherent view of business ethics. The models currently entertained see businesses as profit-driven machines, and governments as devices for redistributing the profit among those who did nothing to produce it. To this bleak vision I cannot help preferring the model that I have been defending. Instead of seeing business ethics as a compromise between two forms of immorality—self-centred profiteering and theft of the results—it recommends that businesses care for their souls as we should care for ours, so as to be upright citizens in a realm that we share.

Bibliography

Berger, Peter (1975), *Pyramids of Sacrifice: Political Ethics and Social Change* (New York: Basic Books)

Berger, Peter (1990), ed., *The Capitalist Spirit: Toward a Religious Ethic of Wealth Creation* (San Francisco: ICS Press).

Cohen, Don and Prusak, Laurence (2001), *In Good Company: How Social Capital Makes Organizations Work* (Boston: Harvard Business School Press).

Collins, Jim and Porras, Jerry I. (2004), *Built to Last: Successful Habits of Visionary Companies*, 10th ed. (New York: HarperCollins, Collins, 2004).

Csikszentmihalyi, Mihaly (2003), *Good Business: Leadership, Flow, and the Making of Meaning* (London: Hodder and Stoughton).

Damon, William (2004), *The Moral Advantage: How to Succeed in Business by Doing the Right Thing* (San Francisco: Berrett-Koehler).

Fukuyama, Francis (1996), *Trust: The Social Virtues and the Creation of Prosperity* (New York: Free Press).

Hayek, F.A. (1982), *Rules and Order*, vol. 1 of *Laws, Legislation, and Liberty* (London: Routledge).

Murray, Charles (1984), *Losing Ground: American Social Policy 1950–1980* (New York: Basic Books).

Novak, Michael (1996), *Business as a Calling: Work and the Examined Life* (New York: Simon and Schuster, Free Press).

Putnam, Robert (2000), *Bowling Alone: The Collapse and Revival of American Community* (New York: Simon & Schuster).

Röpke, Wilhelm (1960), *A Humane Economy: The Social Framework of the Free Market* (Chicago: H. Regnery, 1960; reprint, with a new introduction by Dermot Quinn, Wilmington, DE: ISI Books).

von Mises, Ludwig (1951), *Socialism: An Economic and Sociological Analysis*, 2nd edn., trans. J. Kahane (New Haven, CT: Yale University Press).

Wilson, James Q. (1984), *The Moral Sense* (New York: Simon and Schuster, Free Press Paperbacks).

David Novak

Natural Law, Human Dignity & the Protection of Human Property

Ethics and Business

Being a major component of social life, where so much power is exercised over all of us, business or commerce presents great opportunities to do right and equally great temptations to do wrong. Here the ethical issues are ubiquitous. I shall get to the current ethical crisis in the business world shortly, but first let me tell you how I see the general relation of ethics and business or commerce, which is to my mind anyway, the theoretical aspect of today's crisis. Some very unethical ideas (the stuff of theory) has led and still do lead to some very unethical acts. Our right acts and our wrong acts most often begin in our heads. 'Learning God's law is greater than practice of it, since learning brings one to practice', states the Babylonian Talmud.[1] Here is where concern with business ethics begins.

To my mind, the most basic ethical terms are 'right' and 'wrong' or 'just' and 'unjust'. Most other ethicists, though, consider 'good' and 'bad' (or 'evil') the most basic.[2] 'Good' and 'bad' are primarily aesthetic terms, which are then transposed into ethics by analogy (see Novak, 2000, pp. 12–25).

---

[1] *Kiddushin* 40b.
[2] Note the commonality of three otherwise disparate modern ethicists on the primacy of the term and concept *good* for ethics: Moore, 1903, 1–36; Grisez, 1965; Levinas, 1969, pp. 102–3, 304–7.

So, for example, I can call a picture 'good' *because* its harmonious form gives me pleasure by looking at it. Thus the picture is *good for me*. It is hard to imagine anyone calling an *experience* 'good' if it did not give him or her pleasure, whether tactical, visual, audible, or intellectual. Furthermore, one can call an *act* 'good' if it is done well, that is, if it seems to accomplish what its agent intended it to accomplish.[3] So, in business, for example, one can speak of a 'good deal' as being a transaction skillfully performed, but one could also say this about the deals of thieves, embezzlers, and swindlers.[4]

Thus judgments of 'good' and 'bad' do not in and of themselves involve *ethics* per se. When used in ethical discourse, an aesthetic term like 'good' presupposes an often unstated analogue.

Many people seem to think that the legal level will give us a more satisfactory plane for genuine ethical judgment. I disagree.

The basic legal terms are 'legal' and 'illegal', or 'correct' (that is, 'according to law') and 'incorrect' ('contrary to law'). One can speak of a 'good law' or a 'bad law', yet that can simply mean either a law (or a whole legal system) that pleases or displeases me, or a law that is consistent or inconsistent with the legal system (or constitution) from which it derives its authority.[5] I could be speaking of a law within the Nazi or the Soviet legal system (or, maybe, the Iranian legal system today), or that system in toto. Very unethical acts—indeed, very horrendous crimes—have been justified (or rationalized) by the standards and procedures of such legal systems and the political regimes who have authorized them (Strauss, 1953, pp. 1–8, esp. p. 4, n. 2).

One could say that importing other modes of discourse into business or commerce is artificial, and will probably not affect the people it is supposed to guide. Such importation is what many philosophers would call a 'category error'. To many businesspeople, it seems the equivalent of applying the principles of German grammar to English speech. It seems like foreigners telling them how to run their own country (MacIntyre, 1988, pp. 1–11).

We can avoid this problem, I think, when we see that the most basic ethical terms are 'right' and 'wrong', or 'just' and 'unjust'. When we say that a transaction is 'right', we are not saying it necessarily benefits or pleases me or you. Instead, we are saying: *a right*

---

[3] See Aristotle, *Nicomachean Ethics*, 1.1.1094a1–18.
[4] See Plato, *Republic*, 351D–E.
[5] See Aristotle, *Politics*, 3.10.1286a9. Cf. Finnis, 1980, pp. 266–76.

transaction satisfies the justifiable claims of the parties of the transaction, and the justifiable claims of the society that justice be done. So, for example, when A is to render services to B in return for payment, the transaction is 'right' when A renders his or her services properly and when B pays for these services properly.

The likelihood of the transaction being performed rightly or justly will be far greater if it is performed well—that is, if it is performed harmoniously and if the parties in the transaction see their own respective interests benefited—but the pleasure taken in the transaction does not ethically ground the transaction. A may get pleasure out of being well-serviced by B, and B gets pleasure out of enhancing his or her reputation as a *good* credit risk, but the pleasure each party gets from the transaction itself, which includes the pleasure of personally dealing with competent and honest people, is a secondary accompaniment to the rightful transaction itself.[6] This pleasure, which at best becomes the mutual pleasure of commercial friendship, enhances the rightful transaction.[7] Therefore, pleasure taken in a rightful transaction is right, and pleasure taken in a wrongful transaction is wrong.

Business ethics is not a set of criteria from another discipline that is imported into or imposed upon the business world. It employs general ethical criteria that apply in other areas of human interaction, but the formulation of business ethics arises from within commercial experience itself. One could compare business ethics to biomedical ethics. In biomedical ethics, the questions to be addressed arise from within the whole biomedical enterprise, which leads to the constant search for cogent principles of ethics or 'practical' (as distinct from 'technical') reason. The fact that these principles are usually quite similar to those arising in other areas of human interaction only confirms the truth that universal principles always function within specific situations, and their particular application is *to* and *for* these situations, yet they are not produced by these situations.[8] They are discovered, not invented. Were they discovered in only one area of human interaction, they might be rationalizations for particular practices. If business ethics had nothing in common within any other manifestation of ethics, we could suspect that business ethics is only a rationalization for certain business practices, rather than being a

---

[6] See Plato, *Philebus*, 63E; Aristotle, *Nicomachean Ethics*, 7.11.1152b1–24.
[7] *Ibid.*, 8.3.1156a15–20.
[8] See *ibid.*, 1.6.1096a11–b30.

set of principles that can guide these practices and even be employed to judge them, that is, to conclude whether they are right or wrong.

Natural Law Ethics

Natural law is a kind of ethical formulation. To my mind, it is the most philosophically astute kind of ethics. Since it includes those norms that can be seen to pertain to all humans everywhere at every time, it is discoverable by human reason anywhere at any time, even though the method of such discovery will vary from one culture to another(see Novak, 1998). The 'nature' in 'natural' law is universal human nature; the 'law' in natural 'law' is an imperative that does not depend upon the act of a particular human judge or human ruler to be known or enacted.

Thus 'universal ethics universally knowable' —for example, the type of ethics human rights activists employ (whether they know it or not) — and 'natural law' are interchangeable terms. That equation of universal ethics universally knowable and natural law becomes apparent once we see that the 'universal' here pertains to the humanly inhabited universe or human society per se, and the 'natural' here pertains to what enables human beings to make rationally justifiable, uniquely human, claims upon one another in that society.

We could say that ethics is to business practice what mathematics is to physics.[9] Physics is not deduced from mathematics; instead, mathematics is suggested by physics in the sense that the language of physics, beholden as it is to *material* objects, cannot deal with its *formal* considerations adequately. That is the job of mathematics as theory. Mathematics *informs* physics, giving it an intelligibility it cannot give itself. Although suggested by physics, perhaps even called for by physics, mathematics is brought *to* physics; it does not come down from physics any more than physics is deduced from mathematics. (Even Einstein's highly mathematical physics needed experimental validation.)

Just as physics is not deduced from mathematics, so just business practices are not deduced from natural law. Instead, natural law reasoning is called for by the type of ethical problems that the language of commerce itself, beholden as it is to particular cases, cannot

---

[9] This is based on the insight of the German Jewish philosopher Hermann Cohen (d. 1918) that ethics functions as the logic of the human sciences (*Geisteswissenschaften*, or what we now call the "social sciences", which might very well include "business administration" as well as economics). See Cohen, 1981, pp. 65, 227.

answer, because it cannot provide adequate concepts to deal with their universal or rational considerations. That is the job of natural law as theory. Just as mathematics provides physics with its formal language, natural law provides business practices with their reasons.

Therefore, just as one would not speak of '*the* mathematics' but simply 'mathematics', one should not speak of '*the* natural law' as if it were some sort of object, but of 'natural law', as a form to be applied to any positive human situation. Yet that cannot be done before one is already engaged in that situation. One lives natural law *through* positive human situations, not apart from them. It is a method for clarifying and deepening the moral meaning of these human situations.

This relation *between* ethics and these positive human situations is important to bear in mind when natural law advocates are accused of 'imposing' their philosophical or even their 'religious' views on situations many assume are 'none of their business'. The answer is that we are only using natural law concepts to bring out whatever moral meaning is already latent within these situations themselves. Natural law is not a positive substitute for anything.

The Political Culture of Thieves

Now, what does all this theory have to do with the current crisis of criminal misconduct at the highest levels of American and global business? Do we really need this theoretical background to discern that theft is wrong and thieves should be forced by the law to make civil restitution to their victims, plus have criminal penalties imposed upon them? We do need to think about something deeper. We need to think about a relatively new political culture from which too many of us get our ethics or moral principles. (I use the terms 'ethics' and 'morality' interchangeably here.)

The political culture of which I speak is one that encourages immoral conduct even when it doesn't explicitly mandate it. That encouragement is often a form of implied or tacit approval.[10] It provides no good reason to judge these acts to be immoral rather than just stupid — that is, the stupidity of being too greedy, so that one gets caught for the stupid (in some cases, flamboyant) exercise of greed. This political culture of economic opportunism is antithetical to the political culture that looks to natural law ethics for the formulation and reformulation of its standards, or, if you will, its 'values.'

---

[10] See Babylonian Talmud *Sanhedrin* 27b re: Leviticus 26:27.

Some of our corporate thieves have internalized this political culture and rationalize their immoral acts by its values or standards. Some sympathize with them, perhaps hoping to learn what not to do from their error in getting caught. And others can't summon up any genuine outrage at what they have done. So we need to examine the political culture that has encouraged and rationalized executive thievery, for those who have actually engaged in it, for a larger number who might want to do it more cleverly, and for an even larger number who have no good reason to judge it to be wrong.

What is new is not what these thieves have done or even how they have done it. What is new is the political culture that has deprived them of the capacity for any real agony before they steal, or the capacity for any real remorse after they have stolen, even after they have been caught. What is new is the political culture that has deprived too many of us, who are not thieves, of the capacity to demand any real regret from those who are thieves, because we have lost the capacity to judge thievery with any real opprobrium.

Executive thieves are not like the lone bandits who used to rob stagecoaches. The fact that they are outlaws does not mean they are social outcasts. Quite the contrary. They are very much social insiders. They could not possibly have done what they have done without being participants in a society called a 'corporation', which functions within a larger civil society. These intricate social systems operate according to elaborate rules and procedures, which these executive thieves have had to convince others they fully endorse and subscribe to in order to gain their trust. Without that public affirmation of morality, these thieves could not have gained enough trust from others to be able to deceive them in the way they did. In the Talmud, lying to someone else for the sake of obtaining from him or her what does not belong to one is called *genevat da`at*, that is, 'stealing somebody else's good opinion'.[11] Such deceit enables one to be a thief rather than a robber, because the deceitful thief has so disarmed the victims that they are oblivious to being 'robbed blind', only noticing the theft after, often long after, it had taken place.

These thieves fully endorse and subscribe to social rules in public, but violate them in private, and do so with a sociopath's lack of shame, even when their misdeeds are finally exposed and judged in public to be wrong. This type of bad human conduct is uninformed by the basic norms of natural law. We now need to look at the politi-

---

[11] Babylonian Talmud *Hullin* 94a; Maimonides *Mishneh Torah*: Deot, 2.6.

cal culture that makes such a radical difference between the public and private realms, approving of acts in one realm that it condemns in the other.

Public Virtue/Private Vice

Nobody who has any stake in the successful functioning of their society could deny that society must have institutions to protect its citizens from harm to their bodies, and to their property as an extension of their bodies, and norms that prescribe punishment of those who violate the body or the property of a fellow citizen. This is what Isaiah Berlin famously called 'negative freedom' (Berlin, 1969). The punishment for the violation of this negative liberty is both civil and criminal: civil in terms of arranging for the payment of restitution for the loss of use of one's body or one's property, criminal in terms of incarceration (and, in some societies, even capital punishment) for the suffering caused by the violation of a body or its property.

That is society's duty to its citizens. (Whether society has some more positive duties to its citizens, what Berlin called 'positive freedom', let alone what such rights are specifically, is a question every society must answer for itself (*Ibid.*, pp. 131–4).) When society cannot exercise its duty to protect its citizens from crime (even if does fails unwillingly, because of lack of means), society—in the person of those who have authority in it and for it—cannot expect its citizens to dutifully respect that authority by obeying its laws. In other words, society has a claim upon its citizens that obliges them to accept its protection of their bodies and their property. But the citizens themselves have a prior claim on society that obliges it to protect their bodies and their property.

In this view, the claims of individuals upon society precede society's claims on them, even though historically speaking, society is there before any particular individual comes to it either by birth or by choice. Their claims are, in this view, basically selfish: they require society to protect them and their bodies and their property, in return for which they promise to cooperate with it in its duty to protect the bodies and property of their fellow citizens. The sole reason for one's adherence to social norms is the promotion of what one believes to be one's own good. Citizens need society and its institutions (primarily, the police and the courts) for private self-interest. In this view, we are all private beings, only becoming public beings (law-abiding citizens) to enhance our private interests. This kind of society is primarily a collection of strangers. Nobody is there because he or she desires the friendship or even the company of their fellow citizens. One's interest only includes the members of one's own select interest group, and membership in that group is ephemeral.

There is no idea here of society being a communion of persons, one whose institutions are designed essentially to promote political communion or interpersonal interaction itself as an end in itself.[12] Without a notion of common purpose, which stands over and above individual interest (without obliterating individual economic interest, as was done by Communism) and is more than the interest of the majority (as in utilitarianism), self-interest can be the only reason those having political authority could possibly want it. Their motive in seeking political power can only be that their own self-interest consists of wielding power over their fellow citizens. (All too often, power-seeking politicians loot public funds as a symbol of their political power; hence their misdeeds are more the result of the desire for recognition than of mere physical appetite.)

Politicians of this individualist frame of mind convince their fellow citizens that they exercise power in the citizens' best interest. The citizens may want government protection from criminals domestic and foreign the government to help bring about a higher standard of living. The question is who has political power, how it is wielded, and why anyone would want to wield it. And this problem exists whether the official ideology of the society is socialism, or the unofficial ideology of the society is capitalism. Though at this level, it can indeed be said for the preferability of capitalism that a society with a robust private economy will have greater private scrutiny of public officials than a socialist regime where there is no such economic 'balance of power.' Nevertheless, when governmental scrutiny of the private sector is very much out of balance with the private sector, we get an age of 'robber barons.'

In this notion of a contractual state, there is an exchange made between political authorities and ordinary citizens. That is an exchange between the rights and duties of each side: society's claims *on* its citizens and its duties *to* them, and individual citizens' claims *on* society and their duties *to* society, which is to obey its laws, and to follow the orders of the political authorities when they function in a lawful manner. This exchange becomes manifest at those times

---

[12] See Aristotle, *Politics*, 1.1.1253a9–40.

when each side has to *promise* to live up to its commitments to the other side.

I will now use the first person in the way a phenomenologist attempts to 'get inside' the experience of which he or she is describing.

Who Can Be Trusted?

At the most basic level, the relationship between individuals and society requires trust. I must be able to trust the commitment or promise or pledge of others to me; others must be able to trust my commitment or promise or pledge to them. The question is then: 'Why should I trust you, and why should you trust me?' (see Novak, 2005, pp. 205–12). Following the self-interest theory we have been examining, one could say that I gain the trust of others in my own self-interest. Others would avoid me if they thought that I would steal from them once their backs are turned.[13] Nevertheless, couldn't I gain the trust of others to put them off guard long enough to take more from them than I could if I suddenly and openly robbed them like the lone stagecoach bandit of the Westerns I thrilled to as a child? Thieves who operate this way, by betrayal of the trust others have placed in them, used to be called 'confidence men.'

But what about the law? I know quite well that I wouldn't be able to steal corporate funds if there weren't a elaborate system of law that enables corporations to function in a lawful society. I am not an anarchist (most of whom live in the wilderness or on the streets, not in board rooms). I certainly do not want everyone to do what I am now doing. But the authority of my society and its laws serves my self-interest by doing two things for me: one, it protects my property from being stolen by others with impunity, and two, it enables others to accumulate more property than they could do in an anarchic social situation, thus providing me with more to steal. So while I am grateful to society for providing me with such good opportunities to steal, and providing me such good opportunities to spend and enjoy in public what I have been able to steal privately, I have to consider the fact that I might get caught by 'the law', that I could be impoverished by the fines levied upon me by the court, and lose my liberty by going to prison. When considering this possibility, my only deliberation consists of a cost-benefit calculation. What are my chances of

---

[13] See Plato, *Republic*, 359D–360D.

getting caught? Is the gain I know I can get now worth the risk of the punishment I *might* get later?

The 'remorse' a number of convicted executive thieves have shown (usually between the time of their conviction and the time they are sentenced) seems to be little more than a ploy to get a lighter sentence, than it is an acceptance of true justice. We need to ask: If the remorse shown by those who have imbibed the political culture that judges self-interest to be right *per se* seems phony to us, what sort of remorse would be more genuine? If remorse is the proper expression of shame for having done something inherently wrong, what sort of political culture encourages people to be ashamed of what they have done and be remorseful about it? And in what sort does the fear of being publicly shamed and personally *ashamed* become an incentive not to risk shame? My internalization of the fear of being ashamed of what I could do is what we call 'conscience.' What sort of a political culture encourages the development of conscience?

Conscience and Political Culture

A culture that cannot distinguish between neurotic 'guilt feelings' and genuine shame cannot tell us why remorse is required of those who have done wrong. Lacking a good reason for remorse, it cannot provide the means for anyone who has imbibed its values to express his or her remorse and truly *mean*—that is, honestly *intend* to say—what he or she is saying. Such a culture cannot encourage the development of conscience by its adherents.

At this point, it might be helpful to remember the motto that introduced some of the great codes of Roman law: *Honeste vivere* ('to live with honesty or integrity'); *alterum non laedere* ('not to harm another'); *suum cuique tribuere* ('to grant each his own').[14] In other words, those who live dishonestly, affirming one standard in and for the public and acting upon an opposite standard with and for themselves, such people will usually have no qualms about harming others when that is in their self-interest, and they will usually regard everyone else's property as theirs potentially, that is, as grist for their mill.

The key, then, is to distinguish between a political culture that cogently encourages one to be ashamed of wrongdoing, and a political culture that only pragmatically judges the good or bad consequences resulting from the exercise of one's self-interest or actually approves of what one has done. That kind of culture only pities the

---

[14] Ulpian *Digest*, 1.1.10.1.

criminal for his or her bad luck in getting caught, and especially for having to 'do hard time' in prison. Such pity is born of the sympathy felt for the poor fool about whom it might be said: 'There, for but my good luck, go I'.

I remember a time about twelve years ago or so when my wife and I were invited to a party being hosted by a social acquaintance, a woman whose husband had just been released from prison, having served a short sentence for having defrauded a large number of investors in his company, most of whom were barely indemnified for their losses—if at all. The invitation actually said that this party was a 'celebration' of her husband's 'homecoming', and that he had been 'the victim of an unfortunate misunderstanding'. Knowing him to have been quite civil, even charming, to us in our social interactions with him—and, fortunately, not having invested in any of his business ventures—our first reaction was to accept this invitation. After all, this couple had always hosted great parties in the past.

But my wife, being a better judge of character than I, quickly came back to her moral sense, and just as quickly brought me back to my moral sense. She said that were she this man's wife, she would get him and herself out of town, and maybe even change their name and try to assume a new, anonymous identity somewhere else. But when we didn't accept this invitation, not giving our reasons lest we add to the embarrassment of this convicted felon and those nearest to him, we heard that we were criticized by some of his social circle for being 'moralistic and judgmental'. Apparently, we are adherents of a different culture than this man, his wife, and their friends.

Rights and Duties

Philosophically speaking, where does the error of this political culture of economic opportunism lie? And what is its obverse? I submit that the error lies in a false correlation of the idea of rights and the idea of duties. The political culture that has encouraged executive thievery has a skewed notion of the relation of rights and duties.

Rights are the justifiable claims one person (or persons) may make upon another person (or persons). Duties are the valid responses to the justifiable claims one person (or persons) is obliged to make to another person (or persons) (see Novak, 2000, pp. 3–12). Rights and duties are correlative; that is, you can't have one without the other. Natural law is the set that includes all rights/duties correlations that can be taken as universal in scope and are universally intelligible. Thus an unjustifiable claim—such as 'give me all your money', which I can tacitly take without your knowledge and consent—entails only one valid response, which is my duty to disobey (even though considerations for my own life and safety might well require me to obey such an unjustifiable command). That duty can be fulfilled before the fact by my strengthening my right to keep my own property away from thieves like you. And that duty can be fulfilled after the fact by my filing charges against you.[15] Even when you force me to give you my money (whether at gunpoint or more subtly, say, by economic threats), I can still disobey inwardly, in the sense of not recognizing your 'claim' as a right I ought to honor.

The question is: If rights and duties are correlative, which one has priority? Are duties created by rights, or are rights created by duties? Another way of putting the question is: Do *my* rights precede *your* duty to respond to them, or do *your* rights precede *my* duty to respond to them?

Logically speaking, a right as a claim creates the duty to respond to that claim. If, minimally, a claim is a request (maximally, a command), a request intends a response or an answer to it, even when there is no actual response in fact. (If it continually gets no response, it is futile but not unintelligible.) Thus a claim *initiates* a response, whether successfully or not. But a response when there has been no prior request is meaningless.

The question, though, is how one experiences the order of an exercise of a right and the exercise of a duty. I experience the exercise of your right, your claim upon me for a dutiful response, before I learn how to make my claim upon you for your dutiful response to me. That, of course, assumes that you are there in the world before I am. Hard as it is for children to accept, they come into a world that has been there before them. They must learn how to respond to the claims of those adults already there, waiting for them. Only then can they learn how to make their own claims upon those they encounter in the world.

And, as we know from child psychology, when children's basic experience of claims is the experience of unjustifiable, self-serving claims made by those who are supposed to care for them, they often never learn how to make justifiable claims upon others. Such children become adults who are convinced that making a rights-claim is the equivalent of screaming a threat. They become the type of adults who demand or take what they want because they want it, instead of

---

[15] See Babylonian Talmud *Baba Batra* 40a. Cf. Babylonian Talmud *Shabbat* 88a.

asking and working for what they need because they deserve it and because they can justify—that is, rationally argue for—what they need.

At the most basic level, that just dessert is not because of what a person has done to earn it, but because of who that person is in the world. Jews and Christians formulate the claims of human personhood best when they assert that human nature is most unique in being the *imago Dei*, 'the image of God' (see Novak, 1998, pp. 167–73). *What* the sanctity of human personhood is can only be positively constituted by revelation. But, even without revelation, we can discern *that* human personhood reflects a source beyond the world, and that is why human persons are deserving of respect (see Novak, 2007, pp. ix–xiv). This is what the Jewish tradition calls *kevod ha-beriyot*, 'human dignity'.[16]

I am a 'me' who is addressed by another, before I am an 'I' who addresses others. All such address is based upon need: You need something from me, I need something from you. And there is always a 'you' in the world that becomes *my* world before there is a 'me' cast into this world thereafter. When your rights and my duties, *then* my rights and your duties, are properly correlated, we can intelligently affirm a world that is *our* world. Yet this common world is not our possession. As the biblical story of the Tower of Babel teaches, when humans regard the world as their possession, it inevitably leads to the exploitation of one group of humans by another in the process of robbing God of what rightfully belongs to Him alone.[17]

Because of our mortality, we can only hold some possessions temporarily. And because of our mortality, even what we rightfully purchase (with our money or with our labor) is at best a long-term lease, not a permanent endowment. When we are truly honest with ourselves, we learn that we are just passing through this world, that we are tenants and not landlords. Yet, even as mere transient tenants, we ought to keep up the property as best we can, making it as comfortable for ourselves and the other tenants as possible.[18] Furthermore, when philosophy properly reflects on human nature from our perspective, it can teach us *that* we are transient tenants in the world. But when theology properly reflects on human nature from a divine

---

[16] See Babylonian Talmud *Berakhot* 19b re: Deutronomy 17:11.
[17] See Genesis 11:1–11, also Ginzberg, 1909, pp. 179–81.
[18] See Aristotle, *Politics*, 2.2.1263a25–1263b29.

perspective, from the perspective of the Master of the world, it can teach us *whose* guests we are in the world.[19]

When we have acted as ungrateful guests in the world, taking without giving in return, our place in the world restrains us and punishes us as it must—even if our sub-place or 'counter culture' in the world gives us its approval. Our counterculture has done us no favor when it deprives us of the ability to feel and express remorse, let alone seek an authentic expiation. How can I feel the moral outrage I want to feel at what somebody else has either done to me or is likely to do to me, when I felt no moral outrage, no shame, when I did the same thing or was likely to do the same thing to others?[20] How can I ask for forgiveness from my fellow guest in the world and from the host of the world, if I cannot believe myself to have really done wrong, to have acted against greater social communion rather than for it?

Despite all my action that presumes that I *begin* the world, the truth is that the world *began* long before me, and will endure long after me. Moreover, no matter how wretched my origins may have been, the world did welcome me by affording me the opportunity to survive, maybe even to flourish. That in all honesty I cannot deny. That is why I *owe* the world more than the world *owes* me. Thus I need the means to feel and express shame for my betrayal of my obligation to work for the common good (which can certainly include my own justifiable exercise of self-interest as in my rightful acquisition of private property).

And that means the world's claim on me to benefit it as much as I can is greater than any good I pursue for myself. Without the means to seek expiation from the Master of the world for my ultimate betrayal, I will die unreconciled to the world, which did more for me than I could ever do for it. A political subculture that denies me opportunities for the reconciliation and expiation my being-in-the-world surely needs, that subculture has not only enabled me to harm others easily, it has harmed me by making me, in the deepest sense, 'a restless wanderer on earth' (Genesis 4:14).

Bibliography

Berlin, Isaiah (1969), "Two Concepts of Liberty", in *Four Essays on Liberty* (Oxford: Oxford University Press), pp.122–34.

---

[19] See Leviticus 25:6; Psalms 23:6.
[20] See Babylonian Talmud *Shabbat* 31a.

Cohen, Hermann (1981) *Ethik des reinen Willens*, 5th edn. (Hildesheim and New York: Georg Olms Verlag).
Finnis, John (1980), *Natural Law and Natural Rights* (Oxford: Clarendon Press).
Ginzberg, Louis (1909), *Legends of the Jews*, vol. 1 (Philadelphia: Jewish Publication Society of America).
Grisez, Germain G. (1965), "The First Principle of Practical Reason", *Natural Law Forum* 10, pp. 168–201
Levinas, Emmanuel (1969), *Totality and Infinity*, trans. Alphonso Lingis (Pittsburgh: Duquesne University Press).
MacIntyre, Alasdair (1988), *Whose Justice? Which Rationality?* (Notre Dame, IN: University of Notre Dame Press).
Moore, G.E. (1903), *Principia Ethica* (Cambridge: Cambridge University Press), pp. 1–36
Novak, David (1998), *Natural Law in Judaism* (Cambridge: Cambridge University Press).
Novak, David (2000), *Covenantal Rights: A Study in Jewish Political Theory* (Princeton, NJ: Princeton University Press).
Novak, David (2005), *The Jewish Social Contract: An Essay in Political Theology* (Princeton, NJ: Princeton University Press).
Novak, David (2007), *The Sanctity of Human Life* (Washington, DC: Georgetown University Press).
Strauss, Leo (1953), *Natural Right and History* (Chicago: University of Chicago Press).

Robert P. George

Business and Family in a Decent and Dynamic Society

Business is a calling, even a vocation. It is, to be sure, a way of making a living—sometimes a very good living indeed—but it is also a way of serving. In these dimensions it is like law, medicine, and the other learned professions. And the great schools of business are like the great law and medical schools. Like the other great professional schools, however, many business schools are going through something of an identity crisis. The *Wall Street Journal* recently published an article previewing a soon-to-be-released book by Rakesh Khurana, a professor at the Harvard Business School. Professor Khurana does not spare even his own school from the charge that, as George Anders of the *Journal* puts it, 'M.B.A. training has deteriorated into a race to steer students into high-paying finance and consulting jobs without caring about graduates' broader roles in society.' Anders quotes Khurana as charging that the 'logic of stewardship has disappeared' from business education. 'Panoramic, long-term thinking', Anders says, summing up Khurana's argument, 'has given way to an almost grotesque obsession with maximizing shareholder value over increasingly brief spans' (Anders, 2007; Khurana, 2007).

Business operates in the context of a larger society. It is affected by what happens in other dimensions of the society, and it in turn affects them. The broader society plainly has a large stake in what goes on in business, and business has a large stake in what goes on in society. Business depends for its flourishing on things that it cannot produce. These things are produced, if they are produced at all, by other social institutions. So business has a stake in the health, the flourishing of these institutions.

Decency's Pillars

So far I have been speaking very abstractly, as philosophers are inclined to do. Let me now speak a bit more concretely, in the mode of the sociologist, as it were.

Any healthy society, any decent society, will rest upon three pillars. The first of these is respect for the person—the individual human being—and his dignity. What I mean is that the formal and informal institutions of society, and the beliefs and practices of the people, are such that the human being is regarded and treated as an end-in-himself, and not a mere means to other ends. He is understood to be a subject of justice and human rights, and not an object, an instrument, or a thing. A society that does not respect the person will generally regard the human being as a cog in the larger social wheel whose dignity and well-being may legitimately be sacrificed for the sake of the collectivity. In its most extreme modern forms, totalitarian regimes reduce the individual to the status of an instrument to serve the ends of the fascist state or the future communist utopia. When liberal regimes go awry, it is usually because a reigning utilitarian ethic reduces the human person to a means rather than an end to which other things—including the systems and institutions of law, education, and the economy—are means. In cultures in which religious fanaticism has taken hold, the dignity of the individual is typically sacrificed for the sake of theological ideas and goals.

By contrast, a healthy liberal ethos supports the dignity of the human person by giving witness to fundamental human rights and civil liberties, and where a healthy religious life flourishes, faith provides a grounding for the dignity and inviolability of the human person by, for example, proposing an understanding of each and every member of the human family, even those of different faiths or professing no particular faith, as persons made in the image and likeness of God or bearing a divine spark that is evident in the human powers of reason and freedom of the will. The first pillar of a decent society is present when a society in its institutional commitments and social practices manifests the conviction that human beings as such possess a profound, inherent, and equal dignity, one that in no way varies according to such factors as race, sex, ethnicity, alienage, age, size, stage of development, or condition of dependency.

The second pillar of any decent society is the institution of the family.[1] It is indispensable. The family is the original and best ministry of health, education, and welfare. Although no family is perfect, no institution excels the healthy family in its capacity to transmit to each new generation the understandings and traits of character—the virtues—upon which the success of every other institution of society, from law and government to educational institutions and business firms, vitally depends. Where families fail to form, or too many break down, the effective transmission of the virtues of honesty, civility, self-restraint, concern for the welfare of others, justice, compassion, and personal responsibility is imperiled. Without these virtues, respect for the dignity of the human person, the first pillar of a decent society, will be undermined and sooner or later lost, for even the most laudable formal institutions cannot uphold respect for human dignity where people do not have the virtues that make that respect a reality and give it vitality in actual social practices.

Respect for the dignity of the human being requires more than formally sound institutions; it requires a cultural ethos in which people act from conviction to treat each other as human beings should be treated: with respect, civility, justice, compassion. The best legal and political institutions ever devised are of little value where selfishness, contempt for others, dishonesty, injustice, and other types of immorality and irresponsibility flourish. Indeed, the effective working of governmental institutions themselves depends upon most people most of the time obeying the law out of a sense of moral obligation, and not merely out of fear of detection and punishment for law-breaking. And perhaps it goes without saying that the success of business depends on there being reasonably virtuous, trustworthy, law-abiding, promise-keeping people to serve as workers and managers, lenders, regulators, and payers of bills for goods and services.

The third pillar of any decent society is a fair and effective system of law and government.[2] This is necessary because none of us is perfectly virtuous all the time, and some people will be deterred from wrongdoing only by the threat of punishment. More importantly, contemporary philosophers of law tell us the law coordinates human behavior for the sake of achieving common goals—the common good—especially in dealing with the complexities of modern

---

[1] On the profound and indispensable social role of marriage and the family, see George and Elshtain, 2006.

[2] See Finnis, 1980 esp. chs IX–XII; also see Finnis, 1998, esp. chs. VII–IX

life (see Finnis, 1998, esp. chs. VII and VIII). Even if all of us were perfectly virtuous all of the time, we would still need a system of laws (considered as a scheme of authoritatively stipulated coordination norms) to accomplish many of our common ends (safely transporting ourselves on the streets, for example).

The success of business firms and the economy as a whole depends vitally on a fair and effective system and set of institutions for the administration of justice. We need judges skilled in the craft of law and free of corruption. We need to be able to rely on courts to settle disputes, including disputes between parties who are both in good faith, and to enforce contracts and other agreements and enforce them in a timely manner. Indeed, the knowledge that contracts will be enforced is usually sufficient to ensure that courts will not actually be called on to enforce them. A sociological fact of which we can be certain is this: where there is no reliable system of the administration of justice—no confidence that the courts will hold people to their obligations under the law—business will not flourish, and everyone in the society will suffer.

A society can, in my opinion, be a decent one even if it is not a dynamic one, if the three pillars are healthy and functioning in a mutually supportive way (as they will do if each is healthy). Now, some people believe that a truly decent society cannot be a dynamic one. Dynamism, they believe, causes instability that undermines the pillars of a decent society. So some people, such as the Southern Agrarians, opposed not only industrialism but the very idea of a commercial society, fearing that commercial economies inevitably produce consumerist and acquisitive materialist attitudes that corrode the foundations of decency.[3] And some, such as some Amish communities, reject education for their children beyond what is necessary to master reading, writing, and arithmetic, on the ground that higher education leads to worldliness and apostasy and undermines religious faith and moral virtue.[4]

Although a decent society need not be a dynamic one (as the Amish example shows), dynamism need not erode decency. A dynamic society need not be one in which consumerism and materialism become rife and in which moral and spiritual values disappear. Indeed, dynamism can play a positive moral role and, I would

---

[3] On the thought of the Southern Agrarians, see Ransom, 2006, pp. xli–lii.

[4] On the educational philosophy of the Amish, see Hostetler, 1968, pp. 193–208; see also the Supreme Court's treatment of the case of the Amish in *Wisconsin v. Yoder*, 406 U.S. 205 (1972).

venture to say, almost certainly will play such a role where what makes it possible is sufficient to sustain it over the long term.

That is, I realize, a rather cryptic comment, so let me hasten to explain what I mean. To do that, I will have to offer some thoughts on what in fact makes social dynamism possible.

The two pillars of social dynamism are, first, institutions of research and education in which the frontiers of knowledge across in the humanities, social sciences, and natural sciences are pushed back, and through which knowledge is transmitted to students and disseminated to the public at large; and, second, business firms and associated institutions supporting them or managed in ways that are at least in some respects patterned on their principles, by which wealth is generated, distributed, and preserved.

We can think of universities and business firms, together with respect for the dignity of the human person, the institution of the family, and the system of law and government, as the five pillars of decent and dynamic societies. The university and the business firm depend in various ways for their well-being on the well-being of the others, and they can help to support the others in turn. At the same time, of course, ideologies and practices hostile to the pillars of a decent society can manifest themselves in higher education and in business and these institutions can erode the social values on which they themselves depend not only for their own integrity, but for their long-term survival.

Threatening Forces

It is all too easy to take the pillars for granted. So it is important to remember that each of them has come under attack from different angles and forces. Operating from within universities, persons and movements hostile to one or the other of these pillars, usually preaching or acting in the name of high ideals of one sort or another, have gone on the attack.

Attacks on business and the very idea of the market economy and economic freedom coming from the academic world are, of course, well known. Students are sometimes taught to hold business, and especially businessmen, in contempt as heartless exploiters driven by greed. In my own days as a student, these attacks were often made explicitly in the name of Marxism. One notices less of that after the collapse of the Soviet empire, but the attacks themselves have abated little.

Similarly, attacks on the family, and particularly on the institution of marriage on which the family is built, are common in the academy. The line here is that the family, at least as traditionally constituted and understood, is a patriarchal and exploitative institution that oppresses women and imposes on people forms of sexual restraint that are psychologically damaging and inhibiting of the free expression of their personality.[5] I believe that there is a real threat to the family here, one that must be taken seriously. The defense of marriage and the family in the public debate, including the debate within academia, is critical.

Some will counsel that business 'has no horse in this race'. They will say that it is a moral, cultural, and religious question about which business people as such need not concern themselves. The reality is that the rise of ideologies hostile to marriage and the family has had a measurable social impact, and its costs are counted in ruined relationships, damaged lives, and all that follows from these personal catastrophes. In many western nations, families are often failing to form and marriage is coming to be regarded as an optional 'life-style choice': one among various optional ways of conducting relationships and having and rearing children. Out of wedlock birthrates are very high, with the negative consequences of this particular phenomenon being borne less by the affluent than by those in the poorest and most vulnerable sectors of society. In 1965, the Harvard sociologist and later United States Senator Daniel Patrick Moynihan shocked Americans by reporting findings that the out-of-wedlock birth rate among African-Americans in the United States had reached nearly 25%. He warned that the phenomenon of boys and girls being raised without fathers in poorer communities would result in social pathologies that would severely harm those most in need of the supports of solid family life.[6] His predictions were all too quickly verified. The widespread failure of family formation portended disastrous social consequences of delinquency, despair, drug abuse, and crime and incarceration. A snowball effect resulted in the further growth of the out-of-wedlock birth rate. It is now 69%

---

[5] See, for example, Stacey, August 1993. See also Moller Okin, 1989, pp. 183–6, wherein the author, who before her death was a Professor of Political Science at Stanford University, argued in favor of "genderless" families.

[6] U.S. Department of Labor, Office of Planning and Research, *The Negro Family: The Case for National Action*, by Daniel Patrick Moynihan (Washington, DC: Government Printing Office, March 1965), http://www.dol.gov/oasam/programs/history/webid-meynihan.htm.

among African-Americans. It is worth noting that at the time of Moynihan's report, the out-of-wedlock birth rate for the population as a whole was almost 6%. Today, *that* rate is at nearly 40%.[7]

And these figures are only a small part of the larger story. Many family scholars are observing with particular interest the relationship in Europe between social and legal changes pertaining to marriage and the family, on the one hand, and the decline of birth rates to the point of near demographic collapse on the other. There are fascinating and important issues here, issues of obvious social and economic significance, that deserve rigorous sociological study.[8]

You will have no trouble surmising the consequences for business of these developments. Consider the need of business to have available to it a responsible and capable work force. Business cannot manufacture honest, hard working people to employ. Nor can government create them by law. Businesses depend on there being many such people, but they must rely on the family, assisted by religious communities and other institutions of civil society, to produce them. So business has a stake in the health of the family. It should avoid doing anything to undermine the family, and it should do what it can where it can to strengthen the institution.

As an advocate of dynamic societies, I believe in the market economy and the free enterprise system. I particularly value the social mobility that economic dynamism makes possible. At the same time, I am not a supporter of the laissez-faire doctrine embraced by strict libertarians. I believe that law and government do have important and, indeed, indispensable roles to play in regulating enterprises for the sake of protecting public health, safety, and morals, preventing exploitation and abuse, and promoting fair competitive circumstances of exchange. But these roles are compatible, I would insist, with the ideal of limited government and the principle of subsidiarity according to which government must respect individual initiative to the extent reasonably possible and avoid violating the autonomy and usurping the authority of families, religious communities, and other institutions of civil society that play the primary role in building character and transmitting virtues.

Having said that, I would warn that limited government — considered as an ideal as vital to business as to the family — cannot be main-

---

[7] Report of the National Centers for Disease Control and Prevention: http://www.cdc.gov/nchs/data/databriefs/db18.htm/
[8] On Europe's demographic challenges, see Carlson, 2005.

tained where the marriage culture collapses and families fail to form or easily dissolve. Where these things happen, the health, education, and welfare functions of the family will have to be undertaken by someone, or some institution, and that will sooner or later be the government (George & Elshtain, 2006, pp. 172–96). To deal with pressing social problems, bureaucracies will grow, and with them the tax burden. Moreover, the growth of crime and other pathologies where family breakdown is rampant will result in the need for more extensive policing and incarceration and, again, increased taxes to pay for these government services. If we want limited government, and a level of taxation that is not unduly burdensome, we need healthy institutions of civil society, beginning with a flourishing marriage culture supporting family formation and preservation.

Business's Contributions

I will close with some brief reflections on the ways in which I believe that business has historically contributed to the strength of the other four pillars of decent and dynamic societies. While it is true that some business firms have exploited workers, many firms have enhanced the dignity of individuals by offering challenging and decently paid jobs, providing opportunities for further education, either on the job or in training programs, and encouraging workers to think creatively about how to improve the quality of products and services and the efficiency of production and delivery. Moreover, business has made upward economic and social mobility possible for countless persons. The free enterprise system has given many people the freedom to pursue fulfilling and remunerative careers that would have been unimaginable as options for their grandparents, and provided opportunities for them to become entrepreneurs and investors. Whole societies have been made better off by economic growth produced by market economies. Businesses and successful business leaders and investors have helped to relieve poverty and have advanced many good causes through their charitable giving, and even when government rather than business supplies the money, it is business that is generating the wealth that government distributes.

While some business firms, it is true, have been involved in corruption and have even stimulated it, it is also true that business has in many places been in the forefront of demanding reform of corrupt courts and governmental agencies. Business leaders have helped to shape laws and policies that are suitable for modern systems of production and exchange, and that will enable us to meet the challenges of the globalized economy.

Notwithstanding the hostility to business in some sectors of academia and the elite intellectual culture, businesses and business leaders have been instrumental in supporting education at every level, especially higher education. This is particularly true in the United States, where the tradition of alumni giving is strong and where colleges and universities depend upon it, but it is true in Europe and elsewhere, too. Even where the overwhelming bulk of financial support is provided by governments, it is once again important to remember that governments obtain most of the money they spend through taxation, and taxation at the levels necessary to support modern universities is possible only as a result of the successful efforts of businesses.

So business is a pillar of decent and dynamic societies, it can and must support the other pillars, and it depends on them for its own flourishing. For these reasons, I hope that business leaders, entrepreneurs, and investors will turn their minds to the question of what they can contribute to the cause of upholding marriage and the family in the face of great threats. What business leaders have done in other domains let them now do in defense of this distinctively human and uniquely humanizing institution. Just as the family has a stake in business, which, after all, provides employment and compensation, and which generates economic prosperity and with it social mobility, business has a stake in the family. This will be clear, I believe, if we adopt the 'panoramic, long term view', and follow out (if I may borrow Professor Khurana's phrase) the logic of stewardship.

Bibliography

Anders, George (September 2007), "Business Schools Forgetting Missions?" *Wall Street Journal*, Eastern Edition. Sec. A. p. 1, The Economy.

Carlson, Allan (2005), "Sweden and the Failure of European Family Policy", paper presented at the forum of Focus on the Family entitled "The Family as the Foundation for Social and Economic Development", Washington, DC, 27 July 2005, http://www.profam.org/docs/acc/thc.acc.050727.fof.sweden.htm.

Finnis, John (1980), *Natural Law and Natural Rights* (Oxford: Clarendon Press).

Finnis, John (1998), *Aquinas: Moral, Political, and Legal Theory* (Oxford: Oxford University Press).

George, Robert P. and Elshtain, Jean Bethke, eds. (2006), *The Meaning of Marriage* (Dallas, TX: Spence Publishing Company).

Hostetler, John Andrew (1968), *Amish Society* (Baltimore, MD.: Johns Hopkins Press)

Khurana, Rakesh (2007), *From Higher Aims to Hired Hands: The Social Transformation of American Business Schools and the Unfulfilled Promise of Management as a Profession* (Princeton, NJ: Princeton University Press).

Okin, Susan Moller (1989), *Justice, Gender, and the Family* (New York: HarperCollins, Basic Books)

Ransom, John Crowe et al. (2006), *I'll Take My Stand: The South and the Agrarian Tradition* (New York: Harper, 1930; reprint, with a new introduction by Susan V. Donaldson, Baton Rouge, LA: Louisiana State University Press).

Stacey, Judith (August 1993), "Good Riddance to 'the Family': A Reply to David Popenoe", *Journal of Marriage and the Family* 55, pp. 545–7.

Anthony Daniels

Management and the Corporate State
Private Enterprise Without Enterprise, and Public Service Without Service?

He who would understand the current state of the British public administration must read three authors: Gogol for the absurdity, Kafka for the menace, and Orwell for the mendacity and distortion of language.

From the authors cited, it will be apparent that I will give a descriptive rather than a scientific analysis of the phenomena with which I propose to deal. In any case, it is one of the consequences of the managerialism that now dominates the public administration that the very statistics upon which a scientific account might be based have been deeply corrupted by the very process to be analyzed. The covering of its traces is one of the achievements of managerialism in the British public service.

I will start with a concrete example. In Britain, approximately 95% of healthcare, nearly 100% of emergency services, is funded by the government from general taxation. Thus, if public expresses dissatisfaction with the healthcare it receives, the government is in a very exposed position. He who lives by an assumed responsibility dies by an assumed responsibility.

In the event of public dissatisfaction, therefore, the government can do one or more of several things: it can face the public down with counter-propaganda, it can abandon the whole government-funded system on the grounds that it caused the dissatisfaction in the first place, it can improve the system, it can engage in a lot of distracting activity that makes it very difficult to assess what is actually happening, or it can find a scapegoat. In practice, the latter two are the most expedient, because the easiest, though it is possible that they are engaged upon without conscious intention to deceive.

Here it is worth pointing out that successive British governments have become prisoners, as well as beneficiaries, of an historical myth: that before the institution of the National Health Service there was no healthcare provision for the poor, or none to speak of. In fact, more hospitals were built in the economically depressed years of the 1930s than in the first third century of the existence of the National Health Service (NHS) during times, be it remembered, of general and sometimes unprecedented economic expansion. Shortly after the institution of the NHS, in 1952–53, capital expenditure on hospitals was less than a third of what it had been in 1938–39 (Willman, 1998, p. 54). This is not the place to recall the often glorious history of Britain's voluntary hospitals, expropriated by the state in 1948; suffice it to say that the historical myth is the ultimate justification for the monopolistic state-run system in place today, a myth that has been swallowed whole by the population and that has therefore become an important political factor. In human affairs, you can never get away (even should you for some reason want to do so) from the role of ideas.

The government, wanting to demonstrate its paternal or avuncular concern for the well-being of its wards, the people, and aware that attendance at hospital in an emergency in Britain is a far more unpleasant experience than it need be or is in other, similarly developed countries, thanks to the long delays, decreed that henceforth no member of the public should wait more than four hours after his arrival in the hospital for a place in a hospital bed for further investigations or treatment, should he need it. Furthermore, hospitals would henceforth be judged, and financially rewarded or penalized, and the managers likewise, according to the degree to which they met this target.

The slightest familiarity, actual or theoretical, with the Soviet experience should have been more than sufficient for any sensible person to predict exactly what would happen next. In a highly centralized and bureaucratic system, with no possibility of external monitoring, the main product of targets is lies. Indeed, it makes of lying and all its variants the queen of the sciences, and the key to career advancement and even survival (though in practice a bureaucracy usually looks after its own, and a bureaucrat fired from one position can usually be found a niche somewhere else in the system soon afterwards). The result of target-setting is thus lying organized on an industrial scale, with the concomitant destruction or deformation of the human personality.

The solution adopted by one very famous hospital was ingenious, though very simple. Like patients who want to find reasons for not doing what the doctor suggests, bureaucrats who have never previously evinced any obvious signs of creativity can be induced by their situation to think very nimbly and very fast. The solution was this: that no patient brought to the hospital in an ambulance was to be allowed out of the vehicle into the hospital until such time as he could be guaranteed a bed within the four hours stipulated, should he need one.

The inconveniences of this manner of proceeding, from the point of view of the ostensible purposes of both hospitals and ambulances, may readily be imagined. Perhaps for the first time in the history of the world there was a traffic jam that consisted entirely and solely of ambulances. Since the supply of ambulances in the district was what economists call inelastic, the traffic jam led to delays further upstream in the flow of emergency patients to the hospital. But the target was met, and that was the important thing.

The managers of other hospital adopted different tactics, proving that variety is still possible even in the most centralized of systems. Henceforth, hospital trolleys in corridors upon which patients were required to wait, sometimes for 24 hours or longer before a hospital bed became available to them, were redesignated hospital beds and the corridors as extensions to the wards. Thus was the target laid down by the central power met with triumphant ease, though without any improvement in the service from the worm's eyeview.

Of course, Britain is still a relatively free country, where comment and the exposure of problems are concerned, and publicity was soon given to the practices. The managers then found themselves in a situation in which the four-hour rule, as it was called, had to be obeyed in reality rather than virtually, at least if the target was to be met and the financial rewards obtained and the penalties avoided. The consequences were even worse.

For the first time managers appeared both in emergency rooms and in the wards, in the former to sniff out any patients who, in the technical argot that soon developed, were in danger of breaching the rule, and in the wards to seek out any patients who, in their opinion, might be fit for discharge, at least in the sense that they would not die immediately or embarrassingly soon after they were pushed out of urgency, if not of outright panic, not according to any medical criteria, but purely to increase compliance with bureaucratic imperatives.

One anecdote is worth a thousand statistics, at least in a situation in which the statistics, for reasons that I have hinted at, are completely unreliable and corrupted. A junior doctor of my acquaintance was called to a ward to attend to a patient in need of the most urgent care; but while he was engaged upon saving his life, he was told by a nurse that he was needed in the emergency room because a patient there had been waiting for nearly four hours and was about to 'breach the rule.'

He decided that a human life was worth more than compliance with a rule, and continued his efforts at resuscitation. He received a second, more urgent message, in the form of an order from a manager, which he likewise ignored. When he had finished with the patient who survived he discovered that the manager had moved the patient into a ward on his own authority.

When the junior doctor went to that ward, he discovered that there had been no medical imperative for the patient to be admitted at all, and he discharged him. The manger, far from being abashed, was delighted by the outcome, and felt vindicated. For the patient's short stay in hospital would improve the statistics overall, and make the hospital look even more efficient in the eyes of the central power, which of course would have no knowledge of the cruel absurdity of at least one 'successful' hospital episode.

I could continue almost indefinitely with illustrations drawn from my own experience. I will, however, give only one more. The government, claiming to wish to reassure the public about the level of competence of the medical profession though in reality doing (if not intending to do) the precise opposite, namely raise doubts about its competence and fitness to practice because the profession, like all other professions, constitutes an alternative source of authority to the government's own instituted a system of annual appraisals of senior doctors such as I. The annual appraisal consists of a visit by another senior doctor who is required to ask the appraisee certain pro forma questions. (There are now doctors in the NHS who derive a considerable income from performing such appraisals on family doctors: every regulation is an income opportunity.)

One of the questions to be asked is, 'Are there any concerns about your probity?' The first time I was asked this question, I told my appraiser that I would answer it on condition that he would answer two questions beforehand. He asked what they were.

The first is 'What kind of person would answer such a question?' And the second is, 'What kind of person would ask it?'

The appraiser saw my point at once. We were both knowingly taking part in a process in whose virtue or necessity neither of us believed, but only because it had been mandated by authority as a condition of continued employment, and it was therefore easier to comply than to object. This was bad enough for our sense of our own integrity; but the actual question itself set about brilliantly to destroy the very quality that it was supposedly to enquire about, both of the person who asked and of the person who answered. I know of no doctor who did and does not feel demeaned by the whole time-consuming process, and who does not despise himself, at least a little, for having unresistingly co-operated in it. And professionals who despise themselves are easier to co-opt, coerce, and corrupt than those who retain a sturdy sense of their own independence and probity (though, of course, this too can be exaggerated).

I need hardly point out that the question arises whether my anecdotes are emblematic or representative of widespread processes, or are merely tales of absurdity and malfeasance such as could have been, and have been, told throughout the ages. There is, perhaps, a law of the conservation of absurdity, or at least of discontent, that means that complaint is the one permanent mode of thought about human affairs.

Nevertheless, precisely the kind of complaints I have just made are now made by virtually all the professions in all branches of the public service in Britain. No branch is exempt. Compliance with absurdity or worse is exacted as the price of preferment (which is often very lucrative), dissent or opposition is punished by career stagnation. This, of course, has a leveling effect and promotes groupthink, or at least group-speech, but it also creates the atmosphere of fear that is the natural consequence of a lack of freedom. Self-disgust renders participants ill-equipped to criticize, much less to refuse, orders. They are reduced to apparatchiks, however distinguished in their field they might otherwise be.

The prevalence of the malaise is illustrated by a recent survey of workers in the NHS in Scotland, 80% of whom said that they had been bullied at work, principally by their near and distant managers who, of course, were themselves among the 80% who felt they had been bullied. Of course, the promotion and encouragement of fragility of feeling is one of the ways by which managers increase and maintain their power, and create what is for them a desirable and necessary atmosphere of conflict and anxiety, such that the people under their control are forever looking over their shoulder; for fragility of feeling leads to complaint, and complaint leads to the need for adjudication, and thus to power for the adjudicators.

For example, the definition of bullying adopted by many institutions requires no objective correlates: a person has been bullied if he thinks he has. This results in the creation of a Foucaultian world in which questions of fact are entirely replaced by questions of power and correlates of forces. Extensive and time-consuming investigations are carried out as if they were to establish matters of fact, investigations that not only divert resources from the ostensible but by now secondary purposes of the organization to those of management, but are used to undermine or destroy the authority of those who would once have been considered authoritative because of their intelligence, knowledge, and experience. In other words, a transfer of power has been effected, from a relatively stable and defined professional hierarchy to an unstable, amorphous, and shifting one, whose members themselves live in constant fear and are never allowed to grow institutional roots.

Pride in institutions is another target of managerial destruction: hospitals in the NHS, some of them with very long and distinguished pre-NHS histories, and to which people in the past dedicated their entire working lives, are now merged, de-merged, re-merged, changed in function, closed and re-opened with what would appear insouciance, were it not that insouciance implies a certain light-heartedness, which is not a characteristic of managerialist culture (I use the term CULTURE in its anthropological sense).

Here, for example, is a small straw in the wind: hospitals in the NHS once had their own logos or heraldic devices on their notepaper, but were instructed, by fiat of the Department of Health, to abandon them all and replace them with a generic symbol of the NHS. It is difficult to develop a loyalty to a giant and diffused organization, and in the new circumstances, no one would make the mistake of developing a powerful emotional attachment to his institution or fail to regard it other than as a mere, and perhaps temporary, source of employment. Such pride as still exists in institutions is a shrinking asset of cultural capital.

A Social Revolution

I come now to the question of the origins of what, in my opinion, is a social revolution. Since societies and their histories are seamless robes, it would be both fruitless and ridiculous to attempt to be too precise in this matter. James Burnham noted many of the changes 60 years ago in *The Managerial Revolution*, and his theory was not entirely original even then (Burnham, 1941). The fact is, however, that change has occurred in the British public administration at an accelerated rate in the last quarter century or thereabouts; and I will now speculate on the possible reasons for this, without the hope or expectation of being definitive.

There is the realm of ideas and the realm of interests; the relationship between the two realms is dialectical.

First I want to draw attention to what might be called the sociologization of thought (the fact that I can use such a locution is an indication of how far the process has gone). Human behavior has come less and less to be understood as the result of choice based upon conscious reflection, however fleeting, and more and more as the vector of forces acting upon people, forces of which they may be unaware, and which in any case they are powerless to alter or affect, much less control. Whether this attitude is justified or not, from the purely intellectual point of view it clearly confers upon supra-individual authority, in effect, government increased responsibilities. The government has not merely the right but the duty to read just the forces acting upon people so that they may behave in a better way. Thus is the stage set for the advance of managerialism.

At the same time, there has been a concerted intellectual attack on the very notion of public service. The charge is not merely that public service in practice often fails to serve the public; it is that the very idea is virtually meaningless, or logically incoherent, since every individual in the public service must act in his own interests. The so-called public interest, then, is but a smokescreen for private and sectional interest.

On this view, bureaucracies inevitably increase their own power and extent, the better to appropriate economic resources, because that is what individuals invariably do. As for professions, they are all what George Bernard Shaw called conspiracies against the laity (Shaw, 1911). The motive of the conspiracy, of course, is self-interest: driving up the price of the services provided, behind a smokescreen of concern for professional standards and so forth.

Unfortunately, for political and other reasons, there is an ineradicable need for a public service in modern societies: none is without one. Its size and scope of activities will vary according to the particular circumstances of each country, but no country can eliminate the state sector entirely. How, then, to ensure that the public service actually serves, that is to say, pursues the interest of the tax-paying public rather than its own interest? The question is more urgent the larger the public-service sector becomes.

The solution adopted in Britain or perhaps I should say the pseudo-solution is managerialism, that is to say, control by management. A cadre of managers armed with techniques that are applicable to all institutions whatsoever (management being an abstract science), had to be created. It would discipline the organizations that it managed, that had hitherto retained an amateurish independence that left them free to be inefficient and act in their own interests. The cadre of managers would be disciplined in turn by the setting of targets by what one might call the meta-managers, that is to say, the government.

There was one small problem with this scheme: there was no independent criterion by which the success or failure of the newly managed institutions could be measured, and that was not provided by the managers themselves. We have already seen how easily statistics could be manipulated in a centralized system. The only limit placed upon intellectual dishonesty was that of public unrest, more likely to be aroused by some bad services than by others. For example, there would soon be a public outcry if the emergency services of a hospital failed utterly to succor the ill and the injured, but leaving the children of the poor unable to read or write properly evokes no such protest, and therefore it was (and is) done. The illiteracy rate in Britain is approximately 25%, despite expenditures on education four times higher in real terms than in 1950 (Phillips, 1997).

But this is not the end of the matter. Once in control of the budgets, the cadre of managers found themselves in a position to loot them without fear of legal reprisal. In effect, corruption was legalized, though it was corruption of a peculiarly insidious kind. This happened in both small ways and big. The managers were able to spend large, indeed vast, sums of money on contracting allegedly private and independent services, particularly in the field of consulting, allegedly in the pursuit of perfect or 100% efficiency.

Increased efficiency, of course, required increased quantities of information, and also information systems to process them. Without information, improvements in efficiency could not be measured. But since it was obviously necessary to make all parts of the system equally efficient, the gathering of information became not only a priority, but a task of Sisyphus. Indeed, you could never have enough information; and this had the happy consequence that the numbers of people employed in such administrative tasks had to grow. Another happy consequence was the provision of a rationale for the perpetual interference in the work of professions, whose diversion to non-professional tasks necessitated ever tighter or more stringent management.

Let us return to the phenomenon of consultancy, and world where (in its dealing with government) nothing succeeds like failure. One day my secretary, a woman who had spent forty years as secretary to various doctors, and who was due to retire in three weeks' time, was told by her manager that she had to attend a day's course on how to answer the telephone. She was, in fact, both efficient and obliging; had she not been, it would have been a little late in the day to try to train her. Attendance was compulsory.

What was the meaning of this curious, but in my view emblematic, little incident? In all probability, the organizers of the course were a consultancy firm contracted by the hospital. It the firm would be able to charge according to the number of people attending, so why take the risk of inflating the numbers when it was so easy to ensure real numbers? It was also highly likely that the owners of the allegedly private enterprise running the courses were actually former members of the public service known to the managers of the hospital. Certainly, something has become very common that only a few years previously would have been unthinkable: that the families of high-echelon bureaucrats had interests in consultancy firms whose sole business was consulting with the public service. All corrupt, but perfectly legal.

It must not be imagined that this is a minor phenomenon, or confined to a small scale. A book recently published, titled *Plundering the Public Sector*, suggests that in Britain scores of billions of dollars have been expended on useless consultancies in the last decade, without any obvious improvement (and obvious improvement is the only improvement worth speaking of, since subtle improvements are easily manufactured by statistical legerdemain) in what is provided to the public (Craig & Brooks, 2006).

Corporatist Society

The results are these. A very considerable number of people become directly dependent on managerialism in the public service for their comfortable livelihood. (The expansion of the managerial class also helps to absorb the ever-growing numbers of people with non-vocational degrees produced by our universities, who might otherwise, if unemployed, be a focus of serious and dangerous discontent.) This creates an extremely prosperous and nominally private sub-sector within the private sector, one that is actually utterly dependent on the favors of government and is in turn supportive of the government. In other words, society becomes increasingly corporatist.

Apart from the economic inefficiencies of the system, by far the worst effect is on the human personality. Intellectual and moral dishonesty becomes necessary for survival, and because most people are not by nature scoundrels, who do wrong with open eyes and a glad heart, their very souls undergo deformation. In addition, genuinely talented people suffer frustration and humiliation.

Several important questions are raised by my observations. First, are the processes I have indicated unique to the public service? Second, are they inherent to the enterprise of management itself? Third, if they are not, how are they to be controlled?

I have little doubt that the public service is peculiarly but not uniquely susceptible to the pathologies I have indicated, in large part because it is so difficult to measure success or failure objectively, and because in any case the measurement is largely in the hands of those whose success is being measured. The French Ministry of National Education, for example, which controls the highly centralized French education system, claims great success because more than 80% of children now pass the baccalaureate, whereas only 5% did so in 1910. But since the ministry itself sets the standards required to pass, and changes them constantly from year to year, the real meaning of this 'success' is difficult to assess (Pitte, 2007). Procedurally, perhaps, it is a success, but socially and educationally it is a disaster.

The replacement of real goals by procedural goals is easier in the public service than in the private sector, since in the private sector, absent creative accounting, the balance sheet provides an objective measure of success or failure. When commercial companies become too large, however, no doubt the relation between profit and the activity of large numbers of employees becomes more doubtful, and there is the temptation to replace real goals with procedural ones.

Certainly, I find dealing with my bank just as frustrating, and for the same reasons, as dealing with Social Services on behalf of a patient.

When management becomes a skill and career in itself, unconnected to any other skill or body of specific knowledge, the pathologies will increase. It is essential in the public service that people with technical skills and knowledge should retain considerable powers over management, and not the other way round. Furthermore, there should be considerable oversight from unpaid volunteers in the running of public institutions. This for two main reasons: first, the great majority of professionals, precisely because they have to deal with practical problems faced by actual people, retain a preference for real rather than procedural results, and second, because volunteer overseers have no vested interest in increasing their own powers or the size of their staffs. Public institutions therefore need not professional, but amateur management (which is not the same as amateurish management, of course).

A public service that actually serves will not be produced by bureaucratic control. In the absence of electoral oversight, esprit de corps is the essential quality of such a service. This is not a quality found in giant, centralized organizations, but only in smaller, partially independent ones. Only a degree of trust that most people left alone will try to do a good job is compatible with the independence of public organizations. Managerialism, however, is the firm enemy of esprit de corps. In the prison in which I worked, for example, I was able to encourage the wardens to go beyond their strict duty in assisting me precisely because I ignored completely a specific management directive not to give the wardens any medical advice or treatment. The power of managers in the public service depends upon the formalization of all procedures and relationships, and thus sees esprit de corps not as an asset but as a liability.

In dealing with managers who pass on orders from higher up the command chain, I have often asked them 'What is the instruction that you would refuse to obey on the grounds that it was unethical, or even just harmful to the service?' They have never been able to answer; and the history of the Twentieth Century is not encouraging in this regard. The dangers of unethical obedience to orders is less in decentralized organizations, and where there are fewer monopolies.

In Britain, at any rate, managerialism is triumphant. The great Hungarian writer Sandor Marai published a memoir which begins with the last bourgeois dinner party in Budapest before the arrival of the Red Army. There were fourteen people around the table; there was not much to eat but a little to drink. One of the guests was an enthusiast of the Nazis, and he said that the Hungarians should support their allies to the bitter end. Marai, who was not a Nazi sympathizer, asked him why.

'It's all right for you', replied the Nazi enthusiast. 'You have talent. But we, who have no talent, we need the Nazis.' And as he left the dinner party, he turned to Marai and said, 'Remember, the future belongs to the untalented' (paraphrasing Marai, 2004).

Managerialism is the fulfillment of this prophecy.

Bibliography

Burnham, James (1941), *The Managerial Revolution: What is Happening in the World* (New York: John Day).

Craig, David and Brooks, Richard (2006), *Plundering the Public Sector* (London: Constable and Robinson).

Marai, Sandor (2004), *Memoires de Hongrie* (Paris: Albin Michel).

Phillips, Melanie (1997), *All Must Have Prizes,* (London: Little, Brown).

Pitte, Jean-Robert (2007), *Stop a l'arnaque du bac* (Paris: Editions Oh!).

Shaw, George Bernard (1911), "The Doctor's Dilemma" in *The Doctor's Dilemma, Getting Married, and the Shewing-Up of Blanco Posnet* (London: Constable).

Willman, John (1998), *A Better State of Health* (London: Profile Books).

Wilfred M. McClay

A Strategic Humanist

George Keller, Academic Strategy, and the Management Revolution in American Higher Education

When the humanistic disciplines in particular are in massive disarray, and seem to have lost both their morale and their sense of purpose, perhaps the world of ideas needs a stiff dose of a reality principle that the experiences of business and organizational management can (in their better moments) administer. Of course, faculty in American higher education see the very concept of 'management' as a synonym for manipulation and control, intrinsically inapplicable to the unique work of higher education, and often for good reason.

There is undeniably a certain blend of sentimentalism and self-interestedness lurking behind such suspicion, but there is also something genuine at stake. When the U.S. Department of Education clumsily intrudes itself in the work of higher education to demand standardization of educational 'outputs', as it has recently in the infamous Spellings Report, it misunderstands the character of the very activity it is attempting to regulate and improve.[1] Manage-

[1] U.S. Department of Education, *A Test of Leadership: Charting the Future of U.S. Higher Education*, by the Commission appointed by Secretary of Education Margaret Spellings (Washington, DC, 2006), September 2006, http://www.ed.gov/about/bdscomm/list/hiedfuture/reports/final-report.pdf. The Spellings Report elicited many howls of displeasure from academics who dislike the notion of accountability itself, but for an exemplary response that raises the deeper issues in a memorable way, see the response by Christopher B. Nelson, President of St. John's College (Annapolis), "Remarks before the Cato Institute Forum on the Spellings Commission Report", St. John's College, remarks presented at the Cato Institute Policy Forum entitled "Ivory Tower Overload: How to Fix

ment, rightly understood, is an activity tailored to the thing being managed, and the objectives being sought. Improperly used, however, it is either an obfuscation, which uses high-flown quasi-technical language to conceal the true nature of one's acts, or a form of reductionism, which mistakenly treats the activity of an educational institution as if it were that of an assembly line or a service industry. One must always use the tools appropriate to the task at hand, and one's objective must be the bringing forth of institutional fruit proper to its kind.

Energy in the Executive

David Riesman's 1968 book *The Academic Revolution*, co-authored with Christopher Jencks, identified the rise of the independent power of the faculty, particularly as embodied in the trans-institutional disciplines, as the single most notable change in the structure of modern academia (Jencks & Riesman, 1968). But his identification of that change was far from being a celebration of it. Indeed, by the end of his career Riesman had become convinced that recovery of responsible executive power, and particularly of presidential power, was absolutely essential to the improvement of American higher education. Riesman is well-known as a thinker of extraordinarily wide-ranging interests, whose magnum opus, *The Lonely Crowd* (1950), with its celebrated account of the transformation of American social character in the twentieth century, remains one of the classic works of American sociology (Reisman et al., 1950, see McClay, 1998). Less well-known is the fact that the bulk of his activities from the Fifties onward revolved around the subject of American higher education, and more particularly, by the end of his career, around the college and university presidency, and in the search processes through which such executive position are filled.[2] He was unusual in his understanding of, and sympathy with, the unique problems faced by university presidents, and his impatience with the shortsightedness and turf-defensiveness of faculties. But such sympathy flowed from a larger conviction about the institutional needs of the modern university. He believed that a more general recovery of energy and confidence in the executive office would be essential to the flourishing of academic institutions in the late twen-

---

American Higher Ed", Washington, DC, 27 September 2006, http://www.stjohnscollege.edu/about/resources/06cato.pdf.

[2] See Riesman, 1956, on educational diversity; on the presidency, see McLaughlin and Riesman, 1990, and Levin, 1993.

tieth century and beyond. And such recovery would surely entail a renewed respect, however grudging, for the peculiar skills and insights that go under the rubric of 'management'.

This was, and is, a hard sell. In all too many academic circles, where the permanent antagonism of faculty and administration is regarded as an essential and unchanging fact of life, as permanent as the law of universal gravitation, it is particularly verboten to speak in positive tones about 'modern management' and the administrators who employ it. Consider this not-unrepresentative statement from a 1970 article in the journal *Daedalus*:

> Trustees, presidents, deans, registrars, secretaries, janitors, and the like are not, strictly speaking, part of the university at all... They are ancillary to the real business of the university (Caws, 1970, p. 98).

Few go as far as did Thorstein Veblen, who concluded his influential study, *The Higher Learning in America,* by declaring airily that

> as seen from the point of view of the higher learning, the academic executive and all his works are anathema, and should be discontinued by the simple expedient of wiping him off the slate; and ... the governing board, in so far as it presumes to exercise any other than vacantly perfunctory duties, has the same value and should with advantage be lost in the same shuffle (Veblen, 1918, p. 286).

Such fantasized final solutions, however, reflect the self-delusions of people who never have to imagine how food appears on the table in front of them, or how a signed and non-bouncing check appears in their mailbox at the end of every month, and never give any serious thought to the vast number of institutional supports that they need, simply to be able to do what they do, and to the vast amounts of work, contributed by people performing all kinds of different and non-scholarly tasks, that are required for the institution simply to exist. It is, frankly, the height of narcissism to imagine that the work one does oneself is the *only* work that matters. But the existence of such narcissism is a central peril, not only of academia, and not only of all large bureaucratic organizations, but it is a peril inherent in the division of labor itself, and forms the basis for one of the greatest of all challenges faced by any manager, particularly a good and conscientious and effective one.

This is bound to be true in any organization, no matter its size. In the most ideal settings, the good manager wants to find a way to educate the parts of the organization about one another, so that the organization can maximize the productive benefits of specialized labor without suffering from the impoverishing sense that the parts are permanently set against one another. Such management can no longer be an act of propagandistic mystification, undergirded by constant pep talks and false personalization. We are too suspicious for that, and rightly so. Instead, it needs to seek to expand the knowledge and imaginative apparatus of all workers, not least in helping them understand and appreciate what other members of the organization are doing, and convincing them of the humanizing benefits of living and working in combination with one another—in short, of seeing one's work as an element in the larger life of a collective enterprise.

There will of course be many times when such imaginative expansion is simply not possible. Janitors cannot really comprehend the life-position and work of professors, and vice versa, and many employees simply have neither the desire nor the detachment to understand the other person's problems. Management's task is then one of containment and channeling and temporizing, finding humane ways to contain and deflect and divert the frictions and resentments and conflicts and mutual incomprehensions that inevitably arise in organizational life. In short, to keep the peace and keep the machinery humming. Allowing for such realities, however, we may find it more useful here to think about more ideal situations, precisely because those offer the greatest promise of general reform, something higher education stands in need of. Institutions of higher education promote the human aspiration toward higher ideals, and we should be able to look to them hopefully as exemplars of those ideals and the possibility of realizing them more generally.

A Managerial Answer

How to restimulate thinking about organizational ideals is always a problem, but perhaps especially so in the field of higher education, where the processes of hiring and firing are so convoluted and problematic, where the activities of employees are often so individualistic and tenuously related to the organizational whole, and where organizational objectives themselves are often obscure, even nonexistent. But there has to be a way in which sensible techniques of management can be introduced into such a field without vitiating its core values. The insightful work of educational analyst George Keller, whose death in February 2007 at a very youthful seventy-eight was a very great loss to the cause of educational reform, throws an uncommonly bright light on the subject, although the tasks he set for higher education remain largely unfinished, and even untried.

Keller was a true believer in the high democratic calling of education. Indeed, one could find few better examples of the transformative potential of American higher education than Keller himself, the son of a Latvian father and south-German mother, born in 1928 in working-class Union City, New Jersey, whose life would be changed forever by his encounter with Columbia University, and with the likes of Jacques Barzun and Lionel Trilling, first as a student and later as a colleague and assistant dean. That special milieu of mid-century Columbia, and the lofty vision of higher education it promoted, became his ladder to a wider and richer world, and he never ceased to be grateful for it.

He wanted the same ladders, and also many more various ones, to be available to the coming generations of Americans. Higher education was for him nothing less than an expression of the promise of America itself, in institutional form. Small wonder that he was regularly asked by the citizens of Dickeyville, the charming restored mill town in Maryland where he and his wife, Jane, made their home for the past three decades, to deliver the town's Patriotic Declamation presented on the Fourth of July, a task he gladly performed in 2006 for what he knew would be his last time. It was all of one piece for him. He loved working in higher education because he was an American patriot, and loved his country because of the opportunities for self-transformation it affords.

Keller's *curriculum vitae* was lengthy and unusually diverse, including service as professor and chair of the program in higher education studies at the University of Pennsylvania's Graduate School of Education and as editor of *Planning,* the quarterly journal of the Society for College and University Planning, as well as a stint as a strategic-planning consultant at the Barton-Gillet Company in Baltimore. After retiring from Penn in 1994, he worked as a freelance consultant and writer in higher education, helping to create the journal *University Business* and producing several notable books, including his forthcoming *Higher Education and the New Society,* to be published by the Johns Hopkins University Press.

But his most lasting achievement was his influential 1983 book *Academic Strategy: The Management Revolution in Higher Education,* also published by Johns Hopkins. Crisp and luminous, *Academic Strategy* was the right book at the right time, and few involved in higher-education administration during the 1980s did not find their lives touched and their thinking affected by it. It sold out its first printing in ten weeks, has gone through six more printings, and was named, in a poll of college and university presidents, as the decade's most influential book of its kind. It remains in print, continues to sell steadily, and was even recently translated into Chinese—a clear indication that its value transcends the conditions it was written to address. It has become a canonical text of higher-education management.

Why did a book on such an unsexy subject strike such a chord? It is easy to forget, in these relatively flush times, when announcements of multi-million-dollar capital campaigns are as common as fireflies on a summer night, what a sense of impending doom was then hovering in the air in the late Seventies and early Eighties. 'A spectre is haunting higher education', Keller declared, voicing the sentiments of many, 'the spectre of decline and bankruptcy' (Keller, 1983, p. 3). After many years in which its chief troubles had been those brought on by rampaging growth, American higher education was suddenly in the grip of an entirely different set of difficulties, the characteristic problems of contraction and limitation: declining enrollments, increased competition, ever-inflating costs, diminishing governmental support (with ever more plentiful strings attached to it), and shifting priorities among those who were increasingly being regarded as higher education's 'customers.' The very future of many traditional institutions, especially the venerable but chronically under-endowed American liberal arts colleges, was clearly in jeopardy. But the outlook for even the most well-heeled institutions was suddenly uncertain at best.

The only enduring solution to these problems, Keller argued, would lie in taking a more vigorous and focused approach to the management of academic institutions, using tactics and objectives that could only be developed on an individualized, institution-by-institution basis. His book attempted to explain what such an approach would mean in practice, and the difference it could make.

To begin with, it would mean acknowledging that one size did not fit all. It no longer made sense—if, indeed, it ever had—to treat all institutions of higher learning as if they were essentially the same, and were expected to accomplish the same things and meet the same standards in the same ways. Nor, it need hardly be said, did it make sense anymore to treat the large, expensive, complex, and heavily capitalized modern university as if it were a genteel and genially ramshackle operation, to be governed casually and inattentively, if at all.

Instead, the future flourishing of vulnerable higher-educational institutions would depend upon their ability to identify their particular areas of comparative advantage — the things they did best — and then seek, in a highly conscious and methodical way, to recast their institutional life to emphasize such strengths, and thereby provide a fresh and more competitive profile for the institution. Such reorientation would inevitably mean making the institution more responsive to the academic marketplace, but Keller argued that, far from being a sellout of educational values, this is a very good thing, when done properly. Not only because it would help struggling institutions to survive, but because their survival would be a direct result of their ability to address the needs and hopes of the particular people they serve. Like Riesman, whom he resembled in many ways, he always insisted that the astonishing institutional diversity of American higher education was one of its greatest strengths, and should be preserved and enhanced at all costs.

Clearly colleges and universities could no longer afford to be grandly insouciant about their performance in the educational marketplace, but would such a reorientation undermine the intellectual life of the university? How could modern marketing strategies be introduced without diluting and cheapening the educational mission of colleges and universities, and turning higher education into just another commodity for sale?

Keller urged his faculty colleagues to acknowledge, however reluctantly, that the techniques of modern management would inevitably come to be employed in any economic activity as sprawling and complex and expensive and competitive as American higher education. The real question was the uses to which such techniques would be put. Who would dictate the ends toward which they would be directed? Would it be the accountants and budget officers and the other conquistadors of the spreadsheet or, perhaps worse, the politicians and bureaucrats, as we are now seeing in the misguided initiatives of the Department of Education to establish national outcomes standards, an undertaking that will only subvert the very institutional diversity that Riesman and Keller celebrated? Or, more hopefully, could the new management methods, used properly and judiciously, actually preserve the central role played by the activities of learning and inquiry — by the humanists, scientists, scholars, and student who have always formed the core of the university? Is it possible to understand strategic planning as the sustaining patron of the very best features of the modern college or university?

This may well seem impossible, or at least implausible. But for Keller, strategic planning provided a fresh way of addressing these new kinds of problems. What he proposed in *Academic Strategy* was a process that began with a brutally frank institutional self-assessment. That was absolutely essential. Institutions had to ask themselves where they were strongest, where they were weakest, and how their unique set of strengths and weaknesses positioned them with respect to the ever-shifting requirements of the educational marketplace. Such a view sought a middle ground between the idea of the university as a timeless repository, grandly indifferent to everything but its own internal imperatives, and the idea of the university as a crass commercial operator, seeking above all else to increase its market share.

Neither approach would prove adequate to the new realities, because neither did justice to the complex mixture of the ideal and the practical inherent in American higher education. The university had to stand for something larger and greater than the values of the marketplace, else it ceased to be what it was. But it also had to employ its resources as skillfully and intelligently as possible, and find better ways to meet people where they are, or else it simply would not be able to survive at all.

Radical Ideas

Keller's ideas excited a generation of academic leaders struggling to find new ways forward, but it turned out that they were more challenging, even radical, in their demands than they seemed at first glance. Properly understood, strategic planning meant an institution's finding the strength to say 'No' to many things, even things that had formerly been a part of its settled identity. To adopt a 'strategy' was not merely a question of determining what the institution would do, but deciding what it would *not* do, since others could do it better.

Moreover, even though Keller stressed the need for mutuality and constant institution-wide consultation in strategic planning, such processes had to lead to decisions, and then actions. It was not enough for strategic planning to be *participatory*; it also had to be *decisive*. And the decision-making buck would have to stop in some executive office, preferably the office of the president.

In other words, the effective implementation of any academic strategy would require vigorous presidential leadership, both in setting the institutional agenda and seeing to it that the agenda was enacted. And such presidential leadership has been increasingly hard to find, after many years in which the combination of external demands and internal intransigence has caused presidents' substantive on-campus leadership role to diminish steadily. Changing such a dynamic is easier said than done. The problem is not only that so many presidents do not try to lead boldly and imaginatively, but that so often they are not permitted to. One need only consider the fact that the best-known university presidents of our day are those who have been thwarted and rebuked by their own faculties. Small wonder that so many presidents choose to stay low and keep moving. But the notion that serious and sustained institution-wide reform could ever be led by the faculty is almost entirely fanciful. Serious academic reform will either be pushed forward by strong executive leaders, or it will not occur at all.

Keller roundly disagreed with those who charged that the use of strategic planning treated the college or university strictly as a business. No, he insisted, it treated the college or university as an *organization*. A crucial distinction, but also one that entailed a more radical assertion than it might seem. For it meant that a college faculty needed to be understood as something more than a collection of certified specialists representing the full range of accredited academic fields, and housed under a single institutional roof. It meant that a college's academic offerings amounted to something more than a large vending machine for the dispensing of certified programs of study.

It meant that an ideally functioning college is better regarded as *an organic unity*, a knit-together organizational structure that is animated throughout by a sense of common purpose, a purpose that is qualitatively different from the aggregate ambitions of individuals and the imperatives of their professional disciplines. To be sure, a good college seeks to provide all its employees with the fullest possible range of opportunities for their own achievement and advancement. That is a given. In American higher education, self-realization and institutional service are seen as complementary, rather than opposing, forces. But it also requires something else: a strong sense of the college as a *collegium*, as the institution to which one's most primary professional loyalty is owed.

This loyalty cannot be a mere slogan or a one-way manipulative appeal. A strategic plan depends for its success on the existence of strong centripetal forces binding all individuals willingly, and happily, to the institution, including the institution's leaders. It cannot succeed in a place where institutional loyalty is not cultivated, and rewarded, and reinforced, and exemplified from the top down. It certainly cannot succeed in an atmosphere in which careerist executive leaders are no sooner hired into one job than they are laying the groundwork for their next jump. Keller's idea of academic strategy was actually a quite demanding one, demanding more of both faculty and leaders than, in many cases, they have been willing or able to give.

As this last sentence implies, despite the popularity of *Academic Strategy*, the lessons Keller sought to teach were not entirely learned. Many institutions survived the structural challenges of the Eighties not by strategic concentration but by endless and often indiscriminate internal diversification, finding new constituencies of 'non-traditional' students, inventing new programs to attract them, admitting vast numbers of foreign students, and thereby keeping their enrollments up. Such programmatic additions often included the development of jerry-rigged MBA programs taught by part-time faculty, or poorly conceived and undemanding MLA and other master's degree programs, designed for the certification needs of secondary-school teachers—programs that were fresh and plentiful sources of paying customers, but often had nothing to do with the existing programs of the institution, and that sometimes were, in effect, a corrupt bargain between vendor and customer, a fraud whose perpetration risked tainting the entire product line. Schools also reduced costs by relying more and more heavily on less expensive irregular or adjunct faculty to carry the load of teaching, or by multiplying faculty contact hours by using 'distance learning' or other online instructional methods—a second 'academic revolution' that, by eroding the prestige and authority of the regular tenured faculty, threatened to undo even what was good about its predecessor.

Such innovations sometimes may have reflected creative short-term managerial thinking, but in general these adaptations exacted a price, by eroding institutions' sense of their core academic mission, and making them more and more bottom-line oriented, more and more like diversified corporations of any other kind. In other words, they moved in precisely the opposite direction to that which George Keller was advocating.

Even among the many institutions that embraced strategic planning in theory, far too many merely went through the motions in practice, assembling a wide array of committees and study groups, and soliciting reports and projecting ambitious goals with much fanfare, but lacking the leadership required to make any hard choices. Unless an institution has intelligent and brave leaders willing to make hard choices and stick by them, 'strategic planning' is just another word for endless committee meetings and paperwork and gassy rhetoric, none of it to any good end.

Of this, I can speak with the sad wisdom of personal experience, as an active participant in a massive strategic-planning review conducted by the large, private research university with which I was then associated. Countless meetings were devoted to the setting of the most extravagant goals imaginable, all of which were completely disproportionate to the university's means, and were completely oblivious to the nature of our academic competition. In other words, Keller's first step, the frank, internal self-analysis, was never quite undertaken. The university's then-president made it clear that one of his top priorities for the university was that it would break into the ranks of the top twenty research universities. When asked which of the *current* top twenty his own badly under-endowed and tuition-dependent university would displace, he changed the subject. When asked which programs could be trimmed in order to streamline the institutional mission, he offered none. I came away from our meetings reminded of a brilliant Volvo television commercial of the late 1970s, in which a business executive, clearly patterned upon Lee Iacocca, stood up before a meeting of workers and shareholders and proposed to restore the company's fortunes by ... chanting the word 'Quality!' over and over again. This is was not an exercise in true strategic planning; this was an exercise in self-hypnosis.

Still, some institutions followed the path Keller recommended and have as a consequence experienced an exhilarating rebirth. One of them, Elon University, was the subject of Keller's fascinating recent book *Transforming a College,* which details the steps by which this once-imperiled North Carolina liberal arts college made itself over into a competitive and appealingly distinctive institution, with a bundle of comparative advantages (Keller, 2004).

It may well be the case that Keller's understanding of strategic planning will work best at smaller institutions such as Elon, which are more flexible and more willing to make dramatic changes in order to keep the institution alive and functioning. Large state or private universities with the full plenitude of countervailing forces and 'veto groups' firmly in place—faculties, students, graduate assistants, influential alumni, staff, athletic programs, prospective donors, and so on—may be far more resistant to dramatic change. And it may take severe crises, even near-death experiences, to concentrate an institution's mind, and make it willing to consider the big changes, and support the strong leaders, that can bring new life to a campus. Donors with a keen and genuine interest in the renewal of American higher education should bear in mind the 'comparative advantage' of putting their funds into an institution where those funds have some chance of being genuinely transformative.

Indeed, the fact that Keller's prescriptions seem so much more likely to succeed in smaller institutions suggests in turn the need to disaggregate our thinking, and make stronger distinctions between colleges and universities, and indeed between the great majority of universities and the handful of major research universities, private and public, than we are generally accustomed to making (Graham & Diamond, 1997; Reuben, 1996). As our wealthiest and more influential research universities become more and more deeply committed to being 'producers of knowledge' and incubators for economic development and technological innovation operating in a global context, they seem less and less likely to be effectively answerable to the kind of governance that Keller describes. The task of managing vast institutions such as Harvard or Berkeley is a creature of an entirely different order from that of managing an Elon University.

Necessary Planning

In the end, however, Keller's analyses are more relevant today than ever before to the vast majority of institutions of higher education in the United States, and especially to those primarily devoted to the task of education. Strategic planning in higher education is just as sound an idea as it ever was, because it is, at bottom, about being purposeful, about achieving a deeper understanding of the proper ends toward which an institution's energies should be directed and dedicated. Harvard can afford, literally and figuratively, to operate without such organizational purposefulness. But the Elons of the country cannot.

Although the economic and demographic pressures on higher education have eased, or at least stabilized, the need for institutions to clarify the ends toward which their work is directed is, if anything, even greater, especially when tuitions are higher than anyone 20 years ago would have dreamed possible, and poised to go even higher. I often wonder if the sprawling industry of American higher education dwells inside a bubble of its own, and if the day will not come when the rising cost of higher education will finally have risen too far, and engendered a consumer revolt. Some rumblings to that effect can be heard. The social critic Barbara Ehrenreich argued recently that 'the higher education industry is becoming a racket', one whose implicit come-on — 'Buy our product or be condemned to life of penury, and our product can easily cost well over $100,000' — is being undermined by the steadily declining value of the credentials that such money buys (Ehrenreich, 2007).

Such a view is still an outlier. But it should serve as a warning that the educational aims and benefits of higher education are not obvious to the greater public, and so long as colleges and universities defer the work of making them clearer, both to themselves and to their constituencies, they may find it even harder to make that case when times are not so flush. Such times will come, perhaps sooner than we think. And when they do, the Elons, not the Harvards, will be the more vulnerable, and will suffer the worse consequences.

Those who look for the means to address these problems effectively will hardly be able to do better than to return to the work of George Keller. Whatever the barbarities committed in the name of 'strategic planning', he cannot be blamed for them. Instead, as any reader of *Academic Strategy* can see, and as some of us were privileged to know firsthand, he was a great defender of all that is best about American higher education, an old-fashioned Columbia humanist who managed to learn the language of management without being consumed by it, and had an openness to the possibility that its benefits might extend usefully, and beneficially, to the very realms that are generally inclined to disdain them. He was wise as a serpent, and beneficent as a dove. We do well to emulate him, and follow his advice.

Bibliography

Caws, Peter (Winter 1970), "Design for a University", *Daedelus* 99.
Ehrenreich, Barbara (2007), "The Higher Education Scam", *The Nation*, 14 May, http://www.thenation.com/doc/20070514/ehrenreich.
Graham, Hugh Davis and Diamond, Nancy (1997), *The Rise of American Research Universities: Elites and Challengers in the Postwar Era* (Baltimore, MD: Johns Hopkins University Press).

Jencks, Christopher and Riesman, David (1968), *The Academic Revolution* (Garden City, NY: Doubleday).

Keller, George (2004), *Transforming a College: The Story of a Little-Known College's Climb to Strategic Distinction* (Baltimore, MD: Johns Hopkins University Press).

Keller, George (1983), *Academic Strategy: The Management Revolution in American Higher Education* (Baltimore, MD: The Johns Hopkins University Press).

Levin, Arthur, ed. (1993), Judith Block McLaughlin and David Riesman, "The President: A Precarious Perch", in *Higher Learning in America, 1980-2000* (Baltimore, MD: Johns Hopkins University Press), pp. 179-202.

McClay, Wilfred (Summer 1998), "Fifty Years of *The Lonely Crowd*", *Wilson Quarterly* 22, pp. 34-42.

McLaughlin, Judith Block, and Riesman, David (1990), *Choosing a College President: Opportunities and Constraints* (Princeton, NJ: Carnegie Foundation for the Advancement of Teaching).

Reuben, Julie A. (1996), *The Making of the Modern University: Intellectual Transformation and the Marginalization of Morality* (Chicago: University of Chicago Press).

Riesman, David (1956), *Constraint and Variety in American Education* (Lincoln, NE: University of Nebraska Press).

Riesman, David, Glazer, Nathan, and Denney, Reul (1950), *The Lonely Crowd: A Study of the Changing American Character* (New Haven, CT: Yale University Press).

Veblen, Thorstein (1918), *The Higher Learning in America: A Memorandum on the Conduct of Universities by Business Men* (New York: B.W. Huebsch).

Sean Kelsey & Thomas R. Krause

Leading with Ethics

Making businesses ethical means changing behavior, which in a corporate setting means changing culture. This is the work of leadership, and like all leadership is a matter of turning a vision into a reality. As such, it requires *having* a vision, and being able to communicate that vision effectively.

In a business setting, communicating an ethical vision can be tricky. People who care about ethics have their own personal reasons for doing so, and it is not always easy to articulate them in a vocabulary that will be compelling to an organization composed of individuals with diverse values and points of view. For this reason it is tempting to fall back on the law, justifying a professional concern about ethics by appeal to recent legislation and regulations. After all, the law is an impersonal objective feature of the business and social landscape, visible to everyone. The trouble is that a legalistic approach stands at odds with the vision that business leaders who care about ethics want to communicate. Quite apart from the fact that not everything unethical is illegal, the emphasis on 'law' and 'compliance' fosters the attitude that ethical rules lie outside the mainstream of business conduct and impose arbitrary, artificial, external constraints that make little sense from a business point of view; that although we abide by them when we must, in order to stay out of trouble, they are otherwise annoyances and obstacles to be gotten around.

Another approach, familiar from the academic literature, speaks in terms of a 'theory' on which ethics is part and parcel of business. Think for example of stakeholder theory and Corporate Social Responsibility (eg. Porter & Kramer, 2006) (or CSR) and neo-Aristotelian approaches and their appeals to 'virtue' (eg. Solomon, 1999, p. xxiii). The trouble with these approaches, we believe, is that the theories of business with which they operate are unrealistic and as a result often give rise to cynicism. Reasonable people find it difficult to believe that all the talk about 'community' or 'environment' or 'virtue' is for real, and conclude that it is not for real but about a way to project a certain image. The predictable effect on organizational culture is not a renewed commitment to high ideals, but rather the sinking feeling of finding oneself complicit in a sham.

The challenge then is to find an idiom with which business leaders can articulate their ethical ideals effectively, in a way that appeals to a pluralistic audience and without being false to the nature of the business enterprise. The resources necessary to meet this challenge can be found close to home in reflection upon the origins of business. In brief, our argument is as follows: First, business is a fundamentally cooperative undertaking: an arrangement for the exchange of goods and services, freely chosen, for the mutual benefit of the parties involved. Second, it is not necessary to pretend that business has other, non-commercial, humanitarian objectives—that the aim of business is something other than making a profit. Businesses can articulate and defend their intolerance for bribery, embezzlement, nepotism, extortion, and the like by bringing out how such behavior transforms cooperative relationships into relationships of mistrust, antagonism, and exploitation. Third, we assert, based on strong evidence from empirical research in organizational behavior, that we know how to identify and change the elements of an organizational culture that predictably occasion unethical behavior. This problem has been encountered before, and dealt with effectively, in the form of the challenge to turn the workplace into a safe venue. It is not a pious hope to think that business leaders can make their ethical vision a reality in their own organizations. It is rather a practical expectation based on 30 years of positive experience in shaping organizational culture to foster workplace safety and sustainability.

I

We begin with two stories about the origins of cities, taken from Plato's *Republic*. Cities are the pre-eminent form of human association in Plato; they are the locus not only of politics and law but also of commerce. As such they provide a useful model for thinking about business.

The first story is ostensibly about the nature and origins of justice, but it also tells of the origins of law and of political communities more generally. The speaker, Glaucon, is playing devil's advocate, and his cynical account runs as follows:

By nature doing wrong is good, and being wronged bad, but the bad that comes of being wronged exceeds the good that comes of doing it. Thus when people do wrong to, and are wronged by, one another, and have a taste of both, those who are not powerful enough to do the one and avoid the other think it will profit them to make a deal with one another not to do or suffer injustice. This is the beginning of legislation and contracts; what the law enjoins we call 'lawful' and 'just' and this is the nature and origin of justice—an intermediate between the best, which is to do injustice without paying the penalty, and the worst, which is to suffer injustice while being powerless to avenge oneself. We value justice, which is in-between these, not as something good, but as something to be honored because we are not strong enough to do injustice. No one capable of doing injustice, no real man, would make a deal neither to do nor to suffer injustice—that would be insanity. (358E-359A; our translation)

Regarding Glaucon's speech, we note three things. First, on this telling, human associations arise out of conflict and strife; the pre-existing dynamic between the parties involved is essentially antagonistic and violent. In this respect the passage presages Hobbes's *Leviathan* and his warning that, absent such associations, human life will be 'solitary, poor, nasty, brutish, and short.'[1]

Second, the purpose of these associations is to put a halt to the increasing disintegration of the parties' collective fortunes, which results from the fact that none of them is alone powerful enough to win a decisive victory. In other words, the 'contract' by which the association is constituted is essentially a truce—a compromise between 'the best, which is to do injustice without paying the penalty, and the worst, which is to suffer injustice while powerless to avenge oneself.'

Third, once the association is established, the underlying dynamic remains antagonistic. The 'peace' born of this association is only superficial; it is better than the alternatives lying within reach, but not better than the alternatives we can imagine (and sometimes, sporadically, taste).

This is a fair statement of how a jaded and cynical public nowadays thinks about business. We want to contrast it with a second story, also taken from the *Republic*, but differing markedly in tone from the first. The speaker this time is Socrates, and he is brief and to the point:

---

[1] Thomas Hobbes, *Leviathan*, ch. 13.

> The origin of cities lies in the fact that none of us is self-sufficient, but we all need many things. Thus we ally ourselves, with one person for one need, with another for another; and since the things we need are many, many of us gather into one dwelling as partners and helpers. We call this common dwelling a city, and people give things, and (when they do) receive things in exchange, each thinking this better for himself (369B-C; our translation).

Although both stories locate the origins of cities in a kind of agreement or contract, the differences between them are significant. First, Socrates argues that human associations arise in a situation not of conflict and strife but of need. There is no pre-existing dynamic between the parties—they start out in a condition of comparative isolation. Second, the purpose of these associations is not to halt a decline, but positively to improve the collective fortunes of the parties involved, by means of the creation and exchange of goods for mutual benefit. Third, from the outset, the underlying dynamic in these associations is essentially voluntary and cooperative. Violence, antagonism, and exploitation are completely foreign to the spirit of the original enterprise.

We believe this second story provides manifestly the better model for thinking about the nature and origin of business. 'Better' means not just more salutary, but also more realistic: a truer representation of the spirit of the commercial enterprise. Entrepreneurs do not typically begin their joint undertakings by calling a truce. Nor do the relationships within developing organizations, and those between them and their suppliers, clients, and customers, typically begin in a spirit of mutual antagonism. The underlying original dynamic of the enterprise is not one of mutual violence and exploitation, but one of cooperation for mutual benefit.

Although this is a modest point, it is important. It provides a useful and workable framework for talking about ethics in business.

II

We are all familiar with the tired assertion that the very idea of 'business ethics' is an oxymoron: that talk of 'ethics' and 'morality' is not realistic because ethical norms are at best irrelevant, and at worst inimical to the pragmatic values that organize business practice. It is true that there are pragmatic reasons for businesses to care about ethics. Recent legislation mandates the implementation of ethics programs; recent studies indicate the value of a reputation for fairness, integrity, and trustworthiness to long-term sustainability; the rapid growth of information technology makes keeping malfeasance secret increasingly difficult (see Friedman, 2007). However, it is not hard to see that legislation provides reasons for compliance, but not for genuine ethical reform, and that while the value of reputation and the growth of information technology give businesses a reason to polish their reputations, reputation is often but indirectly related to underlying realities. Thus it is no surprise to find that businesses use most of the resources they spend on ethics on ensuring compliance and projecting a public image. This seems to confirm the tired line that in business the only motive that matters is the profit-motive.

The standard reply to this skepticism is to enlarge our conception of business—to urge that the business of business is not primarily or exclusively making money. After all, it is said, businesses do not exist in a vacuum; they are situated in a larger social environment, an environment that is deliberately structured in ways that permit them to arise and help them to flourish, and along with this favor comes responsibility. It is also said that although many people enter business to make money, many find their professional work fulfilling in other ways as well. It provides them an arena in which they can exercise their talents and realize their values, and for them work becomes not just a way of *earning* a living, but part and parcel of life itself. In this way the values people prize in private life, among them ethical values, become integral to the business enterprise as they conceive of it. The standard reply is, in short, that business and ethics seem related at best indirectly because we are operating with a small-minded and impoverished conception of business—business is not exclusively about making a profit.

We believe this reply at best secondary. Most people enter business and stay in it primarily to make a living, and although societies do take measures to encourage business, they do so primarily because business creates wealth, not because it can save the environment or accomplish other humanitarian ends.[2] Many people *do* flourish in the workplace and find personal fulfillment in their professional avocations,[3] and businesses can and do accomplish things

---

[2] See Friedman, 1970, who argues that individual businessmen lack a mandate to pursue such ends.

[3] Nor do we deny that this is a good thing; given that much of our "free time" is spent recuperating so that we can return to the fray, it would be a shame if work were nothing but labor and toil; we'd be left with virtually no time to spend *living* the living we work so hard to earn.

not easily or efficiently done by individuals or government. Nevertheless, it is important to recognize these valuable side-benefits for what they are: side-benefits.[4] To say that the company's first commitment is to 'social responsibility' or 'virtue and personal fulfillment' is to risk being regarded by serious people as a fanatic, a fool, a fraud, or all three. It is not an effective way to communicate an ethical vision.

We take it as axiomatic, then, that businesses are partnerships primarily for making money — that is their point and purpose. But this does not mean that businesses are somehow intrinsically amoral or immoral. *Making* money is not the same thing as *taking* it by force or deception. That's the difference between business and organized crime. Though both are partnerships for getting money, one simply *seizes* its profits, by theft, extortion, or violence, by hook or by crook, while the other *earns* its profits in exchange for goods and services, on terms that have been mutually and voluntarily agreed upon in advance. Crime is by nature violent and antagonistic: the parties from which it seizes its profits are victims. Business, by contrast, is essentially peaceful and cooperative: the parties from which it earns its profits are willing partners in an exchange for mutual benefit. The fundamental dynamic is not exploitative but cooperative.

In short, to explain why ethics matters in business, it is not necessary to pretend that businesses are something they are not: high-minded, altruistic, social do-gooders or Aristotelian city-states bent on fostering virtue in their citizens. It is enough (and a lot) to insist that although business is all about profits, it is about *earning* profits in exchange for goods and services, on terms agreed upon willingly in a spirit of cooperation and not about *seizing* profits in a spirit of hostility, antagonism, exploitation, deception, and violence.[5] (We do not deny that some forms of global enterprise do vio-

---

[4] Indeed, the fulfillment many of us find at work is bound up inextricably with the narrowly defined objectives we come together at work to pursue in the first place. We enjoy cultivating and deploying our professional expertise, overcoming obstacles, working with others we admire and respect for their creativity, intelligence, efficiency, energy, and perseverance; we derive a sense of satisfaction in being part of something bigger than we are, on a scale beyond the capacities of any one man or woman; we take pride in a spirit of professionalism and a job well-done; and so on. These side-benefits come with being part of a well-run organization, and we risk *losing* precisely these benefits if we take our eye off the task at hand in order to focus on our own personal fulfillment.

[5] See for example the work of Sebastiao Salgado at www.terra.com.br/sebastiaosalgado/.

lence to the people and resources of developing countries.) We may condemn bribery, fraud, deceit, embezzlement, nepotism, extortion, and so on, not just because they are immoral, or illegal, or embarrassing, or short-sighted, but because they are also bad business. They corrode the nature and spirit of the business enterprise by transforming cooperative exchange into antagonism and exploitation; they turn what began as alliances and partnerships—with clients, suppliers, stockholders, supervisors, colleagues, support staff, what have you—into unlawful relationships with accomplices or victims. This result follows even if business is conceived narrowly as a partnership for making money.

In a phrase, the reason ethics matters in business is that ethical norms and values, far from being arbitrary and artificial constraints on cooperation, are its prerequisites. To put the point another way: *ethics is native to business*, not by virtue of its secondary, non-commercial aims, but by virtue of its cooperative form.

III

Most people in business, even those in it principally for the money, will identify with this conception of their enterprise. (Those who don't are criminals, or at least would-be criminals.) That is, they can be brought to see that ethical values are intrinsic to the enterprise *as they themselves conceive of it*.

Some will object (Glaucon-like) that this conception of business as a fundamentally cooperative undertaking is idealistic, not true to life, that it is no more realistic than the familiar academic approaches that focus on 'virtue' or 'social responsibility.' What distinguishes businesses from syndicates of organized crime, the objection runs, is that businesses operate within the confines of the law. When businesses *can* legally seize profits by deceit or coercion, they do so; indeed, even when they can't do so legally, they often do so anyway, when they think they can get away with it undetected, or when they think they can bribe or intimidate potential whistle-blowers. Let's stop pretending, it might be urged, and lift the veil: in both business and crime the controlling dynamic is essentially predatory and exploitative; the only difference is that the one is lawful, the other lawless. But this difference is arbitrary and inessential—both activities are about essentially the same game.

So, the objection concludes, ethics is *not* native to business, not when business is viewed in the clear, realistic light of day. On the contrary, ethics is just what it appears to be: a source of externally imposed *constraints* on business, justified from a point of view business must regard as at best alien and at worst hostile. When businesses operate within these constraints, they do so out of a sense of necessity and compromise; were circumstances more favorable, had they the power to act otherwise with impunity, they would.

We reply that although this is a fair caricature, with few exceptions it is no more than that. The vast majority of businessmen and women are not would-be criminals. This is revealed by the values they prize and cherish, by their understanding of the kind of people they wish to be, and the kinds of lives they want to live. Most people in business are not the sort who would stoop at anything, if only they could get away with it. Their ethical values and ideals are not well-characterized by the vocabulary of 'necessity' and 'compromise.' On the contrary: this vocabulary best describes their attitude toward injustice and wrongdoing (see Toffler, 1986). Glaucon's cynical story has it exactly backwards.

IV

Of course this approach does not solve every problem. Business brings us into contact with many people with whom we are not, properly speaking, doing business. It would be strange to suppose that a just appreciation of our rights and responsibilities in relation to these people will fall out of reflection upon the nature of the business enterprise. The ethical norms governing our non-commercial relationships are grounded in other, non-commercial facts, e.g., that the persons in question are family, or neighbors, or fellow citizens, or human beings. (Our responsibilities as stewards of the environment are likewise rooted in broader considerations.)

How can we talk about these issues credibly in a business setting? It's a mistake to fall back on legalistic, compliance-driven ways of thinking. Even where there is an effective legal system, an emphasis on 'compliance' sends the wrong message: that ethical rules are to be compromised wherever needed and possible. Likewise it is a mistake to pretend that the aims of business are altruistic, humanitarian, and grandiose. If we try to anchor our responsibilities not to coerce or exploit or mistreat other people in some make-believe, altruistic, grandiose, humanitarian objectives, the effect will be to make the former seem as unreal as are (usually) the latter.

Our responsibilities are rooted in (at the very least) in our common humanity. We do not exploit children, because that is inhumane and monstrous.[6] We do not bribe public officials, or murder political leaders, or enslave populations, or prostitute our children, because such actions are vile and corrupt; our humanity cries out against them. Even bribery, though ubiquitous, is done in secret, or under cover of euphemism.

The best way to talk effectively about these issues in a business setting is to take the high road by making a frank appeal to common decency, mostly just by drawing attention to the pertinent facts, not whitewashed and sugarcoated, but told as they are. Business leaders must also deal with the institutional structures that make their people feel compelled to look away from the plain facts, or to suppress or contravene their sense of decency.

Perhaps some will object that this is too idealistic — that, for example, a policy of not paying bribes is in effect a policy not to do business in developing countries. No doubt this is in some cases true, though perhaps not as often as is thought. If paying a bribe is always the easy way out, it is not always the only way out — companies often have more leverage and clout than they exercise. However, even where paying a bribe *is* the only way out, does it follow that we must just roll over and pay the bribe? Everyone draws a line somewhere; virtually no one would prostitute his or her own children as the unavoidable cost, the *sine qua non*, of doing business in a culture that required it.

And if we must draw a line somewhere, what is to stop us from drawing it where it belongs: at offering no affront to human dignity? If we are willing to cross that line, not out of fear and compulsion but from deliberate calculation, we prove ourselves willing to cross any line. And if we cross that line because we turn our eye from the plain facts — if we 'just don't go there' — the effect is just the same.

V

Enough about how to articulate and justify ethical norms and values in a business setting. The practical objective is to make that vision a reality. Is this at all feasible? After all, venality and corruption are permanent fixtures of the human landscape, and they often find fer-

---

[6] Acknowledging that it took at least 100 years of legislation and regulation (roughly 1832–1938) to bring about the effective control of child labor in the US; for a succinct history of child labor laws, see, for example, "Child Labor in US History", Child Labor Labor Public Education project, n.d., http://www.continuetolearn.uiowa.edu/laborctr/child_labor/about/us_history.html

tile soil in the business world. How can the attempt to make businesses more ethical not seem hopelessly quixotic? Though the scandals we hear about with depressing regularity provide little encouragement, the practical problem of reducing or eliminating incidents of corporate ethical malfeasance is a problem we already know how to solve.

Accidents happen and people get hurt. They happen in quarries, they happen in factories, they happen in hospitals. Fatigue, inattention, carelessness, badly designed systems and processes, bad luck are endemic to the human condition. The idea that we could reform our quarries, our factories, our hospitals, so as to virtually eliminate the incidence of life-altering accidents, in a word, to make them *safe* — the prospects of this are about as likely as the prospects of making businesses ethical.

So thought many business leaders 30 years ago, and so think many even today. And yet the fact remains that this pessimism about safety is simply misplaced. In a given industrial setting, we know the types of accident that are most typical and costly in human and financial terms; we know how to isolate and identify the antecedent behaviors that give rise to them; we know how to isolate and identify the specific behavioral elements of the culture that permit these behaviors and even give them incentives; and we know how to implement in a systematic way the changes necessary in order to eliminate these behaviors almost completely. This claim has been demonstrated empirically (see Krause et al., 1999).

Some perhaps will worry that ethics is different. In the wake of recent scandals, businesses have been trying to reform their practices, to make them more ethical, and recent legislation mandating various schemes for reform are being implemented, at considerable cost — with limited success. Often such schemes are met with diffidence or hostility on the part of employees and their supervisors, and so far they do not appear to have been terribly effective.

The reply to this concern is straightforward: the difference between business ethics and industrial safety lies in the *methods* applied in the two arenas. The great progress made in industrial safety is the result of organizational change strategies that aim at leadership, culture and behavior change; in ethics nothing comparable has even been tried. Yet the analogy between ethics and safety is broad and deep. Ethical scandals are the exact analog of industrial accidents. Both are strongly related to cultural influence, which in turn is related to leadership capability. Both have behavioral antecedents; like all behaviors, these antecedents can be observed and are intelligible in light of their perceived consequences. These perceptions in turn can be discovered and measured, and what is more they can be changed, via concrete and specific changes made to the systems and behaviors to which they are the sensible and intelligent reaction. The implementation of such changes can be monitored, as can the perceptions and behaviors they are designed to produce or avoid; interventions can be modified and fine-tuned in an on-going process until they succeed in their intended effects. The time is ripe—companies now have incentives—to begin applying these methods in the area of ethics.

It might be objected that ethics is not likely to be amenable to such techniques, because ethical conduct is not easily quantified. To us this objection seems uninformed. Ethical conduct narrowly conceived—for example, abstention from petty theft, false accounting, or bribery—is no less amenable to definition and measurement than other, broader forms of pro-social organizational behavior, manifesting such qualities as sportsmanship, organizational loyalty, and civic virtue. Yet these and other such behaviors are even now the subject of a flourishing body of empirical research.[7] For this reason we persevere in our confidence that the methods that have proved so successful in improving organizational safety can be similarly successful in improving corporate ethics. If there's a will, there's a way.

VI

If changing an organization's behavior means changing its culture, the way to change culture is, first and foremost, to change the behavior of leadership. Culture involves attitudes and values, not just behavior, but it is behavior that we can directly and objectively define, measure, and change, and it is the behavior of leadership in particular that most determines the shape of an organization's attitudes and values. Thus the way to make organizations more ethical is to cultivate in their leadership the behaviors that strengthen and support an ethical culture.

Though this may seem like a truism, it adumbrates a practical strategy whose effectiveness has been demonstrated empirically (see Krause, 2005). Recent research has identified the factors of organizational behavior that most affect organizational culture and

---

[7] For recent reviews, see Podsakoff et al, 2000; Hoffman et al., 2007.

improve safety.[8] These factors include procedural justice (whether matters are resolved fairly), leader-member exchange (the quality and character of upward and downward communication), management credibility (the consistency of what is *said* with what is *done*), teamwork (the effectiveness of work teams), work group relations (the harmony of team working relationships), and upward communication (the ease of speaking to superiors on difficult matters). These factors have been measured, managed, and coached in many organizations, both domestic and overseas, moving unsafe organizations into a sustainable state of worker safety, and moving generally safe organizations from good to superior conditions of worker safety. Witness Alcoa under the leadership of Paul O'Neill during the period 1987-2002 (see Smith, 2002, also Arendt, 2001, p. 39).

These same dimensions of organizational behavior just spell out concretely what it means in a commercial setting to say that the form of the enterprise is fundamentally cooperative. For this reason they give board members — directors and trustees alike — a way to fulfill their responsibilities to establish and monitor the ethical culture of the companies they serve. They can do so by insisting on the establishment of ongoing mechanisms for measuring, reporting, and coaching specific behaviors, so that they become normal practice and receive consistent, reinforcing feedback from the culture shaped by the organization's leadership. With interventions of the quality, depth, and duration that have improved industrial safety, we can also expect to see material and sustainable improvements in commercial ethics as well.

Bibliography

Arendt, Michael (5 February 2001), "How O'Neill Got Alcoa Shining", *Business Week*.

Dodsworth, M., et al. (January 2007), "Organizational Climate Metrics as Safety, Health, and Environment Performance Indicators and an Aid to Relative Risk Ranking within Industry", *Process Safety and Environmental Protection: Transactions of the Institution of Chemical Engineers Part B* 85, pp. 59-69

Friedman, Milton (13 September 1970), "A Friedman Doctrine: The Social Responsibility of Business is to Increase its Profits", *The New York Times Magazine*, p. 17ff..

Friedman, Thomas L. (27 June 2007), "The Whole World Is Watching", *The New York Times*, Editorial Desk section, p. 23, final edition.

---

[8] See for example Dodsworth et al., 2007; Schein, 1985; Hoffmann and Morgeson, 1999.

Hoffman, Brian J., et al. (March 2007), "Expanding the Criterion Domain? A Quantitative Review of the OCB Literature", *Journal of Applied Psychology* 92, pp. 555–66.

Hoffmann, David A., and Morgeson, Frederick P. (April 1999), "Safety-Related Behavior as a Social Exchange: The Role of Perceived Organizational Support and Leader-Member Exchange", *Journal of Applied Psychology* 84, pp. 286–96.

Krause, T.R., Seymour, K.J., and Sloat, K.C.M. (April 1999), "Long-Term Evaluation of a Behavior-Based Method for Improving Safety Performance: A Meta-Analysis of 73 Interrupted Time-Series Replications", *Safety Science* 32, pp. 1–18.

Krause, Thomas R. (2005), *Leading With Safety* (Hoboken, NJ: John Wiley and Sons, Wiley Interscience).

Podsakoff, Philip M., MacKenzie, Scott B., Paine, Julie Beth, and Bachrach, Daniel G. (2000), "Organizational Citizenship Behaviors: A Critical Review of the Theoretical and Empirical Literature and Suggestions for Future Research", *Journal of Management* 26, no. 3, pp. 513–63

Porter, Michael and Kramer, Mark (December 2006), "Strategy and Society: The Link between Competitive Advantage and Corporate Social Responsibility", *Harvard Business Review*, pp. 78–92.

Schein, Edgar H. (1985), *Organizational Culture and Leadership* (San Francisco: Jossey-Bass Publishers)

Smith, Sandy (October 2002), "America's Safest Companies: 17 Award Winners Share Best Practices", *Occupational Hazards*, pp. 47–62.

Solomon, Robert C. (1999), *A Better Way to Think About Business: How Personal Integrity Leads to Corporate Success* (New York: Oxford University Press).

Toffler, Barbara Ley, ed. (1986), *Tough Choices: Managers Talk Ethics* (New York: John Wiley and Sons).

R. Edward Freeman & David Newkirk[1]

Business as a Human Enterprise
Implications for Education

The challenges facing business education grow out of a fundamental misunderstanding of the nature of business itself: Business is a thoroughly human institution, but business schools and business scholars rarely recognize this. Much current research and teaching treats business as a deterministic phenomenon, and management as a science. By embracing business as a human institution and management as a creative act, we can correct many of the problems identified in the modern critiques of management scholarship and education.

We begin with a brief, stylized history of the business academy, primarily in the United States, where it finds its most dominant form and, historically, its largest audience. We juxtapose this history with the tremendous changes that have occurred in business over the last forty to fifty years, and suggest that the time is ripe for change. Next we demonstrate that recent critiques rest on a faulty and outmoded view of business. Using stakeholder theory, we argue that we need a new approach, most easily characterized as 'business as a human activity.' We suggest two central questions and four problems business education must place front and center. We then discuss how we might draw on all of the disciplines of the academy for a more robust

---

[1] We wish to thank our many colleagues at the Darden School and elsewhere for helpful conversations about these issues. Versions of this paper have been delivered at the Schulich School, York University, and at Copenhagen Business School.

and useful view of business, and more powerful research and educational tools.

I. A Brief History of Business Schools in the United States[2]

Management education is a recent, relatively unexamined, phenomenon. One can identify at least four distinct periods in the United States leading up to the current state of chaos.

The Formative Period.
While there is a great deal of debate about the original purpose of business schools, we argue that their original purpose was grounded in the idea of moral education. According to L.C. Marshall, one of the earliest proposals for a collegiate business school was made by Robert E. Lee, the first president of what is today Washington and Lee University (Marshall, 1928, p. 3). Although the proposal was not put into action, Lee's idea was not confined to the business details of bookkeeping and the like 'but [aimed] to teach the principles of commerce, economy, trade and mercantile law.' At its very beginning the American collegiate business school sought to articulate and teach the basic principles of commerce and economics, as well as their counterparts in the law.

The Wharton School of the University of Pennsylvania was founded in 1881 with funds from the steel magnate, Joseph Wharton, and the number of business schools rapidly increased in the next 40 years in both the United States and Europe. Francis Ruml argued that the existence of business courses in secondary schools and so-called commercial colleges made it easy and natural for the university and collegiate schools of business to focus their attention more on professional and social ends; to place an emphasis upon dealing with the complicated social organization in which the business man does his work; to accept as its objective the training of persons with a social point of view for executives and professional positions in business (Ruml, 1928, p. 47).

Business schools produced several results, such as:

(1) replacing the apprenticeship system, largely dismantled by the industrial revolution

(2) training businesspeople in the fundamentals of scientific management

---

[2] This section is based on Freeman, 1994. We are grateful to the editors and publisher for permission to recast some of that material here.

(3) addressing the growing need for financial as opposed to industrial administration

(4) training an elite capable of managing more complex social organizations (VandeCreek, 1994).

Ruml summarized Joseph Wharton's initial stated purpose as being 'to establish means for imparting a liberal education in all matters concerning Finance and Economy' (Ruml, 1928, pp. 54–5). In his address to the trustees of the newly formed Wharton School, Wharton remarked: 'It is reasonable to expect that adequate education in the principles underlying successful business management would greatly aid in producing a class of men likely to become pillars of the state, whether in private or public life.' And on this original theme of imparting 'moral education' to managers, Ruml approvingly quotes E.P. Cubberly's History of Education:

> As the industrial life of the nation has become more diversified, its parts narrower, and its processes more concealed, new and more extended training has been called for to prepare young people to meet the intricacies and interdependencies of political and industrial and social groups and to point out to them the importance of each one's part in the national and industrial organization (*Ibid.*, p. 53).

The American Assembly of Collegiate Schools of Business (AACSB), founded in 1916, reinforced this idea of a liberal education for business people by requiring accredited schools to require students to take at least 40 percent of their credit hours in subjects other than economics and commerce. In speaking to the AACSB's 1927 conference, Alfred North Whitehead echoed the view that management was ready for professional education, if we only knew what it was:

> Universities have trained clergy, medical men, lawyers, engineers. Business is now a highly intellectualized vocation, so it well fits into the series. There is, however, this novelty: the curriculum suitable for a business school, and the various modes of activity of such a school, are still in the experimental stage (Whitehead, 1966).

To reinforce the argument that that original purpose of business schools was grounded in the idea of moral education, consider Joseph Wharton's original plan. Wharton proposed and implemented a program to take humanities faculty, trained in the liberal arts, and put them in the classroom to teach business subjects. This experiment, tried in 1882, failed miserably, according to Ruml, because the liberal arts professors were resentful and did not necessarily believe that knowledge should be practical. (This attempt to found a business school on the capabilities and resources of a liberal arts institution has been repeated more recently at Yale and Oxford, both of whom recapitulated the history, ultimately replacing professors from the parent institution with dedicated business academics.) By 1883 the Wharton School had hired instructors versed in business, leaving the ensuing 100–plus years barren of meaningful interchange between business and the humanities.

The early history of business schools is rife with arguments about the same controversies that dominate today's discourse. Should faculty be trained in economics? Were graduate economics departments sources of ignorance about business? Could business people be used as adjunct professors, and if so, how many? What was the proper balance between research and consulting? Should the study of business be scientific, or largely storytelling? Was business to be a profession with established ethical norms, or were schools of business merely to socialize students into the practices of business and prepare them for the world of work?

Unspoken are the questions of what is the nature of business itself, and therefore of management and leadership, an essential foundation for addressing the challenge of how best to develop people for these roles. Is management, as Whitehead's comments might imply, a profession, with a body of knowledge to be mastered? Or is it a craft, with skills to be learned?

While these questions are still relevant, the second period in the history of the American business school makes answering them all the more difficult.

The Scientific/Modern Period

Two well-known reports published in the late 1950s gave voice to a crisis of legitimacy in the business school. The Carnegie Report and the Ford Foundation study by R.A. Gordon and J.E. Howell both claimed that business schools needed academic legitimacy, and essentially proposed the adoption of a social sciences approach to the subject matter of business.

According to Thomas Mulligan, writing in an important 1987 retrospective in no less than *The Academy of Management Review,* these reports represented a turning point, where the culture of business schools became overtly scientific and, we would argue, adopted the

positivism that underlay much of the scientific thinking of the period:
> The often unsubstantiated descriptive content of earlier business school curricula and research has been replaced by quantitative description based on rigorous data collection, computer-assisted mathematical modeling, and the foundational concepts of science—testable hypotheses (or, at least, testable networks of hypotheses), correlated observations, and causal explanation (Mulligan, 1987).

The state of business schools, he argued, suggests a desperate need for something like the humanities, but the culture of science that emerged in the business schools has only recently begun to be challenged by the introduction of humanities-based ethics courses.

While Mulligan is correct that the culture of science dominates business schools, there is an alternative to his view that the two cultures of arts and sciences are incompatible. He rightly points out the emergence of 'practitioner' books critical of the scientific approach, but there is more at issue here than practical criticism of academic abstractions.

The Porter/Peters Era

Two seemingly unrelated phenomena from 1980 through the 1990s catapulted business and business thinkers into the center of society and provided a countervailing force to the increasing scientism and irrelevance of business school research. The result was the emergence of another branch of business education, largely through bestsellers, consultants, corporate universities, learning centers, and the like.

The practical leadership in development of management techniques had moved outside the universities. DuPont had pioneered capital budgeting and return on investment calculations in 1903. The Navy created critical path management during World War II. In the fifties and sixties, GE established small business units and the processes for managing them. By the sixties, Bruce Henderson and BCG were offering services built around experience curves and growth-share matrices. All of these managerial innovations were rooted in an analytical view of business (Hamel, 2006).

In the 1970s, economist Michael Porter published his groundbreaking book *Competitive Strategy* on the economic basis of business strategy (Porter, 1980). From this book, offering his theory of 'the five forces of industry analysis', it was easy to reestablish the dialogue between social scientists such as Porter and businesspeople. He had a coherent narrative with real-life implications for executives and how they thought about their business.

During roughly the same period, Tom Peters and his colleagues at the consulting firm McKinsey and Company embarked on a study of why some organizations seemed to be successful year after year (Peters and Waterman, 1982). The report they produced formed the basis for Peters' and Robert Waterman's best-selling *In Search of Excellence*. Its power was, like that of Porter's theory, its systematic, albeit unscientific, narrative about what real companies and real leaders did and did not do to achieve success. *Search* was grounded in the real world and was coherent as a narrative, enhancing its believability.

Our argument is not that the scientific period is over in business schools. The existence of so-called scholarly journals, and the endless arguments in tenure committees about whether a particular journal is an 'A, B, or C' journal, ensures an appetite for trivia in excess of either its production or its value. Porter and Peters show us the power of narrative, of telling a good story about how we can create and manage our organizations. Their financial success also shows the appetite for compelling business narrative. In short, they give us a basis for reintroducing the humanities in business education. The humanities contain powerful narratives and meta-narratives about human societies and cultures. These narratives are more or less coherent and more or less normative, as well as descriptive. Equally important, they are compelling to leaders and aspiring leaders.

The ensuing twenty-five plus years has led to an explosion of the business bestseller, and the seminars and consulting firms telling these narratives. We have been treated to 'business reengineering and process redesign', 'customer intimacy and operational excellence', 'being built to last' and 'going from good to great', 'managing stakeholders and stakeholder engagement', 'supply chain management', 'strategic alliances', and a host of other, oftentimes good and useful, ideas. During this time, the leader him (or occasionally her) self has become the subject of inquiry, with his (or her) successful traits first described then, increasingly, prescribed. Companies have begun their own 'corporate universities', both to teach business skills and to develop leadership, sometimes in conjunction with leading business schools, while the schools themselves have made commitments to executive education as a source of lucrative funding.

Recent Changes to Business and Business Schools

As business schools evolved to become more self-contained and 'scientific', alienated from both practice and from the rest of the university, the real world of business has changed greatly.[3]

Every industry has become more global. The coherence of business strategy is influenced by far-flung and disparate events in many corners of the globe. The purely analytical approach to strategy (such as the one advocated by Porter) has become less and less relevant. The issues of outsourcing jobs, government policy, supply chain management, value chain responsibility, environmentalism, the rise of power of NGOs, are all now central to thinking about strategy. India and China have emerged as serious global players in business, with Russia and Brazil not too far behind. Every aspect of business, from brand values and communications to employee relations, operates in a changing cultural context.

The explosion of the Internet, and the emergence of the dotcom companies laid waste to traditional ideas about how to start a business. Thousands of young people began to develop business plans for companies that were targeted to change people's behavior around basic ideas such as information, shopping, health care, and other basic facts of life. YAHOO!, Google, eBay, LendingTree, *Web*MD, are just a few among thousands of companies started either outside the traditional model of business, often by business school students who were pursuing very different aims from traditional businesses and their narrow 'economics only' paradigm. And many of these start-ups were successful. IPOs were offered often before there was any revenue at all, and this flaunted the traditional way of thinking about a business.

Underneath the bubbling of the dotcom economy, business itself was changing. Information-age institutions looked fundamentally different from their industrial-age counterparts. Businesses seemed to be creating, rather than meeting, consumer needs. Financial resources were less critical than ideas and customers. Products were 'co-created' with customers, and 'extended enterprises' began competing in 'eco-systems.' The 'physics' of business began to change. Companies lost mass through outsourcing. Geography began to dis-

---

[3] These are laid out in more detail in Freeman et al., 2007.

appear, and boundaries between markets became more permeable. And Internet-time seemed to move faster than normal-time. We seemed to be living in a world of creativity and unpredictability, rather than the predictable, repeatable phenomena of the past.

During roughly the same time period, we saw the fall of Communist and socialist regimes all around the world. Bill Clinton's mantra, 'It's the economy stupid', became the watchword for developing capitalist economies, and business took on a renewed importance as a central institution for human interaction.

Concurrently, we have had several waves of scandal, from the Wall Street trading scandals of the late 1980s to the Enron genre of scandals in the late 1990s and early part of this century. Paralleling these scandals have been renewed interest in 'corporate responsibility', 'environmental sustainability', and issues such as 'the public trust of business.'

At the same time, there has been an explosion in the need for quasi-managerial white-collar labor familiar with the vocabulary and techniques of business and finance. There has been an equally rapid growth in the population of business schools to meet this need. As the armies of managers has grown, the MBA has become a qualification for both the officers and the foot soldiers, with little differentiation between the two.

The response of business schools has been to highlight how their MBA programs have been made 'global', largely through exchange programs with students and faculty, or 'field trips', or a week or two in China or India. The schools also have made a token attempt to put ethics into the curriculum, although, repeating Joseph Wharton's experiment on a different scale, often taught by business school faculty untrained in ethics, or philosophy faculty untrained and uninterested in business. Some schools have adopted some new technology for 'distance learning' to help meet growing demand at lower cost. The responses have, for the most part, been traditional disciplinary answers.

At the same time, we have the phenomena of 'ratings' of business schools and the adoption of techniques of corporate branding. To attract students paying higher prices in this more competitive market, schools have begun to worry about their 'brand', their 'image', and the means of differentiating. Business has changed on a massive scale during the last twenty-five years, and we believe that it is fair to say that business schools have simply 'moved the deck.' Consequently there is a malaise, whose true cause is difficult to pin down.

II. Recent Critiques of Business Education

The dominant narrative of business schools, rooted in the Scientific/Modern Period, has a real grip on the hearts and minds of business school professors and administrators, who transmit it to students, so that it becomes self-perpetuating. However, there is some light. A number of recent critiques have begun the process of self-examination.

Jeffrey Pfeffer and Christina Fong[4]

Pfeffer and Fong argue that the MBA is neither necessary nor sufficient for business success, and that a student's grades are not correlated with a flourishing career. Much of what MBAs learn is of limited usefulness, business school research is of limited influence, and true 'evidence based' management is rare.

Many of the bestsellers making an impact on business are based on what Pfeffer would call 'non-evidential approaches.' It is difficult to discern when one reads the entirety of his work whether he believes that the problem is simply a lack of 'good science' in business school research or a more fundamental issue of how research problems are framed at business schools.

In short, Pfeffer and Fong suggest that most business school researchers get 'good science' wrong, and that the resulting MBA is not useful and doesn't much matter.

Henry Mintzberg[5]

In a recent blistering critique of business education, *Managers Not MBAs*, management theorist Henry Mintzberg suggests that for the most part MBA programs have the wrong students, that students in their mid-to-late twenties are simply neither ready nor capable of learning management. He sees management differently from Pfeffer and Fong, as a craft rather than a science. Hence, studying management is a waste of time. One needs to be engaged in the 'doing' rather than the 'talking about doing.' There is simply too much emphasis on the disciplines of business in the business schools, and too much emphasis on the traditional modes of teaching and learning. Consequently, MBAs have become exploiters rather than explorers and innovators. In addition, the managerial class, defined by MBAs, is responsible for a lot of economic misery in society.

---

[4] VandeCreek, 1994.
[5] Mintzberg, 2004.

Mintzberg rightly traces much of the problem back to the Scientific/Modern Period and the emergence of a 'cult of methodology', whereby the worthiness of a particular piece of research is based not on how it allows us to live, but on the 'validity' of the methodology by which it has been executed. However, it is perhaps disingenuous of him to make such a strong claim about the scientism in business school research, as he is routinely lauded for taking empiricism to its logical ends. His early studies of managerial work influenced a generation of students and managers, and have been defended by many as telling us what managers actually do, rather than what they should do to become good managers. His own eschewing of the normative aspects of business research seems to fit squarely into the cross hairs of his critique.

In short, Mintzberg suggests that we get 'management' wrong, and the resulting MBAs do real and lasting damage in the world.

Sumantra Ghoshal

In an influential article titled 'Bad Management Theories Are Destroying Good Management Practices', the late Sumantra Ghoshal argued that the dominant narratives that have taken hold in business schools are the real culprits (Ghoshal, 2005). He singles out the ideologues who, concentrating on the economic and financial aspects of business, propose that the only legitimate purpose of a business is to maximize shareholder value, and those who understand business as a complex agency problem where managers are seen as agents of shareholders. He invokes Hayek's idea of the pretense of knowledge to suggest that we misunderstand the nature of social science. Social science theories become known, 'ideas in good currency' as Donald Schon would say, and students and business people begin to act as if these ideas are true. They enact the dominant narrative. And, in doing so, they create agency problems, and corporations that are immune to any criteria other than shareholder value. He writes:

> In courses on corporate governance grounded in agency theory, we have taught our students that managers cannot be trusted to do their jobs—which, of course, is to maximize shareholder value. ... In courses on organization design, grounded in transaction-cost economics, we have preached the need for tight monitoring and control of people to prevent 'opportunistic behavior.' In strategy courses, we have presented the 'five forces' framework to suggest that companies must compete not only with

their competitors but also with their suppliers, customers, employees and regulators (*Ibid.*, p. 75).

Business school researchers have simply misused the scientific methods by pretending that business is like the physical sciences, with fixed rules and repeatable phenomena. The result is not the useless and uninfluential theory of Pfeffer and Fong, but the highly destructive theory that Mintzberg's MBAs are inflicting on the world. In an incredibly enlightening passage, Ghoshal suggests that the answer might lie in a closer connection between the great thinkers of the sciences and the humanities, adopting a 'scholarship of common sense.' He writes:

> In describing himself and his work, Sigmund Freud wrote: '[Y]ou often estimate me too highly. I am not really a man of science, not an experimenter, and not a thinker. I am nothing but by temperament a conquistador—an adventurer, if you want to translate the term—with the curiosity, the boldness, and the tenacity that belong to that type of being' (in Jones, 1964, p. 171).
>
> Freud's inductive and iterative approach to sense-making, often criticized for being ad hoc and unscientific, was scholarship of common sense. So indeed was Darwin's, who, too, practiced a model of research as the work of a detective, not of an experimenter, who was driven by the passions of an adventurer, not those of a mathematician. Scholarship of common sense is the epistemology of disciplined imagination, as advocated by Karl Weick (1989), and not the epistemology of formalized falsification that was the doctrine of Karl Popper (1968).
>
> To protect the pretense of knowledge, we have created conditions under which this kind of scholarship can no longer flourish in our community. This is true of all social science disciplines, but curiously perhaps it is most intensely true in business schools where, in our desire for respect from scholars in other fields, we have become even more intolerant of the scholarship of common sense than those whose respect we seek (Bailey and Ford, 1996)[6]

In short, Ghoshal suggests that we get theory wrong, management wrong, and social science wrong, and we shouldn't be surprised at the resulting moral decline of business.

---

[6] VandeCreek, 1994, pp. 81–2. Please note references in quotation not available in bibliography.

So What?

The common theme to these critiques is that much malaise in and about business schools is a result of a misguided positivism or scientism, ultimately stemming from what we have called the Scientific/Modern Period of business school history. While there is much truth in this critique, it is difficult to see how such a tightly knit social system is going to change. Indeed, the authors' calls for reform are quite different and do not measure up to the level of passion in their critiques. This helps uncover a deeper issue.

III. Business as a Human Institution

Rejecting the Dominant Narratives of Business

What business schools get wrong is business itself. They may get science, theory, and management wrong as well. But the problem starts with the very idea of business. Intriguingly, little of the management literature and few of the critiques offer a view of what business *is*. And absent a view of business, they are equally unclear on management and leadership.

Implicit in much of the management discussion is a mechanical, deterministic, positivistic view of business—a financial engine controlled by the machinery of scientific management—with managers making judgments about them. (This is most evident in the analytical professions, including consulting and investment banking, which now hire over half the graduating classes of the leading business schools. A consultant's job is often to diagnose and describe a business problem, and an investor's is to predict which stocks will move which direction. Both require rigorous analysis, and both tempt the practitioner to treat the business observed as an independent, determined phenomenon.)

A brief tour of the business school curriculum will find that the basic units of analysis are cash flows, products and services, processes, brands, and other stylized ideas that have acquired a metaphysical reality of their own. As Ghoshal and others suggest, our narrow ideas about value as only economic value to shareholders, our ideas about agency, about the purpose of the firm, and others are all part of the dominant narrative in business schools. And they are all artifacts of human interactions.

Like earlier mechanistic views, the scientific view of management makes it difficult to incorporate the human spirit. It leaves little room for ethics, or for other fundamentally human considerations such as creativity, trust, initiative, and will.

In very few places in business education do we begin with the basic human interactions that make business a profoundly human institution. Business, in its most essential form, is a way that we create value for each other by cooperating and specializing our labor. Business is fundamentally about value creation and trade. Business simply does not work outside of some interpersonal/social/cultural/ethical context, yet most theories of business separate business decisions from this human matrix.

We have only recently separated management as a unique activity and begun treating business as distinct from other social phenomena. 'The identification of management with business management began only with the Great Depression, which bred hostility to business and contempt for business executives. In order not to be tarred with the business brush, management in the public sector was rechristened public administration and proclaimed a separate discipline', as Peter Drucker points out (Drucker, 1998, p. 156).

> It is only the emergence of management since World War II, what I call the 'Management Revolution', that has allowed us to see that the organization is discrete and distinct from society's other institutions (Drucker, 1992, p. 100).

An Example: Challenging Separation from Ethics

This separation of business from more general human activity can be seen most clearly in the popular joke about 'business ethics as an oxymoron.' We might define the 'Separation Fallacy' this way:

> It is useful, first, to believe that sentences such as, 'x is a business decision' have no ethical content or any implicit ethical point of view. And, it is useful, second, to believe that sentences such as 'x is an ethical decision, the best thing to do, all things considered' have no content or implicit view about value creation and trade (business).

This fallacy underlies much of the dominant story about business, and it is reinforced by the approach to research that the critics of business school have decried. Yet almost any business decision has some ethical content. To see that this true, we offer the 'Open Question Argument.' One need only ask whether the following questions make sense for virtually any business decision (the Separation Fallacy would have us believe that these questions aren't relevant for making business decisions, or that they could never be answered):

(1) If this decision is made, for whom is value created, and for whom is value destroyed?
(2) Who is harmed and/or benefited by this decision?
(3) Whose rights are enabled, and whose values are realized by this decision (and whose are not)?
(4) What kind of person will I (we) become if we make this decision?

These questions are always open for most business decisions, and therefore we need a theory about business that answers them. One such answer would be 'Only value to shareholders counts', but such an answer would have to be enmeshed in the language of ethics as well as business. (Milton Friedman, unlike most of his expositors, actually gives such a morally rich answer.) However, to develop that answer meaningfully, we need an ethics capable of engaging the language and issues of business.

In short, we need a theory that has as its basis what we might call the 'Integration Thesis':

> Most business decisions, or sentences about business, have some ethical content or implicit ethical view. Most ethical decisions, or sentences about ethics, have some business content or implicit view about business.

Human Enterprise as a New Narrative

One of the most pressing challenges facing business scholars is to tell compelling narratives that have the Integration Thesis at their heart. Seeing business as a fundamentally human institution means that we can bring to bear on business the full panoply of ideas, disciplines, models, theories, and understandings from literature, the fine arts, history, anthropology, cultural studies, language studies, law, philosophy, the sciences, and other parts of the academy. It involves Sartre's idea that ethics begins with authenticity and the need to justify one's life to oneself and to others. This is no different in today's small businesses and global corporations than it was in post-World War II Paris.

Seeing business as a fundamentally human enterprise means accepting something like the 'Responsibility Principle', which is implicit in most reasonably comprehensive views. It states:

> Most people, most of the time, want to, actually do, and should accept responsibility for the effects of their actions on others.

Without something like the Responsibility Principle it is difficult to see how ethics gets off the ground. 'Responsibility' may well be a difficult and multifaceted idea. There are surely many different ways to understand it. But if we are not willing to accept responsibility for our own actions (as limited as that may be due to complicated issues of causality and the like), then ethics, understood as how we reason together so we can all flourish, is likely an exercise in bad faith.

If we want to adopt the Integration Thesis, if the Open Question Argument makes sense, and if something like the Responsibility Thesis is necessary, we need a new narrative about business. This new story must be able to explain how value-creation at once encompasses both economics and ethics, and how it takes account of all the effects of business action on others.

Such a model exists, and has been developing over the last 30 years by management researchers and ethics scholars called 'stakeholder theorists.' They have challenged much work that is done in the name of 'value-free economics and science.' Indeed they have adopted a critical stance toward much of what the critiques suggest is wrong in terms of the nature of management and its appropriate modes of analyses. But they have also invoked the second sense of the Separation Fallacy to challenge work done by philosophers who have little knowledge of either business or the business disciplines. (Sadly, recognition of their work is missing in most of the critiques of business schools, reinforcing our claim that these critiques are grounded in the dominant narrative.)

We are not going to review the particulars of stakeholder theory. This has been done many times over by many people.[7] We want stakeholder theory to serve as an example of the kind of work that could be done if we truly began to see business as a human enterprise. There is new work to be done to bring the richness of our colleagues' exploration of human activity and intellectual creativity to bear in the domain of management. There are many theories and research programs that could be developed. Getting the 'metaphysics of business' (if you like) right opens up many possibilities. We believe these possibilities offer the only hope for rescuing our business schools.

---

[7] A recent statement that reflects our view is Freeman et al., 2007.

A Valuable Corollary

If business were seen as a human enterprise, business people could again be seen as human beings. (The prevailing view, that business people are a different species, can be seen in our experience teaching ethics to high school seniors. Presented with the ethical decision of whether to read a folder left behind in a negotiation, the students split evenly on whether to read it. But 100% thought business people would read it.) We could encourage students and business people to bring their human sensibilities and judgment into the business setting. Rather than teaching 'business ethics' as a special discipline, whose very existence needed to be defended, we could teach ethics and their application in the business environment.

IV. Rescuing Business Education

If we put the humanity of business into the center of the way we think about it, we must deal with two fundamental questions and four problems of management and leadership in business, even if only by redirecting them. Once these have been addressed, there will remain one big challenge. We appeal to our 'common sense' about business for the legitimacy of what we offer.

Two Fundamental Questions

We simply cannot understand business as a human enterprise without putting these two questions at the center of our inquiry:

(1) What does it mean to be a fully complex human being?

(2) How do complex human beings create value and trade with each other, and what is the meaning of such activity?

We are not arguing for a particular answer to these questions. There can be many. However, we must ask them if we are to understand the real world of business, where there are actual people engaging in relationships and transactions with one other. They cannot be reduced to questions of cash flows, markets, hierarchies, products, role-related behaviors such as consumer behavior, and other sometimes useful but non-foundational ideas.

Four Problems

Having raised these two questions, we must address four problems of management and leadership.

The 'Problem of Authority'

How are we to understand the authority relationships that exist in business, and make sense of them in human terms? Is there a conflict between these relationships and our autonomy as moral agents? How can the work of thinkers such as Philip Zimbardo, Stanley Milgram, Hannah Arendt, Nietzsche, and others be brought to bear on the authority relationships in business? As globalization extends Western models into new cultures, are there other thinkers and models which we must address?

The 'Problem of the Self.'

How are we to understand the role of the self in business? Is the self to be understood as an autonomous agent acting 'for itself', or is it to be understood as a complex interacting set of relationships? What is the role of the history of a 'self'? In particular, what is the connection between the development of self, its engagement in an enterprise, and the relationship of authority? How do race, gender, sexuality, and other 'variables' connect to our ideas about the self? And, how does the concept of the self connect to how we create value and trade with each other?

The 'Problem of Ethics'

Is the history of our ethics a history devoid of the effects of value creation and trade? If human beings have been 'value creators and traders' for a very long time, how could this idea have been absent for most of our discussion of ethics? Would a better first question for political theory be 'How is value creation and trade sustainable over time', rather than, 'How is the state justified'?

The 'Problem of Human Nature'

Is there any such thing as 'human nature'? What do traditional and new narratives about business assume about human nature? Can we have an idea of 'humanity' that transcends individuals without an idea of human nature? What is the role of institutions such as business in shaping our ideas about, or even the facts of, how humans can live? Conversely, should our views about human nature shape what we view to be acceptable, or even possible, business institutions and practices?

Each of these problems is large, and for the most part, all are ignored in the current business school curriculum. The dominant narrative must ignore them. They also must be ignored if Ghoshal and others are correct about the scientism that has taken hold in business schools. These problems simply cannot be addressed solely with traditional 'scientific' or 'social scientific' methods and concepts.

One Big Challenge.

These questions and problems open a rich discussion about the nature of business, management, and leadership. However, they only lay the groundwork for the big challenge:

> What should business schools do—how, when, and for whom—to educate leaders and managers of these human enterprises?

The expanding scholarship of teaching and learning, especially in the liberal arts colleges, rightly draws the distinction between the 'what' of education and the 'how.' Conservatories and creative writing institutes have long understood the differences between criticism and performance, as well as the role of the former in helping to develop the latter. We in the business schools need to understand the balance of our own activities between developing scholars versus practitioners of business, and therefore the best means of achieving this. Here science may offer a better solution, since the laboratory environment develops scientists through apprenticeship rather than lecture.

The foundational questions raised here should give us a better sense of the phenomena of business and possibly how to study them. They may also give us a deeper understanding of the nature of management. This only prepares us to ask the questions about the educational task ahead.

V. An Agenda for Change

If we put these questions and problems at the center of the educational processes for business people, business schools may, over time, come to look very different. We want to suggest five items in an agenda for change. There are many others.

Lead a Conversation on the Connection Between Business and the Humanities

Scholars in the humanities need to become more literate in the real world of business, so that they can offer different lenses to understand value creation and trade. Ph.D. programs in business disciplines need to be broadened to use a wider range of texts and to become more interdisciplinary. Business educators need to look to the humanities for new ways of teaching, especially developing students' judgment and creativity. Above all we need a set of Dewey-like experiments to create new modes of conceptualization.

Rethink the Business Disciplines

We can take each of the disciplines of business and identify concepts that we might call, after Michael Walzer, 'morally thick.' Our goal would not be to drive out the value implications from traditional conceptual schemes, but to welcome them as different lenses.

For instance, suppose that we understood business as a human enterprise and took the two fundamental questions and four problems to heart in marketing. We might ask whether a company's relationship with a consumer is a promise, like the promises that parents make to children, and if the value of its brand is rooted in trust. We might ask whether we should understand customers as ends in themselves, whose projects are important precisely because they are their projects, rather than means to our own ends. We might define our 'value proposition' in terms of our contribution to consumers' own values. We might ask about the moral significance of brands and the effects of brands on civic space or on civil society or on our understanding of the environment, possibly accepting that the consumer as well as the producer has rights regarding the brand.[8]

In finance, we might see markets as having moral relevance and cash flow as a utilitarian measurement of how well a company is creating value for its stakeholders. The challenge raised by Sharia finance might become real, i.e., how does a lender truly participate in the activities funded? Across all of these, we might explore where diverse global cultures should give rise to distinct, locally relevant answers.

Rethink the Disciplinary Matrix of Business Schools

We also need to rethink the disciplinary mix. The world has changed so much that the traditional functionally defined subjects (defined, ironically, by stakeholder group) may no longer be appropriate. Most schools offer courses in marketing (customers), finance (shareholders or financiers), operations (suppliers and production), human resources or organizational behavior/theory or manage-

---

[8] For an analysis of brands as social texts, see Hatch and Rubin, 2006.

ment (employees), and public relations, ethics, or business/government (community).

Where do students learn how to deal with consumers who are employees and shareholders as well? Where do they learn how to create value with NGOs who are critics, often very well-informed critics? Where do they learn how to deal with employees who are community leaders? What standing do traditional disciplines offer to the organizations whose symbiotic products and services are critical to a business's success? What are the thick moral ideas in the new 'disciplines'?

Rethink Research

Here the critics, especially Ghoshal, are surely correct. Researchers need to take responsibility for their theories and for the effects of their actions. Theory needs most often to look more like narrative and only sometimes like 'science.' We need new narratives and new questions that better enable us to engage in value creation and trade, and they should not duck explicitly human, especially ethical, vocabulary. At a minimum, we must rethink the rampant positivism that Ghoshal has identified and debate what constitutes research appropriate to the issues studied. We need to understand how our colleagues in the humanities explore (and contribute to) performance and creativity. We need to redesign the core processes that shape our research, like publication, refereeing, tenure and promotion, and even the ratings game itself, or offer alternatives, to support more appropriate methodologies.

Rethink Teaching

Teaching needs to be very different. We need to design high engagement experiences that allow the student to develop meaningful, theory-informed practices. Management is an art and learning by doing is important, but it is easier to learn with the knowledge of the theory, as music is learned both by practice and knowledge of scales and chords.

MBA programs need their equivalent of etudes, to teach traditional skills in the traditional disciplines as well as to open up these disciplines to insights from the humanities in the morally thick manner we have suggested. But like all performers, business students need to have large experiential and practice components to their education, with teacher as guide and coach, rather than source and judge. Students need to be exposed to at least some of the best thinking and thinkers from across the university, and one would hope these thinkers would also energize their own disciplines with the idea that the business school is more than a morally suspect relative who just won't leave.

VI. Conclusion

Schools that adopt this agenda for reform have a chance to distinguish themselves. But it will not be easy. Business schools are part of universities, which are essentially medieval institutions with high resistance to change. Faculty have high needs for autonomy, among other psychological quirks. Students are driven by their perceptions of what will work in the marketplace. Employers need to fill immediate needs for analysts. And companies and business leaders hire graduates based on particular skill needs in the short term. Deans rarely have the courage to tackle such a project.

To adopt this agenda successfully, a school would have to be aligned around its purpose and have a live conversation about whether that purpose can be realized in the world described by Ghoshal, Mintzberg, and others. Unless schools adopt it, however, they will likely be but a long and uninteresting footnote to Joseph Wharton's failed experiment.

Bibliography

Drucker, Peter (5 October 1998), "Management's New Paradigms", *Forbes*.

Drucker, Peter (September-October 1992), "The New Society of Organizations", *Harvard Business Review*.

Freeman, R. Edward (1994), "Epilogue", in *Business as a Humanity*, ed. Thomas Donaldson and R. Edward Freeman (New York: Oxford University Press).

Freeman, R. Edward, Harrison, Jeffrey, and Wicks, Andrew (2007), *Managing for Stakeholders: Survival, Reputation, and Success* (New Haven, CT: Yale University Press).

Ghoshal, Sumantra (March 2005), "Bad Management Theories are Destroying Good Management Practices", *Academy of Management Learning and Education* 4, pp. 75–91.

Hamel, Gary (February 2006), "The How, Why, and What of Management Innovation", *Harvard Business Review*, pp. 72–84.

Hatch, Mary Jo, and Rubin, James (September 2006), "The Hermeneutics of Branding", *Journal of Brand Management* 14, pp. 40–59.

Marshall, Leon C. (1928), "The American Collegiate School of Business", in *The Collegiate School of Business: Its Status at the Close of the First Quarter of the Twentieth Century*, ed. Leon C. Marshall (Chicago: University of Chicago Press).

Mintzberg, Henry (2004), *Managers Not M.B.A.s: A Hard Look at the Soft Practice of Managing and Management Development* (San Francisco: Berrett-Koehler).

Mulligan, Thomas M. (October 1987), "The Two Cultures in Business Education", *Academy of Management Review* 12, pp. 593–9.

Peters, Thomas and Waterman, Robert (1982), *In Search of Excellence: Lessons from America's Best-Run Companies* (New York: Harper and Row).

Porter, Michael (1980), *Competitive Strategy: Techniques for Analyzing Industries and Competitors* (New York: Free Press).

Ruml, Frances (1928), "The Formative Period of Higher Commercial Education in American Universities", in *The Collegiate School of Business: Its Status at the Close of the First Quarter of the Twentieth Century*, ed. Leon C. Marshall (Chicago: University of Chicago Press).

VandeCreek, Drew E. (1994), "Power and Order: The Ideology of Professional Business Training at Wharton and Harvard, 1881–1933", (master's thesis, University of Virginia).

Whitehead, Alfred North (1966), "Universities and their Function", in *The Aims of Education and other Essays* (1929: reprint, New York: Macmillan).

Kevin T. Jackson

Cultivating the Ethics-Economics Interface

What does it mean to speak of a morally educated businessperson? It means a person armed with core ethical principles, ethical awareness, and ethical reasoning skills, capable of responding to a changing legal and compliance environment as well as complex, conflicting, and sometimes highly problematic interests and opportunities, and moreover prepared to assume the duties and rewards of stewardship, including taking into account multiple stakeholders' concerns before rendering decisions and wielding power responsibly.

A confluence of factors, ranging from the 2008 global economic crisis, the raft of recent corporate scandals to the growth of socially responsible investing, the escalating influence of corporations, a rise in legal and regulatory standards, and mounting forces of globalization, are bringing about an ethics-oriented paradigm for business (Paine, 2003; Trevino & Nelson, 2004). Some business schools are ratcheting up their efforts — a few of them joining forces with corporate executives (Mangan, 2004) — to blend ethics initiatives into their management curricula (Flanigan, 2003; Murray, 2003; Weisman, 2003). Modifications to the AACSB guidelines are prompting business schools to emphasize moral reasoning and personal reflection.[1]

---

[1] AACSB International — The Association to Advance Collegiate Schools of Business, *Eligibility Procedures and Accreditation Standards for Business Accreditation*, 31 January 2007 revision (Tampla, FL: AACSB International 2007). The standards provide, in relevant part: 'The institution or the business programs of the institution must *establish expectations for ethical behavior* by administrators,

I. Re-Examining Assumptions

As one scholar has observed, 'many business schools educate managers to focus almost exclusively on profits and to base their professional careers largely on monetary achievements' (Mitroff, 2004). Business education must challenge the conventional assumptions underlying this phenomenon. One fundamental assumption is that there is a major opposition between economics and ethics. What new viewpoint can supply fresh assumptions about the nature of this relationship? In what ways might business education foster morally educated businesspersons and help them flourish as leaders in today's business environment?

The concept of reputational capital establishes a foundation for a new mindset about business education and business management. This enlightened outlook:

(1) harmonizes financial and social imperatives

(2) deters business misconduct without adopting a compliance-compulsive orientation

(3) infuses moral awareness across disciplines

(4) mediates cross-cultural worldviews to stimulate competitiveness and foster positive social integration.

It establishes a connection between the cultivation of virtuous managers through business education, and the cultivation of virtuous companies through management guided by the moral and economic benefits of reputational capital.

Comparing Shareholder and Stakeholder Conceptions

The idea of reputational capital assimilates both shareholder and stakeholder conceptions, incorporating the best interest of shareholders by harmonizing both ethical and economic mandates. The received view of business is embodied in the shareholder conception advanced by Milton Friedman for promoting a free-market economy. 'In such an economy, there is one and only one social responsi-

---

faculty, and students.' Section 1(E). 'Normally the curriculum management process will result in an undergraduate degree program that includes learning experiences in such general knowledge and skill areas as ... *Ethical understanding and reasoning abilities* ... *Multicultural and diversity understanding* ... *Reflective thinking skills* ... Normally the curriculum management process will result in undergraduate and master's level general management degree programs that will include learning experiences in such management-specific knowledge and skills areas as: *Ethical and legal responsibilities in organizations and society.*' [Italics added.] Section 2(15).

bility of business—to use its resources and engage in activities designed to increase its profits so long as it stays within the rules of the game, which is to say, engages in open and free competition, without deception or fraud' (Friedman, 1962, p. 133).

According to this view, what matters most is beating the competition and maximizing the bottom line; business ethics is an oxymoron. Such a mindset, what R.E. Freeman terms the 'separation thesis' (Freeman, 1994), rejects the idea that economic value is grounded in corporate social responsibility. Economics and ethics constitute polarized forms of discourse for managerial decision-making and business practices. 'Social responsibility' betrays a fundamental misconception about the character and nature of a free economy; makes the interests of all groups other than shareholders impose constraints, rather than goals, on corporate activities; and leaves the proof of payoffs from investing in social initiatives unsubstantiated. The only plausible case to be made for obeying legal and ethical standards, under this position, is to avoid the monetary cost of noncompliance.

The standard alternative view, stakeholder theory, argues that maximizing profits for shareholders is not the sole purpose of a business; but that it serves the larger society, including an array of other constituents: employees, customers, suppliers, and the communities in which the firm operates (Freeman, 1984; Goodpaster, 1991; McDaniel, 1991). The scope of corporate social responsibility is wider than meeting the bottom line for shareholders, and business firms' ethical and discretionary responsibilities go beyond their purely economic and legal responsibilities (Carroll, 1979).

The Pros and Cons

What advantages do these approaches provide? Shareholder theory correctly assumes that corporations are structured to make money—they operate under an imperative to meet the bottom line to survive, not to serve as social-welfare agencies. Stakeholder theory, on the other hand, correctly assumes that corporations must deploy the power they wield in a socially responsible way—corporations should be governed so as to benefit all parties having a stake in the firm's activities (Boatright, 2003, p. 390).

What are their limitations? Shareholder theory neglects the fact that a watchful public, the media, and government will not permit corporations to work exclusively to maximize profit in the service of shareholders while ignoring the ensuing blowback to other constituencies.

Stakeholder theory:

(1) does not give sufficiently rigorous criteria for settling disputes about who or what counts as a qualified stakeholder

(2) lends inadequate guidance as to just how a firm's leaders should balance the competing interests of various purported stakeholders, especially when such interests are conflicting and mutually exclusive (e.g., allocating money to improve workers' wages diverts a firm's resources from giving consumers the same quality product at a lower price)

(3) does not provide a solution to the problem of the extent to which individual firms can be held responsible for a certain outcome when success requires common effort on the part of a sufficiently large number of individual firms (e.g., ensuring cooperation of individual corporations in an anti-corruption policy).

Acquiring New Perspective: The Notion of Reputational Capital

Reorienting business education demands a fresh concept that dismantles the wall between the shareholder and stakeholder theories and links integrity and fair dealing to the bottom line. This new pole-star for business education is reputational capital. Reputational capital is a synthetic notion for three key functions of the stakeholder model: the descriptive, instrumental, and normative (Donaldson & Preston, 1995). The firm's reputation is the stakeholders' *description* of the corporation from the standpoint of their respective roles. Pursuing reputational capital requires that corporate executives care about their shareholders, employees, customers, suppliers, and other affected parties. So the concept of promoting reputational capital *instrumentally* serves as a tool for managers to construct strategic stakeholder relations to generate profit. At the same time, it implicitly reflects a *normative* account of how corporations ought to treat their various stakeholders. A return on reputational capital realizes the 'intrinsic value' of satisfying the interests of all stakeholders (Donaldson & Preston, 1995, p. 67). The more reputational capital a firm builds, the greater the return to shareholders and other stakeholders.

Considering the Value of Intangibles

In the interest of grasping how reputational capital incorporates the best interest of shareholders by harmonizing both ethical and economic mandates, it will be helpful to first examine a conventional assumption about how to determine the firm's economic value. A prevailing view in the finance discipline deems that a company's economic value is measured by its equity (shareholder wealth), in book value (accounting), or in market value (stock price). This measure is somewhat illusory, however, since there are a range of ways to determine the economic value of firms. The task involves choosing whether the interests of just the shareholders, or of all constituents of the firm, or of all groups affected by the firm's activities, matter most, and whether short-term or long-term interests are taken to be paramount. Business decisions that generate short-term profits benefit well-diversified shareholders with a strong risk tolerance and a short-term outlook (Boatright, 1999). But those that cultivate long-term prospects of the firm—building up the firm's reputational capital, for example—advance the long-range interests of risk-averse shareholders as well as various constituencies having a stake in the firm.

If the value of a firm is assumed to be its value as an ongoing enterprise able to create wealth for society indefinitely into the future, managers should not focus on the interests of individual shareholders and on current stock price. Instead, they should weigh and balance the interests of all of the groups that make up the firm and focus on long-term performance. Hence, the real value of a firm lies much deeper than just its financial state. Along with the normal assets and liabilities, firms' balance sheets need to be extended, by adding intangibles running to and from various constituencies (employees, customers, suppliers, strategic partners, investors) and the costs incurred by the firm from damage to these intangibles. The intangibles encompass elements such as credibility, corporate culture, pride, trust, integrity, perception of fair dealing, and dignity.

The chiefly inchoate measurement scale for such intangibles ranges from reputational assets to reputational liabilities. Calculating the difference between these intangibles yields the net reputational capital of the firm. Drawing ethical considerations into the equation has the salutary result of spotlighting a dimension of wealth not captured by conventional financial accounting methodologies. Such a broadened conception paves the way for reckoning a firm's economic value beyond its financial state. Consequently, the economic value of business ethics is realized by an enterprise's strategic, financial, and operational success in establishing reputational assets. Accordingly, here is a practical idea for modern business management anchored to the ancient wisdom of Solomon: 'A good reputation and respect are worth much more than silver and gold' (Proverbs 22:1).

Motivation Matters

Someone might be inclined to ask: if a firm is motivated to do things to improve its reputation purely by the wish to make a profit, can it ultimately be successful in growing reputational capital? In other words, does the profit motivation in business always taint any purported moral motivation that tries to accompany it? Addressing this important question requires some reflection upon two fundamental points.

First, the enterprise of profit-making, when placed in proper perspective — as a process of wealth creation — is itself a source of doing good. There is no necessary contradiction between a company doing good and doing well.

Second, getting reputational rewards from good deeds does require a genuine desire to do good. One-hundred-percent purity is probably not necessary. People know that the typical for-profit company is not Mother Teresa, Inc. But they deplore corporate marketing and PR campaigns masquerading as citizenship and social responsibility initiatives, especially when used to divert attention from a firm's own misconduct. Rolling out ethics training as litigation proofing for senior management or the board dampens any positive outcomes that would otherwise be produced.

In other words, reputational capital is generated from moral action backed by sincere motivation. A company will find it difficult to realize the full financial benefits flowing from integrity and fair play unless it has an explicitly stated commitment to doing right. Attitude matters. Companies that too aggressively promote an instrumental 'it pays to be ethical' attitude undermine their efforts. Taken from a completely financial perspective, one might say that it pays to appreciate the intrinsic value of good business conduct, and that it is most prudent to guide one's actions by this premise.

Admittedly it is often hard to know what is really fueling a company's apparent good conduct. Some act insincerely. Intel lost goodwill by refusing to replace defective Pentium microchips. Intel said that typical users might get a wrong answer once every 27,000 years.

But people simply did not wish to be receiving defective microchips. Initially hit by a wave of negative publicity, Intel eventually agreed to replace the chips at no cost and apologized both for problems caused by flawed chips and its own lack of concern for its customers. But how noble was its motivation? Intel's actions were apparently more a strategic exercise in *ex post* crisis management than as a virtuous expression of day-to-day integrity.

Although some corporations act insincerely, not all do. Paradoxically, the companies that genuinely appreciate the intrinsic value of ethical conduct, as opposed to focusing exclusively on its instrumental value in increasing profits or deflecting attention from misdeeds are most likely to be rewarded financially as people discern that they have a sound reputation rooted, at least in part, in sincere motives.

Indeed the criticism that many corporations act insincerely assumes that it is possible to distinguish disingenuous public relations ploys and pursuit-of-whatever-is-fashionable motives from sincere moral commitments. That is, the skeptic's argument assumes what it wants to deny: that corporations are behaving *wrongly* when they use ethics as an attention-deflecting or fashion-following strategy instead of honoring it for its own sake. If it were true that *all* corporations *always* acted insincerely, if it were not possible for them to act on a higher moral plane, what would be the point of drawing our attention to and condemning such behavior?

The Importance of Trust

Trust is a necessary precondition of legitimate successful business activity. Simply put, if there is no trust, it is exceedingly difficult to secure a deal in the first place, and even more so to preserve lasting, profitable commercial relationships. The world of business simply would not function if each part of every financial transaction needed to be spelled out expressly in writing or delineated in a contract. Furthermore, parties prefer to do business with people who are not out to cheat them. And by sticking with people you can trust, you make gains by cutting down on transaction costs, such as those for attorneys, auditors, and inspectors. There is no substitute for trust in making deals run smoothly.

Thus, because reputation is so firmly grounded in trust and the proper functioning of business transactions requires trust, reputation is a primary attribute of commercial relationships. Building trustworthy relationships with stakeholders accumulates the intangible assets of reputational capital (Jackson, 2004). The value of shareholders' investment increases commensurately (Roman et al., 1999; Verschoor, 1998; Waddock & Graves, 1997).

It is critical to distinguish a morally educated businessperson from ethical opportunists—those bent on tweaking the firm's short-term attributes, such as corporate image and identity. Moreover, although it is common to use the terms 'corporate identity', 'corporate image', and corporate reputation' interchangeably, these concepts are not the same. A firm's identity and image relate to elements of its 'personality', such as corporate name, logo, advertising slogans, and brand image, which are targeted primarily at consumers. The reputation of the firm, by contrast, pertains to deeper attributes of the firm's character and integrity. Thus, unlike image and identity, yet somewhat akin to individual virtue, corporate reputation requires consistent moral behavior over a period of time to develop. And reputation is associated with all aspects of a company, cutting across all of its departments and divisions.

A morally educated businessperson is deeply aware of how reputation is cultivated, earned over the long term by attention to integrity, respect, authenticity, and fair dealing. She grasps its potential for bringing specific strategic advantages. She knows there is no column on the balance sheet that assigns a monetary value to a firm's reputation, and no item on the income statement that gives a financial return for reputational capital.(7) Yet equally she knows that having a strong reputation magnifies the worth of a business enterprise beyond the book value of 'goodwill' contemplated by accounting rules.

II. Rethinking Goals

What are we to take the legitimate goals of business education to be? During a presentation on ethics education I gave at an AACSB conference a few years ago in New Orleans, one side of the audience believed that business schools should be motivated to invigorate ethics instruction to keep future MBAs out of jail. An opposing side stressed the importance of enlightening businesspeople to attain excellence and promote socially responsible and sustainable business. It seemed to me that the divisiveness with which the discussion played out betrayed an unbalanced conception within institutions of higher learning and corporate ethics offices alike of what it is to be a morally educated businessperson.

Pitting Practical Against Abstract

Business practitioners normally take the perspective of business law and specific ethical rules to be paramount. They take a hard-nosed, practical approach to management education. Inculcating crisp directives for right conduct into future business leaders will clean up the moral landscape of corporate America. The emerging mandate referred to in the Introduction, that business schools expand the teaching of ethics in their programs of study as a response to widespread business scandals is one manifestation of this approach.

Others hold that, strictly speaking, there is no '*business* ethics' per se (Maxwell, 2003). Ethics and morality are almost exclusively a matter of following the most fundamental, abstract, and universal principles. Such a mindset is reflected in the following passage from a well-respected textbook on business ethics:

> Business ethics is not a separate ethics that constrains business in a way that other human and social endeavors are not constrained. Nors does it permit business to do what one is not allowed to do in other areas of life. It is part of the general field of ethics and only within that wider sphere can it be properly understood (De George, 1999, p. 19).

The first perspective consists of following specific norms. For example, the rules imposed by the Sarbanes-Oxley legislation and rules governing 'yield burning' and 'pay-to-play' in the mutual-bond industry. It forms a moral code of convention or customary practice. The standards are spelled out in corporate ethics programs such as voluntary codes of conduct and legal compliance regimes (Aaronson, 2001; Donaldson, 2000). The second perspective consists of more abstract principles and goals by reference to which critical thinking about the first level takes place. Goals and principles are used to understand and evaluate specific rules. Examples include the goal of maximizing the total net utility in society and the principle that corporations should maximize wealth for shareholders.

In debates about the goals of business ethics education, almost always either the practical approach (focused on laws and rules) or the abstract approach (focused on reasoning-with-principles) is relegated to an inferior, or at least unimportant, position.

What Does Reality Dictate?

Effective management in the real business world requires coordinating the two levels on which moral thinking and ethical judgment take place. This realty should drive business education to achieve the right balance between both. The morally educated businessperson knows and obeys 'the letter of rules'—specific norms. A legal rule-oriented approach equips the student with knowledge of norms and facilitates her taking prudent actions in specific contexts. At the same time, she also complies with 'the spirit of rules'—going beyond specific norms by garnering reasoning skill and ethical awareness based on her own self-accepted core moral standards.

Goals, Conventions, and Duties

Let us take it as given that some universally valid abstract principles and goals exist. For example, that everyone has a right to equal respect And that net-total utility ought to be maximized. In many cases, such principles and goals by themselves fail to establish concrete rules. They require coordinated action on the part of many people if they are going to fly. And two or more mutually incompatible plans of action may each advance the same principle or goal.

Here is an illustration. Suppose it is a fundamental goal that employees get financial support in retirement. What concrete duties can be derived from this goal? Does each company have a duty simply to support its own employees with pensions and no one else? Or does each individual (or corporation) have the duty to make a contribution to a social fund (social security), which will then be used to support retirees? Is every person obligated to contribute to his or her personal retirement account? A determinate answer could only be derived through a social convention coordinating everyone's actions.

If it is generally understood that everyone will contribute to a social fund, the goal will be adequately advanced if a sufficient number make their contributions, but it might also be adequately advanced if every business supported its own employees. At the same time, if one follows a rule different from the prevailing convention, the result might be to make no contribution or excess contribution to advancing the goal. To act in accordance with two or more of the rules might be to make sacrifices beyond what could be reasonably expected of any individual person or firm. In short, we often need to know what actions we can expect of others if we are to know what effect our individual actions will have.[2]

---

[2] I am indebted to the late Prof. Conrad Johnson for this idea as well as the example that illustrates it.

Having some convention or custom at hand can lend assistance to this interaction problem by providing people with mutual expectations about each other's conduct. The existence of a convention also makes publicly known what we can reasonably expect of one another, and when our actions or failures to act make us the proper object of external sanctions such as criticism or blame, or internal sanctions of conscience. In other words, the presence of convention provides conditions for the existence of specific duties.

A degree of arbitrariness lingers in business ethics in the sense that there are different and incompatible codes around which business conduct can be coordinated to advance fundamental, universal ends. Which codes happen to get drawn up by various companies is largely arbitrary. That is, the codes are more arbitrary than the fundamental ends. Whatever may be the best way for arriving at valid universal principles, there remains the need for a code of fairly specific (though not necessarily formally promulgated) rules for implementing those principles.

Fitting Specific Rules Within Broad Principles

Laying stress on the letter of rules clearly hasn't stemmed the tide of corporate scandals. Neglecting to improve confidence in business integrity while cranking out more laws is counterproductive. Over-regulated firms channel tremendous energy toward compliance, meaning loophole-hunting, while gliding over the spirit of the rules (Jennings, 2003).

Today's business is dynamic and calls for forward-looking leadership. A 'reasoning with principles' approach helps to guide the student into taking a moral position.

Looking to a broad principle or theory can give coherence and unity to specific rules, and helps in correctly applying the rules. Consider this rule, a version of which is found in most banks: 'Don't process your own personal bank transactions, and don't have relatives or close friends process them either.' Just what is a 'close friend'? Precisely how distant does a relative have to be? It is trying to avoid a conflict of interest, because conflicts of interest can interfere with one's legitimate contractual role at the bank and put stakeholders at inappropriate risk. We need to know the point of the rule to apply it intelligently. Taking a moral position means being willing to be bound by a principle acceptable to all other affected parties, give good reasons when that principle is challenged, and make a good-faith effort to reach a mutually acceptable position and to stick to it without making ad hoc or opportunistic exceptions just to advance one's own interests or ideals. This is not to say that all of what is involved in being a morally educated businessperson is exhausted by being disposed to adopt and act on principle. As proponents of an 'ethic of care' are keen to point out (Noddings, 1984; Noddings, 2002; Tronto, 1993), the moral person sees and identifies with the feelings and interests of others.

Recapitulation

Looking back at this section by way of summary we see two sets of arguments. The first applies to those advocating a rule-oriented approach to ethics initiatives. Although recent scandals have prompted a turn to specific rules to increase corporate accountability, many business situations are too complex for a straightforward application of specific rules. One needs judgment and discernment to apply them. But judgment and discernment in turn depend upon an understanding of the goals and purposes of the rules. Ultimately these derive from the principle level. Therefore, a morally educated businessperson needs an appreciation of the abstract realm of principle.

The second set of arguments speaks to proponents of broader, principle-oriented ethics initiatives, such as courses in applied moral reasoning. The weakness of such an approach becomes apparent when one reflects that, at the end of the day, business education aims more at teaching business leaders how to successfully work in the real world than, say, illuminating aspiring philosophers as to the value of knowledge for its own sake. Plus, the depth of corporate scandals and attendant stepped-up legal standards requires detailed legally compliant responses.

Some Practical Recommendations

Educators need to develop both kinds of skills and be familiar with both areas. Business professors might want to consider taking courses to keep them current in the more detailed rule-dominated regions. Teach-the-educator courses could be developed along the lines of continuing legal education courses, covering specific fields such as securities regulation, employment discrimination, information technology, and so on.

Business education should arouse a motivation to not only obey the law but also to go beyond that to obey the spirit of law. This is so for two good reasons. First, business leaders will not grasp the point of going beyond bare minimum legal requirements (into ethics) unless they first know what the law is. Second, maintaining and building a good reputation demands following both the letter and the spirit of law (Jackson, 2003).

A path needs to be charted that avoids potential perils from two extremes. On the one hand, a business curriculum should not let, say, philosophy or theology courses mischaracterize business ethics issues by removing those issues too far from their essential business habitat (e.g., ignoring concerns for meeting the bottom line and maintaining a competitive edge). On the other hand, a curriculum should not let business law courses portray business ethics merely as a matter of legal compliance.

III. Re-constituting Disciplines

The challenge of bringing ethics education into business schools is often framed as a choice between having a separate business ethics course and using an 'infusion' approach, with instructors from each discipline expected to raise students' awareness of ethical issues as they pertain to each of these disciplines. (A school can pursue both approaches simultaneously [Treviño & Weaver, 1994].)

There are several shortcomings with using traditional academic business fields as vehicles for teaching business ethics. Just directing a marketing or a finance professor to 'raise ethics issues' that come up in the course does not ensure that any systematic examination of the issues takes place, even if the instructor has the best intentions for doing so. And such an approach does not necessarily lead to deep and lasting solutions to the ethical challenges of the new paradigm.

Even worse, it can become a pretext for not doing anything. Faculty may lack expertise in the finely detailed nuances in rules, or in linking the rules to broader matters of principles. They may feel they have a hard enough time getting the essentials of their own material across without taking a time-consuming detour through ethics. On the other hand keeping business ethics restricted to a separate course has its own shortcomings, especially if the course is taught outside the business school, say, in the philosophy department. That arrangement can keep business ethics isolated from real world challenges.

By itself the deployment of abstract moral reasoning fails to provide satisfactory resolutions of many practical ethical dilemmas in business (Badaracco, 1997). A regimen of moral reasoning may also fail to cultivate moral imagination (Johnson, 1993): 'the ability to perceive that a web of competing economic relationships is, at the same time, a web of moral relationships ... searching out places where people are likely to be hurt by decision making or behavior of managers' (Carroll, 1987, p. 13) and the 'awareness of various dimensions of a particular context as well as its operative framework and narratives ... [t]he ability to understand that context or set of activities from a number of different perspectives, the actualizing of new possibilities that are not context-dependent, and the instigation of the process of evaluating those possibilities from a moral point of view' (Werhane, 1999, p. 5).

Moreover, it does not necessarily help students leverage a firm's limited cash flow to achieve the moral ends they have come to appreciate so profoundly. Faced with specific problems in the real world, such a student finds that they do not come neatly packaged as the 'ethics dilemmas' framed in his course book of case studies.

So how should business education cultivate a student's ability to respond to the dynamic business scenarios one confronts in the real world? How can business ethics courses be made more practical and down-to-earth? How can students be motivated to continue lifelong learning about the ethical dimension? How can what's going on in abstract case studies be linked to what students are going to be facing in the real world?

Working Across Disciplines

One way is to develop interdisciplinary business ethics courses. For instance, a course could use risk-control methodologies from the finance area to explore methods of controlling ethical risk. Or it might compare the conventional metrics of a company's financial success, such as earnings-per-share or revenue growth, with the various non-financial criteria that are figuring into the equation of corporate success (corporate citizenship, quality management, ethical leadership, responsible governance, fair marketing, brand equity). When integrated into business performance, these non-financial facets can be leveraged to build long-term reputational capital for the firm. Such intangible assets make up a substantial part of a company's net value.

Another possibility to consider is a course that merges ethics with marketing and communications to stimulate students' thinking about stakeholder relationships. They could be challenged to enlighten marketplace participants about the significance of non-financial factors such as integrity and fair dealing in creating value for business organizations. A significant ethical challenge for public relations and advertising is to move beyond just 'relationship building' to meeting the demands of conducting honest, open, fair, and compassionate business. Another is to find the proper degree of proactivity in getting the word out about what a firm is doing in terms of its commitments to the fundamentals of running an ethical enterprise.

Finally, business courses can be affiliated with psychology. Such a course might explore the questions raised by research exploring how cognitive limitations and personal biases influence ethical decision-making:[3] How is a person's perception of and judgment about ethical dilemmas influenced by workplace pressures (e.g., time and money) and demands (e.g., an overbearing boss)? Does having a self-interest in transactions tend to make people rationalize unethical behavior? Are there unforeseen consequences of being too stringent and diligent in enforcing legal and ethical compliance, such as causing people to act irrationally, prompted by excessive fear of sanctions?

It is interesting to note a similarity between the compartmentalization issue as it arises in business schools, and its appearance within the business firm itself. Parallel to the debate about where ethics should be placed in the curriculum is a debate about whether there should be a separate ethics officer, a separate chief reputation officer (CRO), or whether such functions should be infused throughout the organization.

Some companies opt to appoint a CRO or a CRA (chief reputation adviser), whose chief task is to protect the company's intangible reputational assets. The CRO's responsibilities entail oversight of advertising; corporate contributions; employee, customer, and media relations; quality; legal compliance; investor relations; and public affairs. The CRO usually works with specialists from each field, helping them to acknowledge the consequences for the company's reputation of decisions. Should a firm use a CRO, or have all of its responsibilities handled by the CEO? Setting up a distinct CRO function can put up walls, when what is really needed is to integrate the firm's character into its actions. Smaller firms normally do not need to establish a CRO position, but whether a firm opts for a CRO or not, it should make everyone in each department of the firm a guardian of the company's reputation.

---

[3] Gaudine & Thorne, 2001; Trevino & Youngblood, 1990; Midlarski & Midlarski, 1973; Lowenstein, 1996; Derry, 1987.

The board of directors has legal and fiduciary duties toward shareholders. Since reputational capital is a significant form of wealth from a stock-growth perspective, the board should also shoulder responsibility for fostering conduct that builds and protects this valuable asset of the business enterprise.

IV. Re-defining Context

In our globalized business world, increased contact between different cultures escalates conflict and the need for inter-culture and inter-region cooperation. Differences of moral conviction notoriously give rise to a special kind of conflict of interests. Whether some practice affects their own liberty or economic prospects, or their interests in some narrow sense, people do, as a matter of fact, often take an intense interest in the convictions and behavior of corporations.

The expansion of multinational corporations, booms in emerging markets, and culturally diverse workplaces (Davids, 1999; Donaldson, 1996) raises the question for business education: Is it better for future businesspeople to be more tolerant, or less so, in dealing with the moral conflicts posed by a multicultural world?

Business educators should be mindful of their purposes in teaching ethics in the multicultural context. I submit that some central legitimate purposes are: enhancing students' business skills for different cultural environments, not separating people but seeking to integrate them; improving corporate competitiveness; finding creative solutions to the pervasive 'when in Rome' versus 'righteous American' dilemmas (De George, 1993); and arousing students' awareness about the rationality (or irrationality, as the case may be) of their own and others' moral preferences and aversions.

Challenges of Pluralism

Today's pluralistic world embodies major differences in preferences and aversions, together with ever-shifting expectations about corporate social responsibility. Generally speaking, Wal-Mart is viewed positively in Asia yet negatively in Germany (Armour, 2003). Starbucks is widely adored in Asia but despised in some parts of Europe, in particular, France (Wyatt, 2004). Consequently, such companies confront obstacles to entering countries skeptical of the social value it may bring.

People's moral preferences and aversions are embedded in global capital, consumer, and labor markets—what Thomas Dunfee calls 'marketplace morality' (Dunfee, 1999). Moral desires are reflected in capital markets with mutual funds engaged in socially responsible investing and people screening their personal investments (say, eschewing gambling or tobacco stocks). They are reflected in consumer markets when consumers support their preferences for a clean environment by paying more for pollution-reducing fuel even though the law does not force them to buy it. Canned tuna sales increased for companies that switched to suppliers that protected dolphins, even though the switch elevated prices. Consumers voice disapproval of a company's practices by joining boycotts. They are reflected in labor markets, when job seekers choose jobs according to their perceptions of ethical work environments.

People from one culture may have a strong aversion to what they perceive as another culture's denial of equal rights for women, deprivation of freedom of speech and political and religious expression, use of child labor or forced prison labor of political dissidents, or liberty-restricting family policies. They may link these aversions to the idea that companies have a legitimate interest in addressing such behavior, whether by internal governance systems, lobbying efforts, criticism, economic boycotts, employee indoctrination, or proper moral development.

To express moral anger or resentment is to take the position of speaking, not just for oneself, but for one's organization, for society, in defense of some legitimate collective or individual interest. (By 'legitimate collective or individual interest' I mean that some behaviors may hurt many people, but not significantly hurt any one person, as insider trading hurts investors but not an individual investor. In suppressing such behavior, society would be protecting no significant individual interest but a collective interest.) This is one reason why moral thought and language in transnational business contexts strikes many as imperialistic. If business students are encouraged to 'moralize' in the sense of thinking of virtually all of their preferences and aversions as the legitimate object of corporate involvement and/or society's protection, the resulting conflict may be inconsistent with building the foundations of cooperation and mutually shared principles needed in a pluralistic business world.

Virtually any activity that multinational enterprises undertake, even if the firm intends to do good, raises someone's ire it seems. H.B. Fuller Company, known as a good corporate citizen in Minnesota, was chastised for not doing more to prevent street kids in Central American countries from sniffing its product, Resistol glue, as an intoxicant, and seriously injuring themselves (Bowie & Lenway, 2008).

Rational Scrutiny of Preferences and Aversions

What qualities are needed of morally educated businesspersons, if they are to advance the productivity, stability, and enlightenment of a pluralistic world? The morally educated businessperson will have the developed capacity to sort out those preferences and aversions that, although intensely felt, can be dismissed as irrational or unimportant and those of rational and of fundamental importance (Brandt, 1979). Some aversions are simply grounded in ignorance, or percolate up from early, submerged experiences which, if brought to light, vanish. Others, though neither irrational nor capable of being eradicated, are not sufficiently important to be the basis for moralizing about the behavior of business organizations. It can be instructive to reflect upon Jesus' admonition 'Judge not, that you may not be judged' (Matthew 7:1), and remember that it takes a good moral character to know when to raise the moral issue (Dewey, 1944, p. 354; Dewey & Tufts, 1908, pp. 254–8).

It is important that the morally educated businessperson reflect on whether her moral judgments represent interests so fundamental, rational, and indispensable as to justify attacking the reputations of, or laying a significant claim on, not to say outright deprivation of, the liberty of people and businesses in other cultures.

The Idea of Reputational Sanctions

What are the sources of reputational liability in the new paradigm? Here a legal analogue is helpful. Whereas courts of law enforce sanctions for legal rules, reputational sanctions are created by both what we may term the 'court of key constituencies' (the stakeholders: the employees, suppliers, business partners, clients, investors, and so on) and the 'court of public opinion.' Unlike the judgments of legal tribunals, their judgments carry no right to an appeal. Companies have no due-process rights, no rights to confront witnesses, no presumption of innocence. In today's Internet and CNN world, a firm's conduct—whether it is exemplary or unscrupulous—is instantaneously broadcast to everyone, everywhere. And if the groups comprising the court of key constituencies form negative judgments about a firm's comportment they will simply withdraw support and give it to competitors to whom they ascribe a more favorable reputation. The Rainforest Action Network called for an international boycott of Burger King, alleging that the chain used cattle that grazed on pastures formed by denuding South American tropical forests. The company initially ignored the charges. Yet within two years Whopper sales had dropped nearly seventeen percent. While it is not possible to know exactly how much of that decline was attributable directly to the boycott, the company eventually abandoned the practices in question.

Just because expectations of ethical conduct, social responsibility, and good citizenship for firms are rising, it does not follow that *all* of the expectations are legitimate. Some basic questions to consider are:

- Is the purported moral standard universal, or is it only relative to a particular culture (or subculture)?
- What kinds of financial constraints and pressures is a firm operating under? Do such factors excuse or justify its conduct?
- Is a purported moral violation of a firm significant or trivial?
- Is the firm really just violating a pointless norm, one without a rational basis or useful social purpose?

Regarding the first question, people in one culture may believe that fundamental human rights are abstract, universal moral principles; but people from another culture may see human rights as culture-specific rules. Moreover, cultures differ as to the degree to which legal norms figure into a shared understanding of what is right and what is wrong. For instance, in highly legalistic cultures, the law is often leaned on to dictate how companies ought to behave, whereas non-legalistic cultures frequently depend upon more diffuse forms of social pressure to guide business conduct. Appreciating distinctions between theory and practice, between ideals and reality, matters. Should a firm abandon its operations using child labor in Bangladesh on the ground that this is violating human rights? What if closing the factory will catapult many families into complete poverty, since their children's wages are their only income? It is hard to address such questions in the abstract. We need to know what the conventional business practices in a given culture or country are, what the local law is, and whether it's enforced, and how its people expect each other and U.S.-based businesses to behave.

An illustration of how the second question gets engaged is seen in debates about corporate inversions. Some companies reincorporate in Bermuda and similar offshore locations to cut their worldwide tax bills. Although some arrangements are outright illegal, critics allege that even the technically legal moves amount to unpatriotic, tax-dodging tactics. On the other side, some argue that firms are justified in pursuing offshore reincorporations as a response to overly burdensome U.S. tax laws.

The third question harkens back to the legal analogue of sanctions. Just as the law makes distinctions among degrees of offenses in meting out punishments, the court of public opinion and the court of key constituents assigns reputational rewards and penalties to business behavior according to both its general level of significance and its bearing on the character of the enterprise in question. Areas of corporate behavior most advantageously governed by public, collective moral rules—violations of which would reasonably justify impositions of substantial reputational penalties—are areas in which:

(1) firms and the people working in them are tempted by interests that conflict with, not only with impersonal good, but with the rights of other firms and individuals

(2) a single public criterion applying to all is needed to ensure efficiency and to forestall self-serving rationalizations

(3) judgments must be raised to the level of public discussion, pressure, and collective sanctions, the appropriateness of which can be efficiently decided in public moral debate (paradigm cases include the use and holding of other people's property, injury of other persons, and gaining unfair advantage)

(4) the efficacy of some rules, such as those imposing environmental controls and insider trading regulations, requires that all firms obey them.

In devising and implementing competitive strategies for building a company's reputational capital, a morally educated businessperson will seek innovative ways to advance such moral norms, particularly those carrying high relevance to the core identity of the firm. Consider initiatives undertaken by Interface Carpets. In 1994, its CEO, Ray Anderson, resolved to turn all of the firm's factories on four continents into environmentally sustainable operations. It set out to recycle wherever possible, reduce pollution, and cease dumping in landfills. The firm had been using over 500 million pounds of raw material annually. It released about 900 tons of air pollutants, 600 million gallons of wastewater, and 10,000 tons of garbage each year. Within two years the company obtained twenty-three percent more efficiency from recycling, and trimmed forty million dollars in costs. The savings aided Interface in capturing the winning low bid in 1997 to carpet the Gap's new headquarters. The Gap was prompted to solicit Interface's bid due to the carpet company's bold environmental initiatives.

Human Rights Obligations of Corporations

What about international human rights and reputational capital? For several decades, attention to the responsibilities of business for human rights has been growing. Following Shell's experience in Nigeria, and Levi Strauss and Co.'s deliberations about sourcing in China, the United Nations (UN) instituted a Global Compact for Business in 2000, which enlists corporations to uphold human rights. More recently, the UN has launched other human rights initiatives, including a code of ethics for transnational corporations. And at a meeting in Switzerland of the Caux Round Table—a body of business leaders from firms in Europe, Japan, and the U. S.—the group subscribed to an international code of ethics, providing a global framework for conduct and ethical standards.

On the positive side, numerous opportunities for building reputational capital present themselves for multinational companies willing to advance human rights and fundamental freedoms. A company might opt to sponsor a park beautification initiative in a foreign country, earning political support and public trust while thwarting requests for bribes from government officials. Or a firm could commit to eliminating child labor from its production chain. In cases where unemployed children and their families would be hurt by this, a company could set up benefits programs that provide medical care and education for child laborers. Levi Strauss took a creative step by paying children's school tuition, providing uniforms and books, and offering each child a job at age fourteen. Other companies, such as Adidas, are requiring suppliers that hire children to agree not just to keep them in school, but also to pay the children normal wages while attending school.

On the negative side, significant reputational liability exists as investors, customers, employees, and human rights advocates press companies about their direct and indirect dealings with governments that systematically violate human rights.

For example, the government of Sudan is funding an Islamic militia in Darfur that is committing genocide against non-Islamic people. An estimated 400,000 people have died, and four million have been displaced. United States Trade Sanctions imposed under the

Clinton Administration in November 1997 banned direct business operations in Sudan. Harvard University divested its stock in the Chinese oil companies PetroChina and Sinopec after a committee of faculty, alumni, and students examined the issues: the genocide itself, the importance of oil to the Sudanese government, the effect of PetroChina (wholly owned by the Chinese government), one of the largest companies operating in Sudan, which generates massive revenue for the Sudanese government. Yale, Stanford, and dozens of other universities followed Harvard's lead. California and other states' legislatures approved a divestment plan. Barclay's Global and Northern Trust are marketing Sudan-free investment funds. Canadian oil firm Talisman Energy pulled out of the country in 2003, and Siemens and ABB, Ltd. left in 2007.

The divestment campaign is now targeting Fidelity, the biggest investor in PetroChina. Fidelity responded by delivering passing-the-buck statements such as the following:

> We believe the resolution of complex social and political issues must be left to the appropriate authorities of the world that have the responsibility, and capability, to address important matters of this type. And we would sincerely hope that they would do so wisely on behalf of all of the citizens of the globe (Wasik, 2007).

The company is giving two excuses for keeping clear of human rights. First, the firm deflects responsibility away from itself to 'appropriate authorities.' This stance reflects the traditional 'accountability argument', which holds that, since firms are private institutions, they are subject to a lower level of accountability than are public institutions. Without clear guidelines and accountability the argument goes, even well-intentioned corporate pursuits of socially responsible activities might distort the governance process. However, whereas the accountability argument claims that it is dangerous to unleash the power of corporations from the discipline of the market, the new mindset for business brings in the counterargument that *not* using corporate power for social betterment itself poses a moral issue. So corporations act unethically by choosing not to get involved in matters where they could have a positive impact.

Second, Fidelity alleges it lacks the capability to address human rights. That assertion embodies the traditional 'expertise argument', holding that corporations should mind their own business, focusing on profit-making instead of social agendas. After all, companies enjoying expertise with their product or service lines do not necessarily have expertise in identifying and analyzing moral issues or in promoting socially beneficial activities. Corporations attain success in the market by identifying and satisfying customer needs. Yet that ability does not necessarily carry over into non-business areas. But that argument is also out of sync with the new paradigm for business. While a company certainly may lack the expertise to solve every social ill, it has an obligation to at least confront social problems that (as here): relate to the company's conduct, affect significant numbers of people, and can be addressed with the corporation's resources. Moreover, many government agencies (especially those in less-developed countries) themselves lack the expertise to effectively cure social problems. So corporations are able to pursue joint-action with nongovernmental organizations and other businesses in launching corporate citizenship projects. The Danone Group sponsors employees in Spain to work with a local organization, SOS Children's Villages Network, to support homeless or orphaned youth. Enlisting the assistance of UNICEF, Proctor and Gamble developed products aimed at alleviating malnutrition in poor countries.

The upshot is that Fidelity faces potential reputational sanction by not following the patterns of corporate conduct established in previous disinvestment initiatives, such as in South Africa, for example, and patterns being established by its competitors with respect to the Darfur region. Dodging responsibility for human rights adversely affects a company's reputation, and ultimately its reputational capital—the most valuable intangible asset it has. Today it is expected that companies will take a leadership role in promoting human rights. Meeting the demands of that role requires that business schools cultivate morally educated businesspeople with the very competencies and sense of accountability Fidelity says it lacks.

Conclusion

This chapter examined how business education can foster morally educated businesspersons who can:

(1) embrace a new paradigm in which businesses must follow social mandates as well as financial imperatives

(2) comply with an increasingly legalistic, compliance-focused approach to ethics triggered by major business scandals, while venturing beyond compliance

(3) integrate ethics into all areas of business

(4) mediate the conflicting forces of tolerance versus intolerance occasioned by multiculturalism.

Section I urged that, since a company's reputational capital directly affects the bottom line, business education should present a broader conception of economic value than has traditionally been offered—one that accords legitimacy to intangible assets as well as tangible ones—and integrate the ethical dimension into the teaching of business strategy. Students should be encouraged, when studying cases, to explore opportunities for firms facing ethical dilemmas to cultivate reputational capital through integrity and fair play.

Section II demonstrated that business ethics education should preserve the essential rule-principle duality of moral thinking and judgment in the business world. Neither the rule nor the principle side should dominate. A morally educated business person will understand that to achieve lasting success, firms need not only to maintain reputation by legal compliance but also to magnify reputation through deeper commitments to the spirit of law, informed by the realm of principles. Business schools should not lean on law courses as an exclusive vehicle for advancing business ethics education, while those teaching ethics must be fluent in both the practical-conventional and the abstract-philosophical domains and teach students to move adroitly between the two levels. Using case studies combined with ethical theory and critical thinking is a good way to do this.

Section III gave suggestions for designing interdisciplinary ethics courses that will help the morally educated businessperson function in the real world.

Finally, Section IV showed that the morally educated businessperson must know how to discern standards of global marketplace morality by examining their appearance in capital, consumer, and labor markets. Just as important, a morally educated businessperson will seek the wisdom to strike the right balance between values that are of such fundamental social importance that their advancement and protection warrants moralizing—and adopting whatever relevant behaviors are demanded—and those values that are not.

Bibliography

Aaronson, Susan (March-April 2001), "Oh, Behave! Voluntary Codes Can Make Corporations Model Citizens", *The International Economy* 15, pp. 40–7.

Armour, Stephanie (10 February 2003), "Wal-Mart Takes Hits on Worker Treatment", *USA Today*, sec. B, p. 1.

Badaracco, Joseph (1997), *Defining Moments: When Managers Must Choose Between Right and Right* (Boston: Harvard Business School Press).
Boatright, John (2003), *Ethics and the Conduct of Business* (Upper Saddle River, NJ: Pearson, Prentice Hall).
Boatright, John (1999), *Ethics in Finance* (Oxford: Blackwell).
Bowie, Norman, and Lenway, Stefanie Ann (2008), "H.B. Fuller in Honduras: Street Children and Substance Abuse", in *Ethical Issues in Business: A Philosophical Approach*, eds. Thomas Donaldson and Patricia Werhane (Upper Saddle River, NJ: Pearson, Prentice Hall, 2008).
Brandt, Richard (1979), *A Theory of the Good and the Right* (Oxford: Oxford University Press, Clarendon Press).
Carroll, Archie (March-April 1987), "In Search of the Moral Manager", *Business Horizons* 30, p. 13.
Carroll, Archie (October 1979), "A Three-Dimensional Conceptual Model of Corporate Performance", *Academy of Management Review* 4, pp. 497–505.
Davids, Meryl (January-February 1999), "Global Standards, Local Problems", *Journal of Business Strategy* 20, pp. 38–43.
De George, Richard (1993), *Competing With Integrity in International Business* (New York: Oxford University Press).
De George, Richard (1999), *Business Ethics* (Upper Saddle River, NJ: Pearson, Prentice Hall).
Derry, Robin (1987), "Moral Reasoning in Work-Related Conflicts", *Research in Corporate Social Performance and Policy*, vol. 9 (Greenwich, CT: JAI Press), pp. 5–50.
Dewey, John (1944), *Democracy and Education* (1917; reprint, New York: Free Press).
Dewey, John, and Tufts, James H. (1908), *Ethics* (New York: Henry Holt).
Donaldson, Thomas (13 November 2000), "Adding Corporate Ethics to the Bottom Line", *Financial Times*, p. 6.
Donaldson, Thomas (September-October 1996), "Values in Tension: Ethics Away From Home", *Harvard Business Review*, pp. 48–62.
Donaldson, Thomas, and Preston, Lee (January 1995), "The Stakeholder Theory of the Corporation: Concepts, Evidence, and Implications", *Academy of Management Review* 20, pp. 65–91.
Dunfee, Thomas (Summer 1999), "Corporate Governance in a Market with Morality", *Law and Contemporary Problems* 62, p. 143.
Flanigan, James (10 September 2003), "Instilling Boardroom Ethics, Starting in the Classroom", *Los Angeles Times*, sec. C, p. 1.
Freeman, R. Edward (1984)), *Strategic Management: A Stakeholder Approach* (Boston: Pitman).
Freeman, R. Edward (October 1994), "The Politics of Stakeholder Theory: Some Future Directions", *Business Ethics Quarterly* 4, pp. 409–22.
Friedman, Milton (1962), *Capitalism and Freedom* (Chicago: University of Chicago Press).
Gaudine, Alice, and Thorne, Linda (May 2001), "Emotion and Ethical Decision Making in Organizations", *Journal of Business Ethics* 31, pp. 175–87.
Goodpaster, Kenneth (January 1991), "Business Ethics and Stakeholder Analysis", *Business Ethics Quarterly* 1, p. 553

Jackson, Kevin (2004), *Building Reputational Capital: Strategies for Integrity and Fair Play That Improve the Bottom Line* (New York: Oxford University Press).

Jennings, Marianne (Spring 2003), "A Primer on Enron: Lessons From a Perfect Storm of Financial Reporting, Corporate Governance and Ethical Culture Failures", *California Western Law Review* 39, p. 163.

Johnson, Mark (1993), *Moral Imagination: Implications of Cognitive Science for Ethics* (Chicago: University of Chicago Press).

Lowenstein, George (1996), "Behavioral Decision Theory and Business Ethics: Skewed Trade-Offs Between Self and Others", in *Codes of Conduct: Behavioral Research Into Business Ethics*, eds. David Messick and Ann Tenbrunsel (New York: Russell Sage Foundation).

Mangan, Katherine (30 January 2004), "Business Schools and Company CEOs to Create Ethics Center", *The Chronicle of Higher Education*.

Maxwell, John (2003), *There's No Such Thing as "Business" Ethics: There's Only One Rule for Making Decisions* (New York: Warner Books).

McDaniel, Morey (Fall 1991), "Stockholders and Shareholders", *Stetson Law Review* 21, p. 121.

Midlarski, Elizabeth, and Midlarski, Manus (June 1973), "Some Determinants of Aiding Under Experimentally Induced Stress", *Journal of Personality* 41, pp. 305–27.

Mitroff, Ian (October 2004), "An Open Letter to the Deans and Faculties of American Business Schools", *Journal of Business Ethics* 54, pp. 185–9.

Murray, Sarah (23 June 2003), "Values Should Go Beyond Rules and Regulations: Amid New Financial Regulations, Business Schools are Putting Greater Emphasis on Professional Ethical Conduct", *Financial Times*, p. 2.

Noddings, Nel (1984), *Caring: A Feminine Approach to Ethics and Moral Education* (Berkeley, CA: University of California Press).

Noddings, Nel (2002), *Starting at Home: Caring and Social Policy* (Berkeley, CA: University of California Press).

Paine, Lynn (2003), *Value Shift: Why Companies Must Merge Social and Financial Imperatives to Achieve Superior Performance* (New York: McGraw-Hill Companies, McGraw-Hill, 2003)

Roman, Ronald, Hayibor, Sefa, and Agle, Bradley (March 1999) "The Relationship Between Financial and Social Performance: Repainting a Portrait", *Business and Society* 38, pp. 109–25

Treviño, Linda and Nelson, Katherine (2004), *Managing Business Ethics: Straight Talk About How to Do It Right* (Hoboken, NJ: John Wiley and Sons).

Treviño, Linda, and Weaver, Gary (April 1994), "Business Ethics: One Field or Two?", *Business Ethics Quarterly* 4, pp. 113–29.

Treviño, Linda, and Youngblood, Stuart (August 1990), "Bad Apples in Bad Barrels: A Causal Analysis of Ethical Decision-Making Behavior", *Journal of Applied Psychology* 75, pp. 378–85.

Tronto, Joan (1993), *Moral Boundaries: A Political Argument for an Ethic of Care* (New York: Routledge, Chapman, and Hall).

Verschoor, Curtish (October 1998), "A Study of the Link Between a Corporation's Financial Performance and Its Commitment of Ethics", *Journal of Business Ethics* 17, pp. 1509–16

Waddock, Sandra, and Graves, Samuel (April 1997), "The Corporate Social Performance-Financial Performance Link", *Strategic Management Journal* 18, pp. 303-19.

Wasik, John (29 January 2007), "Buffett Can Follow Harvard, ABB Lead on Sudan", *Bloomberg.com*, http://www.bloomberg.com/apps/news?pid=20601039&refer=columnist_wasik&sid=aDBiT.cG_7Rw.

Weisman, Robert (30 December 2003), "Harvard Raises Its Hand on Ethics: 1st-Year M.B.A. Students Must Take New Course", *The Boston Globe*, sec. C, p. 1.

Werhane, Patricia (1999), *Moral Imagination and Management Decision-Making* (New York: Oxford University Press).

Wyatt, Caroline (15 January 2004), "Starbucks Invades Parisian Café Culture", *BBC News*, http://newsvote.bbc.co.uk/mpapps/pagetools/print/news.bbc.co.uk/2/hi/europe/3401637.stm.

Edwin M. Hartman

Teaching Business Ethics with Aristotle

Can we who teach ethics make our students more ethical? If not, what good are we? Is it really the job of those who teach business ethics to make their students ethical? Isn't it enough if we show them how to be ethical if they want to be? After all, accounting professors teach their students how to be accountants if they want to be; no professor is required to make students want to be accountants.

We have a complex challenge. We are supposed to teach our students ethics, and we are supposed to convince them that they have reason to learn ethics and to be ethical. But to begin with, we do not agree on ethical principles: we cannot be sure what the right ones are, where they come from, or how to apply them to complex situations, especially if they seem to conflict. Our students feel comfortable in expressing their familiar sophomore relativism by asking, 'Who's to say what's right or wrong?' Second, even if we agreed on what one ought to do, we might still not know why an agent has any self-interested reason to do it. Business students want to learn accounting, finance, management, and so on because it will make them successful and prosperous in business. It is not clear that learning ethics will benefit them, or that they will want to be ethical if they see no benefit. It does not look like a competitive advantage, particularly for the individual.

If we cannot deal with either of these problems satisfactorily, we can hardly expect success in teaching business ethics to students who are typically skeptical about ethics.

Perhaps it is not surprising, then, to find evidence that business students are less honest than those in other disciplines (McCabe & Treviño, 1996; cited in Pfeffer, 2005). It appears to be a problem that feeds on itself: if our students learn not to trust other businesspeople, they will themselves be less trustworthy. The cycle will continue, and honesty will become an ever less viable policy, and compliance a more expensive matter.

My claim is that Aristotle helps us deal with these difficulties. He succeeds in part because his aims are modest. He acknowledges that ethics does not offer the level of certainty that we find in mathematics, and that one should not demand that level of certainty of a field that does not have it to offer.[1] But it is not an arcane discipline. He bases his ethical views largely on common sense, supplemented by what he calls science. In his view, if we can arrange the deliverances of intelligent common sense and science into a coherent whole, we (or at any rate the best of us) can indeed make sound ethical judgments, and we can show that there is good reason to act accordingly.

Aristotle's Views

Aristotle takes ethics to be primarily about character, which we may define as one's standard pattern of thought and action with respect to one's own and others' well-being (Kupperman, 1991, p. 17). Character includes virtues and vices, and involves certain values, and the right emotional makeup as well. (Aristotle does not use the term 'values', but he does countenance desires for the most important human goods. He would surely hold—quite correctly—that one may value something unimportant or even something not good.)

Having a virtue involves having what Frankfurt calls second-order desires: one not only is but wants to be motivated by a certain sort of consideration (Frankfurt, 1982). Values involve our higher-order desires, especially those concerning the sort of person one wants to be, which may be good or bad. To have a strong character is to have values that consistently guide one's actions. (Aristotle attends to some personal features that are not clearly moral: a sense of humor, for example.) Character determines your identity in that maintaining your character is tantamount to continuing your life.[2]

Aristotle does not reject principles; in fact they play an important role in his ethics. A courageous person, for example, will act on the principle that one should take appropriate risks to achieve some good result. But principles are secondary, in the sense that we act on principles of courage because we are courageous, and not the other

---

[1] Aristotle, *Nicomachean Ethics*, 1.3.1094b12–14, 23–27.
[2] *Ibid.*, 9.4.1066a13–29, b7–14.

way around. If you are a courageous person, your immediate thought in rescuing a friend from a pit bull is not that one ought to be courageous in a case like this, but that Smith needs help. A friend's peril is a reason for action, from your point of view.

Aristotle and other virtue ethicists do not, however, believe that we can find principles that will tell us exactly how much trouble the friend should be in before we help her, or how much of a risk we ought to take, nor any algorithm to prioritize competing principles. The principle that one should take appropriate risks to achieve some good result is vague, and cannot be made less vague without provoking arguments.

Having a virtue is not a matter of being able to produce an air-tight definition of a virtue. It is more like having certain enduring desires that can serve as reasons to act because they have to do with one's well-being or other important concerns and commitments. A person of generous character acts generously, wants to do so, and thinks it good to do so. If you are generous, you are and want to be the sort of person who is normally motivated by thoughts like this: 'Jones is in need, so I'll give him what he needs.' To be a person of truly generous character entails having and wanting to have a settled disposition to assist needy friends, and emotions to match—in this case, sympathy. The next best thing, though short of a truly generous character, is acceptance of one's obligation: 'Jones is in need and I'm his friend, so I ought to give him a few dollars.'

Note that one's generosity may not only justify one's action but also explain it. If you help Jones out of generosity, your generosity is causing you to help him. You are not doing it to show off or because you want to get leverage over Jones or because you are drunk.

Virtues involve attitudes and emotions in an essential way. Aristotle does not claim that you can make yourself feel grateful on a particular occasion, but you can in time become the sort of person who is grateful on appropriate occasions.[3] Good parents raise their children to be honest, hence to be strongly inclined not to lie, to feel a sense of repugnance when lying even in circumstances that justify it. In this respect he sets a demanding standard.

He believes that growing up in a good community is the primary way to become a virtuous person, in part because he believes that common opinions about ethics are on the whole correct, and in part because he believes that the needs of a good community help deter-

---

[3] *Ibid.*, 1.3.1095a2–13.

mine what counts as virtuous. One comes to apprehend courage first by being told as a child that some acts are courageous, and some others are cowardly. Over time one gets into the habit of acting courageously, and comes to have a pretty good sense of what courage looks like. Then through a process that Aristotle calls dialectic, which we shall discuss, one may acquire a fuller understanding of courage and its contraries, cowardice and foolhardiness, and can reliably identify instances of them.

But a virtue is more than a disposition.[4] Rationality is involved as well. Acting courageously just by imitating courageous people will not suffice. To be truly courageous one needs a clear idea of what is most important to one, and concern about the kind of person one is. Not knowing one's values means that one cannot assess the importance of anything, and therefore cannot rationally consider the appropriate level of risk to accept to protect what one values. Courage and recklessness are psychologically similar but morally different, and the rationality required to act on the first rather than the second is rare. Still, a courageous person need not give an unassailable definition of courage or prove conclusively that a certain act is courageous.

Though ethics involves rationality, it is not like geometry.[5] It is more like navigation or medicine or comedy.[6] One has to develop a feeling for navigation and medicine. There are rules, but they are not as definite as those of geometry. Yet there are still right and wrong answers, and the wrong ones can be catastrophic.

Aristotle's approach requires some elaboration and defense. First, we need to see why he seems to think it self-evident that being ethical serves the agent's best interests — that in fact ethics is principally about the agent's best interests. Second, we need to understand how he uses dialectic to shore up common sense. Third, we need to see how Aristotle's virtue-based ethics deals adequately with morally complex situations.

Character and Interests

Utilitarianism, like other typical principle-based ethical theories, purports to tell us what we ought to do, but it does not even try to show that an agent is better off for being ethical. If it will be truth for-

---

[4] On this and related points I am indebted to the work of Alzola, 2008.
[5] *Nicomachean Ethics*, 1.7.1098a29–34.
[6] *Ibid.*, 3.3.1112a5–7 and 4.8.1028a23–34.

ever on the scaffold, wrong forever on the throne, then business ethics is a mistake, if not an oxymoron. This is a serious matter. If acting ethically makes the agent worse off, we are going to have a difficult time persuading our students to take business ethics as seriously as they take subjects that will indeed serve them well. There is some evidence that ethical organizations do well, but most studies make facile assumptions about what an ethical company looks like and offer correlations instead of causes.[7]

Utilitarian theories do not usually characterize the good life that ethics is supposed to promote, while Aristotle does: it is a matter of living according to nature—humankind's communal and rational nature—and so flourishing, to use the now popular rendering of the word *eudaimonia*. Since human beings are social and rational creatures, the good life is a matter of living according to reason in a congenial community.

Let us be clear: according to Aristotle, ethics is about the good life of the agent. Insofar as you are virtuous, unless you are unlucky in some important way, your life is good, satisfactory, happy, flourishing. It is significant that Aristotle claims that *phronesis*, which normally translates as prudence or practical wisdom, is coextensive with virtue as a whole. As 'practical wisdom', *phronesis* is appropriately self-interested and is not theoretical as mathematics is.

This leaves unanswered any question about the relationship between personal happiness and what we today would say is the subject matter of ethics: the interests of others. Aristotle seems to believe, moreover, that there is some self-evidently good state toward which every substance develops, and that humans will flourish when they have achieved a state of maturity that includes rationality and sociability. A skeptic will deny that human beings tend toward some identifiable end state, and will not accept that we can know that our natural end, if such there be, includes rationality and sociability.

We cannot entirely rehabilitate Aristotle's teleology, but we can create a plausible and generally Aristotelian view on which ethics and happiness overlap. I want to make three broad points in so doing. First, we are indeed social creatures whose happiness depends to some degree on our sociability. Second, rationality of a certain kind is a necessary condition of our well-being: we are better off if we are in a state of psychic and logical harmony. Third—and

---

[7] The criteria for being an ethical company are questionable as well. More pseudo-science.

this point is closely related to the second—the satisfaction of our desires is a good thing only insofar as we have desires that, from a broader and longer-term point of view, we want to have.

That humans are in some important sense social creatures seems beyond doubt. Hence the good life involves living satisfactorily in a congenial community and being the sort of person who fits well into a good community. Your happiness depends in part on your being a productive and congenial member of the community. Desires that are at odds with this can create serious problems. You have good reason to be virtuous, and not merely to act sometimes as though you were.

Aristotle claims that your character is a matter of what you enjoy doing: good things if you are a good person, bad things if you are a bad one.[8] Good character is not just a matter of doing the right thing, but of having the right desires and emotions.[9] You should be grateful for kindnesses, angry if and only if you are seriously wronged, sympathetic toward the wretched, glad to help your fellow citizens. Emotions of the right sort support good character.

It does not follow that one is better off being virtuous; the argument shows only that people of good character enjoy being virtuous. Aristotle attributes virtue to the one who gladly does the right thing, but not all who consider ethics and happiness would agree. Kant does not require that the good person act on inclination; in fact, the 'dear self' seems to be a kind of natural enemy of the good will. St. Paul, a tormented man, is eloquent on the battles of the (bad) flesh against the (good) spirit, whereas Aristotle takes the second to be the form of the first, and the flourishing of the virtuous to be psychic harmony rather than torment.

Aristotle does take notice of the situations in which we steel ourselves to do the right thing against inclination. In those cases, however, we exhibit self-control, which is ethically inferior to temperance, in which inclination does not oppose virtue. There are costs associated with virtue. Acting courageously is often unpleasant: after all, one may be risking one's life, and one is not being courageous if one holds one's own life to be worthless.[10] But whereas self-control is a matter of choosing to do the right thing in spite of

---

[8] *Nicomachean Ethics,*2.3.1104b5ff.
[9] *Ibid.*, 10.8.1178a9–24, etc.
[10] *Ibid.*, 3.9.1117a34–b17.

wanting to do the wrong thing, courage is a matter of choosing to perform an act that essentially includes fear.[11]

Yet we may wonder whether Aristotle can give a convincing argument against those who claim to enjoy being successfully rapacious rather than just. One possible answer would be that in the long run your unscrupulousness will catch up with you, perhaps because your reputation will repel people with whom you want to negotiate or work. Indeed it might, but it also might not.

We need to look closely at Aristotle's claim. Since a good person enjoys doing the right thing and has the right desires, when you are asking yourself whether you want to be a good person, you are asking yourself what desires you want to have. To put it another way: given that you want to serve your own interests, *what do you want your interests to be?* Now that is a profound question—a question about a higher-order desire. Do our students want to be people who can enjoy only great financial success? Or do they want to be people who enjoy a life in which work plays an important but not dominant role and offers challenge, fun, association with interesting people, and compensation that lets them live comfortably? The question is not which one business students prefer. It is a higher-order question about *which one they would choose to prefer* if they could choose their preferences. It would be difficult to answer that question by reference to self-interest, since it is difficult to see what would count as a straightforwardly self-interested answer to the question, 'What do you want your interests to be?'

Is there any reason at all to prefer one of those two answers? One reason for preferring the second is that you are more likely to get what you want. Most students who give it are indeed happier in the end than those who give the first.[12] Great wealth is hard to achieve, and many who achieve it turn out to enjoy it less than they expected to. A good life must be achievable and sustainable. It is not good for you to value something that you are unlikely to be able to get and keep.

It may seem impossible to decide what one is going to prefer, but there is a sort of situation in which one in effect does. If students learn how a strong organizational culture can affect one's character, they will know that the choice of an employer is a most important

---

[11] This interpretation, which I owe to Garver, 1980, is controversial. Fortunately my thesis does not require getting this passage exactly right.

[12] Belk, 1985; Kasser & Ryan, 1996, cited in Haidt, 2006.

one. I may (depending on the organization) like being the sort of person who enjoys acting ruthlessly, or the sort who maintains a professional attitude. Choosing an employer, like choosing any sort of community, may in effect be choosing which desires to cultivate, hence to some degree choosing a character.

On what basis can a student choose to have one sort of character or another? Certain choices will cause the student to develop certain desires that are likely to be frustrated, while others will lead to a life easily attained but so narrow and impoverished as to be not worth attaining. This leaves an existential choice, one not made in a way an economist would recognize as rational, but surely not irrational.

Making a decision about one's employment may be such an existential choice. A vulnerable character can be overridden — that is, people can be made to act out of character — but over the long haul one's higher-order desires may change to adjust to one's organization (Milgram, 1974; Zimbardo, 2007; Hartman, 1996). On the Aristotelian view, that is a significant change in character. So choosing to take a job with Company A may cause Jones to want to be highly professional, honest, and so on, but taking a job with Company B may cause him to want to be ruthless and very rich and to feel contempt for the dullards and wimps who toil for honest pennies. But perhaps if Jones had taken the job at Company A, 10 years later he would have been contemptuous of the racing rats at Salomon. The choice is between two options that are not comparable; it cannot be made rationally in the standard sense. (For one thing, we often do not know how much we shall enjoy some experience, or for how long, and it is probably even more difficult to predict the results of a significant change in higher-order desires (Gilbert et al., 1998).) It is possible that Jones will eventually be happy with either choice, in which case ethics can be the tiebreaker.

It will not do to try to convince Jones that a particular kind of life will be best for him. We ought to recognize a great variety of forms of satisfying life. At the same time we ought to respect the limits on that variety implied by our rational and social nature. As business students plan their lives, we who teach business ethics should encourage them to consider their strengths and limitations, their opportunities, and what they can and cannot learn to enjoy. Let us not encourage them to assume ahead of time that whatever they happen to want is possible, or that they will enjoy it if they get it.

Rationality and Psychic Harmony

Aristotle has arguments in support of his conception of the good life, and therefore of ethics. He believes that the good life will have a certain wholeness, rather than being a series of unconnected experiences. Happiness requires desires that are rational in the sense of being consistent with one another, and actions that are consistent with one's desires.[13] Hence a happy person is in a state of psychic harmony: the faculties of the soul are working well together, as they are supposed to.

Aristotle clearly does not regard rationality as just a matter of the efficiency with which a means leads to the satisfaction of some desire, as Hume and many mainstream economists hold. Surely there is something irrational about desiring (say) health while eating and drinking to excess, smoking, and avoiding exercise. It is also irrational not to desire health, physical or psychic, at all: these are goods, desirable for anyone. And it is at least arguably irrational to accept near-term gratification rather than postpone greater gratification—a form of weakness of the will.[14]

Consistency of desires is not sufficient for good character or for happiness, but it does seem to be necessary. There are difficulties in prizing both idleness and personal achievement, or heavy drinking and fitness, or feeling free to offend and having many friends. But can't you do well if you hide your hostility or rapacity? Aristotle says no: if you do it for strategic reasons, as when people are watching, you will be doing something that you do not enjoy.[15] You will be in a state of disharmony. In any case, you are going against your sociable nature. How many true friends are you going to have? Will you be a happy citizen of your community? A satisfied employee?

Leon Festinger was the most important pioneer in investigating cognitive dissonance. He and his followers found that people will go to great lengths to maintain a coherent set of desires and principles (Festinger, 1957). In particular, they will interpret their own judgments and sometimes the facts of the case to keep their words and actions consistent with the principles that they want to hold. We suffer not only because we are not as good as we claim to be, but from

---

[13] *Nicomachean Ethics*, 9.4.1066b7–11.

[14] To understate, the nature of rationality is a matter of controversy. Rationality has a normative aspect, and differences in definition reflect different views of how we should think. I shall not discuss objections to the standard views about consistency and transitivity.

[15] *Nicomachean Ethics*, 9.4.1066b7–14.

the inconsistency between what we claim to be and what we are. This is evidence in favor of Aristotle's view that we are uncomfortable with psychic disharmony.

We might object that Aristotle does not show that integrity of the sort that he has in mind is sufficient for good character. Some have argued that one may have this kind of integrity but be a bad person, because rationality in the sense of coherence of beliefs and desires is not enough to guarantee an ethical life, though it might be sufficient for a happy one. But remember that Aristotle claims that, as humans are social beings, the satisfactions of family, friends, and community — necessarily reciprocal — are not optional. They are essential human goods: if you do not desire them or cannot bring yourself to act on your desire of them, your desires just will not be coherent.

Good character is essentially a matter of the healthy state of one's own soul. It is natural to wish to achieve psychic health, which is self-evidently a good thing. It is not a state that nature reliably brings about — not everything flourishes — and it is not the final state of most people. It is a state in which one is not at war with oneself, torn by inconsistent desires, constantly frustrated by life, cognitively dissonant. It is attractive to almost anyone, surely including most business students, if they consider it.

From Aristotle's point of view, to say that there are no right or wrong answers in ethics is to say that there is no difference between happiness and unhappiness, or between a fulfilling life and a miserable one. That is truly absurd, an affront to common sense. And Aristotle takes common sense very seriously.

Common Sense

Plato and many philosophers since have doubted that common sense could be the basis for ethics, or much else worth knowing. Questions like 'What ought I to do?' and 'What reason have I for doing what I ought to do?' were thought to be beyond the reach of common opinion — to be the sort of thing that philosophers should tackle.

Aristotle does not think this way, in part because he does not demand ironclad certainty and because he starts with common sense — with familiar and widely shared opinions — and makes it coherent. He does not put forward radically new conceptions of courage, justice, or friendship. He does not suggest that becoming a good person is a superhuman achievement, though it is not easy or even very common. The effect of the *Nicomachean Ethics* is not to undermine our ideas about ethics but to refine and rationalize them.

There is much to be said for Aristotle's fidelity to common sense. If an ethical theory generates conclusions at variance with our common and firm convictions, we have reason to question it. For example, if Kant's ethical theory implies that one ought not to lie to the Nazis even to save the lives of innocent Jews, we have reason to question his theory. On the other hand, insofar as Aristotle countenances slavery, as most of his contemporaries did, we should recall that morality is not merely a matter of consensus.

Aristotle's process of dialectic starts with common opinions, with the intention of finding principles that are consistent with most of those opinions and explain them, or improve on them insofar as they can be shown to be inadequate in some way.[16] In the best case, one's beginnings (*archai*) form a coherent whole. The *archai* with which we begin thinking about ethics are particular moral judgments or intuitions. Aristotle seems to have in mind something such as John Rawls's (Rawls, 1971, pp. 48–51) reflective equilibrium. There are no unassailable propositions that serve as the foundation of all ethical knowledge. One compares one's principles (which Aristotle also calls *archai*, unfortunately) and one's considered judgments about particular cases, and if they do not form a coherent whole, adjusts one or both to create an internally consistent set of principles that are also consistent with most of our judgments on ethical cases. In the case of what Daniels has called wide reflective equilibrium (Daniels, 1979), we bring in pertinent science, settled beliefs about human nature, and other facts. Wide reflective equilibrium seems close to Aristotle's view that at our moral best we have a set of background beliefs, intuitions, and principles that cohere, with emotions to match. Rawls has in mind logical rather than psychological coherence, whereas Aristotle seems to be thinking of both, although he does not sharply distinguish them.

We—amateurs as well as professionals—still talk about ethics in this way. We test and sometimes reject an ethical theory because it generates strongly counterintuitive results. We will reject a standard form of act utilitarianism that would violate fairness and undermine rights, but we will also reject a certain claim about people's rights because permitting it would have catastrophic consequences, on the theory that ethical action does not normally have catastrophic consequences.

---

[16] See *Nicomachean Ethics*, 7.1.1145b4–8, for example.

Aristotle does not claim that those who go through the process of dialectic will find principles that apply perfectly to complex situations. Ethics still is not geometry. But the principles that one does have will be clearer and more defensible, though possibly somewhat more complicated and not always easily applied, and one will have better and more trustworthy intuitions for those situations in which principles compete or are hard to apply. In particular, one's intuitions will lead one to apprehend the situation under the right principle rather than under principles that social pressure forces on one or that rationalize one's preferred behavior.

Consider large stock options for executives, for example. Proceeding on the basis of intuition, consistent with some egalitarian principle, liberals are likely to claim that they are unjustifiably generous; conservatives will defend them as being what the market dictates, and as being a good way to align the interests of the executives and the stockholders. Liberals might take executive pay to be a counterexample to the notion that we ought to determine pay by reference to markets, or they might deny that the CEO's friends on the board constitute a market. Conservatives will reject the egalitarian conception of fairness that liberals embrace. How might the standoff be resolved? Conservatives could suggest that we consider the likely consequences of eliminating stock options—a typical utilitarian argument. The liberals might take the position that fairness trumps utilitarian considerations.

Part of the background for the conservative position is agency theory: we can count on executives to work effectively for the stockholders if and only if they are paid to do just that. This view presupposes a particularly pure and narrow form of self-interest that motivates executives, and its proponents do not exactly offer a sophisticated argument for it.[17] But if agency theory is what we teach our students, then they may come to believe uncritically that the presupposition is true. It is all the more important that we examine the presupposition.

Agency theorists tend to be utilitarians. I once heard Jensen give a talk in which he scornfully asked, 'What is justice, anyway? Where do I find it?' He seemed to have little difficulty in defining and finding utility, with no thought of whether his view of utility was adequate from a moral point of view. Thus suitably reduced, utility fits comfortably into economic theory. In a characteristically dialectical

---

[17] Jensen & Mechling, 1976, cited by Ghoshal, 2005.

conversation we might challenge this form of utilitarianism and offer considerations based on justice and rights. We might seek a way to make considerations of utility, justice, and rights fit together and fit our intuitions as well. Reducing justice and rights to the economist's notion of utility is a facile way to do it: it will make a poor fit with other principles that we hold, with many of our views about the nature of the good life, and with our intuitions.

Many of us have heard economists say something like this: executive compensation is an economic issue, not an ethical issue. We might take this to mean that it is a matter to be handled by the sort of utilitarianism that standard economic theory presupposes. But as our students should discover in discussing matters such as this, there are many different ways in which a situation may be described or framed. A law limiting stock options might be framed as preserving fairness or as an unwarranted diminution of corporate autonomy, or as a way of undermining managerial effectiveness. We hope that our students become better at understanding and describing these multifaceted situations correctly, and therefore at making better judgments. This is a way to improve their ethical perception.

Ethical Perception Done Correctly

Aristotle claims that the person of good character perceives a situation rightly—that is, notices and takes appropriate account of its salient features. The faculty of imagination (*phantasia*) enables you to understand what a perceived object is, or to grasp the ethical quality of an act.

You are morally responsible for perceiving the act correctly—that is, for framing it right. To frame it incorrectly by failing to apprehend the ethically salient features of the situation is a mark of a bad character.[18] A person of good character can perceive that a certain act is courageous rather than foolhardy, generous rather than vainglorious, right rather than wrong, and will act accordingly. Aristotle seems to believe that emotion helps us frame properly (an irascible person will take offense inappropriately, for example), but weakness of the will is sometimes the result of wrong framing.[19] *Moral imagination* is the name we now give to the ability to frame ethically significant states and events (see Werhane, 1999).

---

[18] *Nicomachean Ethics*, 3.5.1114a32–b3.
[19] *Ibid.*, 7.3.1147a32–b6.

People may make judgments and act on the basis of how they describe a complex situation to themselves. You can frame eating a doughnut as a pleasurable experience or a fattening act, but a person concerned with health should take the second as salient. A good accountant will frame the Enron-related tricks as misrepresenting the financial position of the firm rather than as good client service. Those who teach business ethics face the task of teaching students to do better at ethical framing. A typical business course will not normally put an ethical frame around the problems and issues that it covers. It will present them as economic issues, and not ethical ones. Its language is about items such as incentives rather than obligations, and it is a powerful language. Insofar as a business ethics course helps students become more fluent in the language of right and wrong, it enriches their moral imagination and increases the probability that they will give salient descriptions of morally significant situations.

Our students' environment will influence the way they frame a situation: they will likely do it as others do it, as is the custom in their profession, as the client wishes, etc. Ethical behavior depends upon the employee's ability to recognize ethical issues, and this ability appears to be a function of corporate culture more than of individual employees' attributes (Chen, et al., 1997).

Consider the Milgram (1974) experiment, in which experimental subjects willingly administered what they believed to be painful shocks to innocent people who had given wrong answers. At least some of the participants did not see themselves as causing pain to an innocent subject, but instead as following directions and helping Dr. Milgram in his important work. Your ego will be influential as well: you are likely to describe your failure to confront the boss as a piece of thoughtful diplomacy, whereas others will see it as self-serving and cowardly. Your interests will influence the framing too: you tend to argue for the moral rightness of actions that favor you, and to describe those actions accordingly. Rationalization to evade cognitive dissonance is depressingly common. No doubt this sort of thinking afflicted the Arthur Andersen accountants working for Enron.

How can we help our students improve their framing? At the very least, we ought to show them that there are alternative ways of framing situations without giving the impression that one way is as good as another. It will be helpful to teach business students about social psychology. Those who understand organizational culture, for example, will be able to take its possible effects, on framing in particular, into account. Former students who have learned about the Milgram experiment in a business ethics course testify that they do sometimes think of it when they are in similar situations, and act accordingly, show that people can be protected against crowd-induced culpable indifference by being taught to recognize the crowd's influence and to act appropriately despite it (Beaman et al., 1978; Slater, 2004, pp. 109f).

If managers are aware, as Aristotle was, of how easily stray desires and emotions and social pressure and unexpected emergencies can divert us from our most rational intentions, they should try to avoid getting into those situations in which they are vulnerable. This is 'self-management' (Elster 1984, 1985). Finding ways of protecting the company from the kind of bad behavior that pressures and emergencies encourage is a corporate form of self-management. Graduate school is not too soon for thinking this way, and a business ethics class is a good place to consider how foreseeable but unforeseen emergencies and other pressures may sway those whose character is vulnerable — that is, most people.

How, then, does a person of good character make a decision in a complex situation? The kind of person you are will have as much to do with the decision as will your reasoning about it. Dialectic will give you somewhat sharper, though still not perfectly sharp, principles and intuitions and improve your reasoning about because you are better at noticing and evaluating aspects of the situation that people of less character do not handle so well. Your decisions will seem intuitive, in part because you will not be able to defend them in a way that convinces everyone. But the intuitions of a person of good character, sharpened by experience and by dialectic (perhaps in a business ethics course) are a good basis for action, although they will not necessarily protect you from bad culture or rationalization.

In part because one cannot accurately calculate with all the variables in mind, and in part to avoid rationalization, people of good character will often stick with certain nearly unexceptionable rules, such as, 'We don't lie to our employees. Period.' They may say, 'We're just not that kind of company', or 'That's something I'm just not prepared to do.'

Ethics and Strategy

One way to help students learn to see business issues as moral issues and to grasp their salient features is to discuss case studies with them. In a typical strategy course the students consider cases that challenge them to apply principles to a real situation. This is the beginning of developing their intuitions about strategy. There are principles for strategists to follow, but in real-life corporate strategy there is much to be said for trusting the intuitions of an intelligent person with a good track record. There will be some easy cases, but there will also be some hard ones, when the experienced and wise manager makes a decision that relies on intuition to a significant degree. Some managers are consistently better than others at framing these situations appropriately. So, for example, one might see a business as low-profit or high-cash-flow, and the strategic situation may determine which description is salient. Successful strategists often cannot say in any detail how they favor one frame over another, or how they rank pertinent considerations.

Case studies in ethics substitute to some degree for experience. In particular, they develop the students' moral imagination. Properly taught, complex cases exercise students' moral judgment about particulars, as when justice and economic efficiency conflict. In looking at a case and considering the many ways in which one can frame a situation and which ways of framing capture its salient features, students are developing moral imagination and thus practical wisdom and thus good character.

One might say that in strategy we can assess the strategist's skill by reference to the track record, but in fact the track record does not always prove very much. Rosenzweig has argued that it is a mistake —one made by Peters and Waterman, Collins and Porras, and many others—to look at successful companies and try to identify the features that account for their success (Rosenzweig, 2007). The standard diagnosis is that a real winner has a supportive culture, focuses on customers, cleaves to a widely understood mission, and so on. But many such companies, having been held up as examples of what you, too, can do to succeed, perform much less well after the book in question is published.

The problem with the diagnosis, says Rosenzweig, is that people in successful companies are likely to say that their culture is supportive, their focus on customers, and their mission before everyone's mind: profitability has a halo effect; everything else looks good. It is no doubt true that having a culture of mediocrity, ignoring customers, and lacking a mission will do a company little good, but the rules that the strategic gurus have identified are almost trivial as stated.

The economic and competitive environments have effects that the gurus ignore.

Rosenzweig has something like a virtue theory of strategy. His shining examples, Bob Rubin and Andy Grove, know that deciding on a strategy is a matter of dealing with uncertainty. What is needed, in addition to the ability to gauge the probabilities insofar as you can, is something like courage: you take a leap into the unknown with the appropriate amount and kind of fear; and if things go wrong, you are ready to weigh the odds and do the same thing again next time. You do not worry about looking bad; you do not retreat to the safety of doing nothing or of groupthink. You have the courage to act rationally. Things may go wrong: fortune is not always on your side, and you may incur short-term obloquy, which will be unpleasant. But failure does not undermine your satisfaction in having done the best you can do, or your confidence on the next attempt. That attitude is more effective than any principle that a strategist is likely to propound.

Courage can help a strategist make deals, but there are usually new deals to be made tomorrow. What really tests character is to make decisions on which the future of the company depends.[20] The virtues of courage, wisdom, farsightedness, honesty, fidelity to the stockholders, respect for the cautionary opinions of other senior managers, and so on do not guarantee success, and sometimes the strategist does not get another chance.

Can students also gain in critical understanding of their values? Can we help students find and stick with good values, whatever their career choices? At the very least, we can encourage them to reflect on what is most important to them and how to protect it.

Reading fiction is a way to do this. In fact, Richard Rorty argues that literature is better for this purpose than is philosophy. Sometimes non-fiction will do equally well (Rorty, 2006 and elsewhere). Michael Lewis's *Liar's Poker* (1989), for example, can help students to reflect on their values as they consider the addictive Dash Riprock and the predatory Human Piranha, and ask themselves why selling equities in Dallas should be inappropriate for anyone with any self-respect. Considering Salomon or the Milgram experiment may enable them later to stop and reflect, and to undertake moral reasoning rather than rationalization. A measure of self-knowledge, a component of good character, will lead them to protect their best values not only by choosing a congenial environment but by avoiding if

---

[20] My colleague Bruce Buchanan made this point in conversation.

possible and resisting if necessary the pressures to do the wrong thing wherever they are.[21]

Conclusion

Becoming ethical is not a matter of discovering arcane principles that ground our decisions in certainty, for ethics is neither arcane nor certain. Being ethical is primarily a matter of being a person of good character, with virtues, emotions, values, and practical intelligence to match. The ethical values that experience teaches us are at least the beginning of wisdom about ethics. Ethical progress is a matter of refining and adjusting these values, learning to bring them to bear in making decisions, and protecting them from hostile environments. Our part of the project is to encourage reflection on values and offer exercises in putting the values into practice. Then perhaps our students will go on to flourish.

Bibliography

Alzola, Miguel (March 2008), "Character and Environment: The Status of Virtues in Organizations", *Journal of Business Ethics* 78, pp. 343–57.

Aristotle, *Nichomachean Ethics*, trans. Terence H. Irwin (Indianapolis, IN: Hackett Publishing Company, 1985).

Aristotle, *Ethica Nicomachea*, ed. Ingram Bywater (Oxford: Clarendon Press, 1894).

Beaman, Arthur L., et al. (July 1978), "Increasing Helping Rates through Information Dissemination: Teaching Pays", *Personality and Social Psychology Bulletin* 4, pp. 406–11.

Belk, Russell W. (December 1985), "Materialism: Trait Aspects of Living in the Material World", *Journal of Consumer Research* 12, pp. 265–80.

Chen, A.Y.S., Sawyers, Roby B., and Williams, Paul F. (June 1997), "Reinforcing Ethical Decision Making through Corporate Culture", *Journal of Business Ethics* 16, pp. 855–65.

Daniels, Norman (May 1979), "Wide Reflective Equilibrium and Theory Acceptance in Ethics", *Journal of Philosophy* 76, pp. 256–82.

Elster, Jon (1984), *Ulysses and the Sirens: Studies in Rationality and Irrationality*, rev. edn. (New York: Cambridge University Press).

Elster, Jon (1985), *Sour Grapes: Studies in the Subversion of Rationality* (New York: Cambridge University Press).

Festinger, Leon (1957), *A Theory of Cognitive Dissonance* (Stanford, CA: Stanford University Press).

Frankfurt, Harry G. (1982), "Freedom of the Will and the Concept of a Person", in *Free Will*, ed. Gary Watson (New York: Oxford University Press), pp. 81–95.

---

[21] For encouraging evidence of the possibility of doing this see Haidt, 2001, and Beaman et al., 1978.

Garver, Eugene (1980), "Aristotle on Virtue and Pleasure", in *The Greeks and the Good Life*, ed. David J. Depew (Indianapolis, IN: Hackett Publishing), pp. 157–176.

Ghoshal, Sumantra (March 2005), "Bad Management Theories Are Destroying Good Management Practices", *Academy of Management Learning and Education* 4, pp. 75–91.

Gilbert, Daniel T., Pinel, E.C., Wilson, T.D., Blumberg, S.J. & Wheatley, T.P. (September 1998), "Immune Neglect: A Source of Durability Bias in Affective Forecasting", *Journal of Personality and Social Psychology* 75, pp. 617–38.

Haidt, Jonathan (October 2001), "The Emotional Dog and Its Rational Tail: A Social Intuitionist Approach to Moral Judgment", *Psychological Review* 108, pp. 814–34.

Haidt, Jonathan (2006), *The Happiness Hypothesis: Finding Modern Truth in Ancient Wisdom* (New York: Perseus Books, Basic Books).

Hartman, Edwin M. (1996), *Organizational Ethics and the Good Life* (New York: Oxford University Press), pp. 143–65.

Jensen, Michael and Mechling, William (October 1976), "Theory of the Firm: Managerial Behavior, Agency Costs, and Ownership Structure", *Journal of Financial Economics* 3, pp. 305–60.

Kasser, Tim and Ryan, Richard M. (March 1996), "Further Examining the American Dream: Differential Correlates of Intrinsic and Extrinsic Goals", *Personality and Social Psychology Bulletin* 22, pp. 280–287.

Kupperman, Joel (1991),*Character* (New York: Oxford University Press).

Lewis, Michael (1989), *Liar's Poker: Rising through the Wreckage on Wall Street* (New York: W.W. Norton).

McCabe, Donald L., and Treviño, Linda K. (1995), "Cheating among Business Students: A Challenge for Business Leaders and Educators", *Journal of Management Education* 19, no. 2 (1995), p. 205.

Milgram, Stanley (1974), *Obedience to Authority: An Experimental View* (New York: Harper and Row).

Pfeffer, Jeffrey (March 2005), "Why Do Bad Management Theories Persist? A Comment on Ghoshal", *Academy of Management Learning and Education* 4, p. 99.

Rawls, John (1971), *A Theory of Justice* (Cambridge, MA: Harvard University Press), pp. 48–51.

Rorty, Richard M. (July 2006), "Is Philosophy Relevant to Business Ethics?" *Business Ethics Quarterly* 16, pp. 369–80.

Rosenzweig, Phil (2007), *The Halo Effect…and the Eight Other Business Delusions that Deceive Managers* (New York: Simon and Schuster, Free Press).

Slater, Lauren (2004), *Opening Skinner's Box: Great Psychological Experiments of the Twentieth Century* (New York: W.W. Norton).

Werhane, Patricia H. (1999), *Moral Imagination and Management Decision-Making* (New York: Oxford University Press).

Zimbardo, Philip (2007), *The Lucifer Effect: Understanding How Good People Turn Evil* (New York: Random House).

James O'Toole

Aristotle and the MBA
The Odd Couple

A Harvard MBA on vacation hired a fishing guide named Joe to help him land a marlin. Joe lived in a modest house by the sea with his wife and children. Every day, he rose when the sun was warm and took a swim in the ocean with his family. Three days a week he took clients to sea in his boat. The other days he would lie in his hammock and read from breakfast until lunch with his wife.

Almost every afternoon he picked his kids up after school and took them on 'an adventure'. After a long dinner, en famille, Joe and his wife would walk to a nearby café where the locals gathered every evening.

Joe's fishing expeditions were first-rate. The MBA explained to Joe how to put together a group of venture capitalists to 'build your underperforming business.' Instead of inefficiently taking one client out at a time, he could have a fleet of large, high-tech fishing boats. With a little strategic advice he could branch out into related businesses, perhaps build a high-rise hotel on the beach.

Most important, Joe could go on TV and become the 'marketing face' for his business, creating a 'brand' that could be franchised at other sleepy fishing communities: 'A guy like you could become a celebrity.' The MBA then delivered the clincher: 'When that happens, we have an IPO and you get rich!'

Joe asked 'And what then?' The MBA answered: 'Well, you retire to some nice place on the beach, do a little fishing and reading, and get to spend some time with your wife and kids.'[1]

---

[1] Story circulating on the Internet

Over the last few years, MBA programs have come under increasing criticism from scholars, environmentalists, business journalists, investors, and (some) corporate leaders for:

- ignoring the 'soft side' of business, particularly social, moral, and ethical concerns
- being overtechnical and narrow, not the generalist programs they were originally intended to be
- failing to develop true leaders with relevant skills
- encouraging their students' tendencies toward arrogance and greed
- enculturating short-term thinking among executives who then cannot build sustainable enterprises (Bennis & O'Toole, 2005; Mintzberg, 2004).

A good place to start addressing these concerns is with the first, and arguably most profound, of Western philosophers to consider what we today call organizational leadership. The moral concerns Aristotle addresses in the *Politics* and *Nicomachean Ethics* are largely absent from the curricula at most major U.S. business schools.[2] Absent, in particular, is a focus on how leaders create ethical and sustainable corporate cultures, although research shows that the values of corporate executives are the prime determinants of a corporation's culture, and that culture in turn drives organizational behavior (O'Toole & Lawler, 2006).

The world according to Aristotle corresponds remarkably with contemporary thinking about human capabilities and meritocracy, and about how business organizations should be structured to maximize effectiveness. He also was concerned with what we today call social responsibility. His ideas are consistent with modern economic concepts, particularly the linkage of rewards to contributions.[3]

Aristotle's Assumptions

Aristotle's writings are practical, but they are hard-slogging for modern readers. Hence, it is helpful to keep in mind that his moral philosophy resets on five fundamental precepts:

---

[2] Aristotle is not the final word in philosophy. He is wrong about many things—slavery, for instance—and business students would do well to read Heilbroner, 1999, for a marvelous introduction to a range of serous philosophical thought relating to economic matters.

[3] Aristotle is the focus of a large number of books and articles by business school professors, including Hartman, 2006; Bragues, 2006 and Solomon, 2006.

(1) The capacity to reason is the essence of being human.

(2) The highest forms of reasoning are abstract and moral thought, including choosing between the right and wrong ways both of living one's own life and of organizing human institutions.

(3) Personal virtue comes from developing the capacity to reason. That is, we fulfill our humanness by developing our naturally given potential.

(4) Everyone is capable of learning and of development. The good life comes from the process of *filling*, and not from the impossible end of having *fulfilled* our capacities.

(5) While developing one's natural capacities is the 'highest good', it is not the 'complete good.' We do not develop ourselves for selfish reasons, but to better contribute to the good of the communities of which we are members.

The measure of the importance of an activity is the degree to which it requires the highest-order, most abstract, mental capabilities, and we can assume that Aristotle would have placed the leadership of modern business organizations at, or near the top, of his hierarchy of human endeavors. The highest-order, most-human activities are 'politics and philosophy' because they require the greatest deployment of abstract reasoning. 'Philosophy' includes what we call the sciences, arts, and learned professions. Thus, engineers, lawyers, and doctors are 'philosophers', as are journalists, teachers, playwrights, and so on. Likewise, 'politics' includes not only serving in elected office, but the leadership of business organizations.

The important thing to Aristotle is not a person's job, but the extent to which that person is using his or her higher-order mental capabilities. His concepts of philosophy and politics should be thought of as inclusive: a factory worker who participates in problem-solving is using those higher-level capabilities as much as the company's CEO.

Aristotelian Microeconomics

An astute economist, Aristotle anticipated Adam Smith's work on the division of labor by over two thousand years. People should be engaged in tasks where they can make the maximum social and economic contribution. It would do the people of Athens no good if those who possessed the greatest aptitude to design and build large structures, such as the Parthenon, were not doing so because they were denied the opportunity to develop their engineering capabilities. The reason Athens was such a highly developed society in 400 B.C., while most other places in the world were mired in subsistence agriculture, was because the Athenians had freed their most-talented individuals from the tyranny of toil and given them the leisure to develop science, medicine, engineering, and the arts. No wonder barbarians didn't create acropolises: they treated everyone as equals.

How could justice be served if those with limited capabilities were made leaders of society, or the bosses of enterprises, while those with the greatest natural capacities were held down at the bottom carrying out orders? Aristotle concludes that what we would call meritocracy is the most just form of governance since everyone benefits from the rule of the most competent.

Paradoxically, Aristotle's point of reference is the good of the community. He believes the natural hierarchy of humans should not serve as an excuse to reward those at the top for having been born with advantages, but that the people at the top are responsible for making it possible for those lower down to lead good lives. When they do, everyone benefits from inequalities based on real capabilities and economic contribution. Who would want to work at Microsoft if equality were its main goal, and the company's executive team had an average IQ of 100, while Bill Gates and Steve Ballmer were assigned work as security guards? Individuals capable of making greater contributions should be treated differently—but only in some respects. In particular, they should be freed from lower-level work so they can concentrate on activities making maximum use of their potential.

The question then becomes: how large a share of the bounty produced by an organization are those at the top entitled to reap? Below I examine several Aristotelian tests of fairness of the distribution of rewards, but suffice it to say here that corporate leaders such as Gates and Ballmer are rewarded justly for their contributions if they have:

- contributed value
- increased the overall wealth of the community
- made it possible for everyone in their organization to develop their full potential. Note that the MBA curriculum generally focuses on only the first of those three criteria.

Modern Perspectives

MBA students often have told me that their goal in life is simply 'to be happy', a condition they associate with beer, beaches, blondes, and Beemers. Aristotle argued, instead, that happiness is the objective result of how we live. His highest good, *eudaimonia*, has little to do with feelings of pleasure and contentment. What he means by happiness is something more like 'the deep sense of satisfaction one gets when one grows as a human being.' Yet he complicates matters when he elaborates on the nature of the good at the top of his hierarchy:

> If happiness is activity in accordance with *virtue*, it is reasonable that it should be in accordance with the highest virtue; and this will be the *best thing in us ...That activity is contemplation.*[4]

Contemplation is the only activity that is absorbing 'good work' for all one's life. It includes what former California Governor Jerry Brown did when he meditated and what Einstein did while creating elegant equations and other forms of positively absorbing mental work: playing a piano, woodworking, solving a business problem, writing a scholarly paper.

If going to the beach isn't the best use of our time, shouldn't we spend it developing our greatest talent? Aristotle answers 'yes and no'. Yes, a person who is born with a high aptitude for science, mathematics, and spatial thinking obviously should study to become the best engineer she is capable of becoming, and never be satisfied with the depth of engineering knowledge she possesses. But no, she will still would be uni-dimensional if she fails to develop her potential in the arts and social sciences. While her potential may not be as deep in those fields, she nonetheless has almost unlimited potential in terms of breadth: She can study Chinese, history, ecology, psychology, anthropology, and learn to play the piano.

There is no limit to the contemplative challenges awaiting her if she chooses to grapple with such profound questions as 'Am I leading a good life?' and 'Am I doing the right thing?' To Aristotle, men and women who devote as much of their lives as possible to fulfilling their potential in such ways are engaged in true leisure, which he called philosophy, and are on their way to being happy.

Instead of doing what we have always done, writing yet another academic article or playing another round of golf, Aristotle encourages us to stretch ourselves, try new things, learn new skills, and

---

[4] The quotes are my own (often simplified) translations, found in O'Toole, 2005.

learn about new places. Each of us must pursue happiness in our own way. Growth for an artist may entail starting a business, and growth for a business executive may entail becoming an artist. Yet, Aristotle says, even such adventurous personal choices are not enough to constitute a good life. In addition, virtuous men and women pursue what he calls 'the complete good'.

The Complete Good

Aristotle argues it is not enough merely to *possess* the capacity to reason, and not even enough to *develop* it. In addition, to be virtuous, humans must use our reasoning capacity to meet the needs of our communities. We are 'political animals' and virtuous men and women engage in the practical world of politics in addition to philosophy.

With that two-pronged requirement in mind, we may summarize Aristotle's philosophy of virtue, excellence, and happiness: There is a moral difference between just living and living well. Individuals become virtuous to the extent that they strive for excellence, choose to develop their many talents and capacities, particularly their highest-order reasoning abilities. They 'complete their virtue' to the extent that they, as leaders of communities and organizations, provide conditions under which others can pursue happiness and achieve excellence.

The Role of Money

Among the panoply of instrumental goods needed to pursue happiness, the foremost and most morally complex is money. Without wealth creation, we cannot have food, clothing, shelter, and other necessities. And because we are not beasts, we want to enjoy good food, nice clothes, and a safe and secure home, not to mention an occasional trip to Paris. So work is a natural activity and, like the wealth it produces, is instrumental to a higher end: We work to live, we don't live to work.

But Aristotle asks, 'Is it enough merely to live, or even to live comfortably?' No, he answers: 'What we really want is *to live well*.' Living well must mean doing things so blissful we do them for their own sake, not for the sake of any extrinsic compensation. Aristotle doesn't categorize professional activities as *work*: computer nerds are not working when they are hacking, scientists are not working when they are doing research, and professors are not working when they are writing, because they would do those activities even if they weren't paid to do them. Such contemplative activities are *leisure*.

If we are not fortunate enough to have intrinsically 'leisurely' professions, Aristotle says we have to find a way to free ourselves from work-work in order to make time to contemplate. Ergo, we need money to afford the leisure time required to pursue happiness. Money isn't the root of evil; it is actually a good *when* it is instrumental to the higher end of creating the opportunity for leisure.

In some ways, the Aristotelian goal is to carve out a life-style and work-life much like the one enjoyed by the Internet's fictional 'Fisherman Joe.' Because Aristotle had known people who behaved like Joe, he concluded almost everyone is free and able to choose to live the good life, even if they do not have great educations or oodles of money.

The issue isn't material goods vs. the free 'best things in life.' It is about how we will live, and the sign of virtue is to act consciously, choosing one's ends rationally and from the 'proper disposition' of seeking excellence. The key to virtue is 'to deliberate well.' Virtuous people are introspective, self-critical, rational, and curious, not necessarily affluent.

So, How Much?

Today we face the same ethical question people have been asking themselves since the glory days of ancient Greece: *How much is enough for me?* Aristotle offers the barest outline of an answer: We need enough wealth not to worry where the next drachma is coming from. Further, we need enough to be comfortable and to have adequate savings, for without a sense of security we won't have the peace of mind needed to concentrate on higher pursuits. On the other hand, he explains:

> It seems to some people that good fortune is the same as happiness. But it isn't. It is actually an impediment when it is excessive and, in that case, perhaps it is no longer right to call it good fortune. For wealth has a limit in its relationship to happiness.

In sum: too little money and one is unable to develop one's self effectively; too much money and one may become lost in materialism.

The Golden Mean

In answering the question 'How much is enough?' Aristotle warns us not to expect precise answers from philosophical inquiry. Ethical analysis is not scientific; it does not produce clear and quantifiable results (which may be a reason why philosophical discussions are not part of the MBA curriculum), but 'has as much clearness as the subject matter admits of.'

What matters more to Aristotle than the conclusions we reach is how we construct, and think through, such problems. When we answer the question 'How much is enough?' he doesn't care what amount we arrive at, but whether we engage in a disciplined moral analysis.

To begin that process, we must pose our question in an appropriate context. We should start with a definition of the good life. We always must keep the highest end in view to think effectively. We should also engage in honest dialogue with friends who are also struggling with the question, and try to answer the objections of those who disagree with our conclusions. The one person we typically fool in moral analysis is ourself.

Aristotle offers a disciplined process by which we can decide. First, we must distinguish between needs and wants. We need incomes that cover the costs of necessities, of raising and educating our children, of leisure activities such as travel that help us to grow, and of investments sufficient to provide income for our retirement. But we do not need everything we want. Second, we must avoid the defects of want and of excess. On the one hand, we must be realistic and not underestimate what we need. The precise amount one needs depends on such factors as age, interests, family situation, and place of residence. Older, single people who live in rural areas do not need as much as younger couples raising kids in Manhattan. On the other hand, we must also avoid conspicuous consumption. We need clothes and art, but we don't need Brioni suits and original Picassos.

Objections, Reasonable and Otherwise

Implicit in Aristotle's reasoning is the conclusion that a great many more people can afford to start pursuing happiness now than are currently doing so. But should everyone spend less time toiling, and more time engaged in philosophy and politics? There are two reasonable objections to that claim.

First, some, perhaps many, people are perfectly happy pursuing more, and prefer their material goodies to the (nonexistent for them) benefits of contemplation. People who dedicate their lives to making money are already leading full lives, and Aristotle is a condescending elitist to say otherwise. But Aristotle is not trying to impose his views on anyone. He is responding to the wealthy and powerful people who asked, 'Is that all there is?' In response, he suggested to all those capable of doing so to consider what it would mean for them to live a fuller, more interesting life. He asked everyone to do this because he worried that too many bright, hard-working people will miss out on the greatest joys in life because they get caught up in the pursuit of material goods.

The struggles that matter aren't those between practical people and intellectuals. Virtuous people are, again, introspective, self-critical, rational, and curious, and Aristotle thinks practical people also possess, and benefit from, those traits. He even doubts they can prosper in their business affairs for long without them. Virtuous, practical people ask tough questions about what is right for themselves, and for others. When they do so habitually, they come not only to understand what is right for themselves, they also do what is right.

The second objection is more substantive and complex. This is a version of Adam Smith's belief that individual unhappiness breeds productivity: economists would say Aristotle is naive to assume there is a limit to the amount of wealth people should accumulate. They ask what would happen to the economy if everyone said, 'That's enough': Wouldn't growth and innovation stop, jobs cease to be created, and the economy collapse?

In fact, Aristotle doesn't disdain wealth, and doesn't condescendingly argue the rich should be social workers instead of entrepreneurs. He wants to help those who are well-off *also* to live well. He sees no reason a practical-minded businessperson can't live a full life. To that end, he argues that people shouldn't unnecessarily foreshorten their horizons, limit their activities, narrow their experiences, and use only a part of the potential they were born with. The professor who churns out narrow, technical articles year after year is no more leading the good life than is the business person who spends an entire career only pursuing wealth.

There is nothing wrong with making more money—unless doing so eclipses other, morally higher, concerns. In fact, the issue isn't economic at all: We aren't going to quit being Homo Economicus. The issue is that we are *also* social, political, and philosophical animals. So Aristotle asks us to consider how we might spend our time in useful and rewarding ways in addition to making money.

Here is Aristotle's answer to the second objection: Habitually deliberative people are more likely to hit on what is right for themselves, their business, and their communities. Although they will choose to limit their wealth, entrepreneurial activity will not (and should not) cease.

Practical Wisdom

MBA students are taught technical skills, and Aristotle says it is right that they are. A 'statesman' (a leader, and this would include those in business) needs special traits and skills, among which are intelligence and technical knowledge. To gain such intelligence one needs first to master some discipline, whether a science or an art. People who do so effectively are said to possess *intellectual excellence*, a trait measured by their skill in calculations (such as designing a computer chip) or in theoretical reasoning (such as making investments in futures markets). Possessing, then developing and effectively using, this kind of intelligence is necessary to succeed at work, make contributions to knowledge, create wealth, and realize one's personal potential.

But Aristotle adds that more importantly, a leader needs *practical wisdom*, which has nothing to do with science, theory, disciplinary knowledge, or knowledge of facts in any way. It is concerned 'neither with eternal and unchangeable truth' but 'with matters where doubt and deliberation are possible', and in particular, with 'how things can be other than they are.' It requires 'the use of one's faculty of opinion in judging matters' relating to what is right and wrong for a business, or society as a whole.

Such practical wisdom is the prerequisite of 'moral excellence', the *sine qua non* of *leadership*: 'That is why we say Pericles and men like him have practical wisdom. They have the capacity to see what is good for themselves and for humankind.' Pericles used his practical wisdom to identify the policies that would make Athenians collectively happy and create a good society characterized by justice for all. Hence, while virtuous leaders have skill-based *intellectual excellence*, more important, they possess the *moral excellence* that derives from practical wisdom.

At all times, the conscious goal of a just leader is to help followers achieve what is good for them (which, on occasion, may be something different from what they think they want). In other words, leaders must have both technical skills and the practical wisdom to be effective, with effectiveness defined as the capacity to discern and provide justice. (In contrast, business schools teach 'contingency', an amoral theory of leadership.)

The Social Contract

Aristotle writes that the unwritten constitutions, or social contracts, of the small-scale societies he observed were the prime determinants of the degree to which people led good lives. In the few just societies he observed, the constitution provided opportunity for people to develop their natural abilities and thus pursue happiness.

The leader's duty is to create conditions under which followers achieve their potential. Political leadership is therefore a task and responsibility rather than a privilege, right, or reward. Aristotle says, 'It is the mark of a man of practical wisdom to be able to deliberate well about what is good and expedient for himself . . . and about what sorts of things are conducive to the good life in general.'

But how does a leader know what is conducive to the good life for others? This is a tricky business. On the one hand, Aristotle believes Platonic paternalism is morally wrong and impractical, while, on the other, he says it is virtuous and practical for leaders to place the good of others above their own narrow self-interest. That is a fine line to draw. Usefully, he then shows how leaders begin the process of deciding what is in the interest of others *without* dictating how they should behave. A virtuous leader starts by putting himself in the place of his followers, asking 'How would I want to be treated if I were a subject of this state?' Because the welfare of the community takes priority over the interests of individual members, a virtuous leader asks a second question: 'What form of social contract would allow all members of our community to develop their potential in order that they each may make their greatest contribution to the good of the whole?'

How is this to be determined? Because wisdom is never the sole province of any individual, the practical and just way to determine the conditions of a social contract is through discussion among all the participants in the system. This should not be confused with political democracy. Aristotle was no enthusiast of democracy, believing that only the virtuous few who actively pursue both the highest and the complete good are fit to participate in political decision-making. Yet his political oligarchs are not tyrants.

In his model of governance, all qualified people in a community come together to discuss rationally the issues and problems they face. While that participation is limited to virtuous individuals, all those so qualified are equal in terms of their right to participate. These equally enfranchised participants nonetheless will be unequal in that some will be smarter, some wiser, some more articulate, and some will have more technical knowledge in particular fields. But all participants would be equal in terms of being able to ask questions and then to evaluate the various policy ideas put forward by experts. No one person would dominate every discussion because political issues are so complex and varied no one ever has all the information needed to make the best decisions in all cases, and no one ever has a monopoly on wisdom.

Aristotle was not naive: He understood people have real and legitimate differences of opinion, and that they are divided by competing and conflicting interests. Still, he could not imagine a situation in which qualified people who come together to achieve justice for their community could not, after free and rational discussion, eventually arrive at a rough agreement about matters that affected them.

The Aristotelian Workplace

How does this apply to business? Extrapolating from the Ancient's writings on politics, a modern Aristotelian workplace would have four primary characteristics:

(1) it provides a real opportunity for all workers to learn and to develop their talent and potential

(2) all employees participate in the decisions that affect their own work

(3) all employees participate in the financial gains resulting from their own ideas and efforts

(4) the leaders are virtuous.

The second and third points are inextricably linked: Participation in decision-making without participation in financial gains is unjust because the fruits of employee contributions are reaped by others (executives and shareholders). And participation in a company's financial gains without participating in decision-making also is unjust because workers are powerless to influence the conditions that determine the size of their paychecks. Importantly, the first three characteristics derive from the existence of the fourth, virtuous leadership.

Modern workplaces are the moral equivalent of Aristotle's small-scale communities. As political societies grow more complex, workplaces become the arenas in which modern men and women expend most of their energies, and in which they have the most influence. Hence, business leaders have inherited the ethical roles, tasks, and responsibilities of Aristotle's virtuous political leaders.

But few modern workplaces are Aristotelian, in at least three ways. First, the terms of our employment contracts tend to be greater determinants of our lifestyles than provisions in the social contracts we have with our city, state, and national communities. Modern businesses have the greatest power to create conditions under which individuals can realize their potential.

Second, research on group behavior reveals that Aristotle's face-to-face model works when the number of people involved is very small and that in small groups most people will behave rationally and cooperatively, as he posited (Lawler, 1986). However, when the number exceeds 20 or so, as it does in most businesses, the group starts to break into factions, participants stop listening to each other, and the strongest individuals come to dominate.

Third, Aristotle believes the ability to reason is the main qualification for participation in decision-making, and would believe the modern organization's criteria—status, titles, salary, power, ego, and the like—are unjust and irrelevant. Since the goal of governance is to determine 'the good' and the best means to achieve it (in business terms, the right strategy, structure, policies, and products), work organizations should tap into all sources of practical wisdom. Useful ideas from middle managers, or even front-line workers, should be as welcome as those from the executive suite.

If Aristotle is right that the good life entails developing one's potential, leaders of work organizations have a moral responsibility to provide conditions in which employees can do so. Organizations that deny them the chance to develop their potential deny them the opportunity to realize their humanity. Hence, business leaders have inherited the ethical roles, tasks, and responsibilities of Aristotle's virtuous political leaders. Virtuous business leaders serve not to make themselves rich, famous, adored, or powerful, but to provide society with the goods and services it needs in an economically efficient manner while at the same time providing the environment for the intellectual and moral development of employees. Like Aristotle's political leaders, their task is to make 'the good' of the company commensurate with the good of its employees; in fact, to make the two mutually reinforcing.

Hence, the first challenges of virtuous business leadership are to create:

(a) processes for eliciting and evaluating ideas from across the organization

(b) systems of governance in which all employees find themselves in groups small enough for all to have a meaningful say in decisions directly affecting their own work.

Workplace Applications

Here is an example of these principles in action. In the early '70s, a corporate executive wrote the following Aristotelian words:

> The employer's obligations to society, stockholders and workers [are] intricately interrelated. One cannot, in effect, serve society at all if he does not serve its people. One cannot serve shareholders effectively if he does not act to make business itself an agent for human growth and fulfillment (cited in O'Toole, et al., 1973, p. 25).

At the time, he was cooperating with the United Auto Workers in a workplace experiment in an old, unproductive facility where auto mirrors were manufactured. Workers were given the opportunity to manage themselves, even though most of them were relatively uneducated and came from disadvantaged backgrounds. The workers produced x mirrors per day. The workers, the union, and management agreed that, whenever they produced x+n mirrors, they would be free to:

(a) go home

(b) continue working and earn a bonus

(c) attend a company-sponsored school where the courses offered ranged from work-related subjects to basic education to the piano. Fully a third of the workers chose to attend the company school on their found time.

Workers were allowed to find ways to organize their tasks in almost any way they wished, and allowed to redesign plant conditions to make their tasks less tedious and more interesting. The work itself became a learning experience, and the workers began making changes, experimenting with better, faster, more efficient ways to make mirrors. Ultimately, they improved their productivity to the point where they were reaching their quota around mid-day. Moreover, as they gained confidence and experience, they began to suggest ways to redesign other jobs in the plant, and they invented imaginative ways to share in cost savings resulting from the changes they either initiated or supported. This was an Aristotelian workplace, designed not only to be successful economically, but, equally, to allow for worker self-fulfillment, learning, and growth.

Similar Aristotelian efforts have been implemented to make work into learning experiences and, in particular, to permit blue-collar and other front-line workers to find the kind of intellectual rewards in their jobs that professionals and managers often find in their 'leisure-work.' In the early '80s, Jack Stack, CEO of the rust-belt SRC Holdings, taught all of his employees, mostly blue-collar workers with no more than high school educations, the financial skills he learned when he had earned his MBA. When they were as adept as he was at reading the company's cash-flow statements and balance sheet, he gave them full authority to act on their knowledge and shared with them the gains resulting from their ideas and efforts. For the last 20 years, every SRC employee has had access to all financial and managerial information, and the net effect, in the words of the company's CFO, 'is like having 700 internal auditors out there in every function of the company' (O'Toole & Lawler, 2006). This example illustrates how leaders can create ethical, sustainable corporate cultures. Unfortunately, learning how to design such high-involvement workplaces is not in the curriculum of major business schools.

Developing Managers and Leaders

Many current CEOs claim the mantle of virtue based on their apparent commitment to the development of their top management teams. The problem is that their egos, and the related misuse of their power, prevents their effectively creating other leaders. Aristotle, according to philosopher Richard Kraut, believes great leaders observe 'decent limits' to the use of their power and allow others to lead and develop: 'No virtuous person wants to be best if this turns his equals into people who are predominantly passive recipients of his moral feats' (Kraut, 1989, p. 127).

In practice, celebrity CEOs sometimes behave as if there were only one leader, themselves, and not only garner credit for all good decisions, but amass for themselves the best opportunities to learn through leading. Worse, they dismiss executives who challenge their authority, particularly upcoming stars who shine too brightly and thus threaten their CEO status as the sole source of organizational enlightenment. Here we might recall Aristotle's assertion that political leaders, even effective ones, who amass too much power should be exiled because they limit the opportunity for others to participate in decision-making and, thus, to develop fully. Note that the advantages of such shared leadership are seldom taught in top tier b-schools.

One need not be a CEO to be concerned with the issue of employee development. Whatever our level in any organization, public or private, many of us have the authority to affect positively the quality of life of those who work for us, or with us. If we choose to lead them virtuously, here are some questions Aristotle might say we need to ask ourselves:

- To what extent do I consciously provide learning opportunities for everyone who works for me?
- To what extent do I encourage full participation by all my people in the decisions affecting their work? To what extent do I allow them to lead in order to grow?
- To what extent do I measure my own performance as a manager/leader both in terms of my effectiveness in realizing economic goals, and in terms of using my practical wisdom to create conditions under which my people can seek to fulfill their potential in the workplace?

In business schools, such Aristotelian measures are often dismissed as inappropriate, impractical, and irrelevant to the task boards hire executives to do: create wealth. MBA students are taught that their responsibility is to shareholders, not employees, and if employee development interferes with profit-making, then 'trade-offs must be made'. Aristotle would answer that virtuous leaders have responsibilities to *both* their owners and workers and, if there is a conflict between the two, it is their duty to create conditions in which their interests can be made the same. He would remind us that, while most leaders measure themselves solely in terms of their effectiveness at obtaining and maintaining power, virtuous ones also measure themselves by ethical standards of justice. It is appropriate that business leaders be evaluated by their effectiveness at generating wealth for shareholders, but also by their ability to provide their followers meaning and the opportunity for development in the workplace.

Just Distribution of Rewards

In light of recent corporate scandals, it is dismaying to find many executives still concerned that they might be getting less than their fair share of the wealth produced by the companies they lead. To them, the measure of what they are entitled to receive is the amount executives in comparable companies earn. As often noted, this has little to do with their performance or with their relative contributions to their organizations. Instead, it has everything to do with power and leverage.

Looking at the *Fortune 500*, the average CEO currently takes home over $10.8 million per year—in real terms, some 20 times more than in 1981, and some 400 to 500 times what their front-line workers earn. Even moderately well-paid CEOs of large corporations make about as much in a day as their workers make in a year.

While boards and investors may say this growing disparity is acceptable, the Ancient says being willing to take less than the share a contract permits one to take is a sign of fairness and virtue. By definition, one never takes less than one's fair share when one does so voluntarily. Thus, there would be no question of a CEO receiving less than his fair share if he were to voluntarily choose to absorb some of the costs of the increase in, say, his employees' insurance premiums, or grant some of his stock options to others in his organization who have none.

Harder to reckon is what is just and fair. But it is not impossible to do so. For example, Disney's board compensated its CEO, Michael Eisner, with $285 million between 1996 and 2004. We don't have the data required to decide how much Eisner deserved, but, thanks to Aristotle, we have a question that a virtuous member of the Disney board's compensation committee might have asked: 'Is our CEO's proportionate contribution to the organization 10, or 100, or 1,000 times greater than that of a cartoon animator at our Burbank studios or the operator of the Space Mountain ride at Disneyland?' While asking such a question is practically unheard of in the boardrooms of giant companies, a few small- and medium-sized companies have done so, and have gone on to establish ratios as low as 20:1 between the compensations of their highest-paid executive and their average worker. While that may sound unrealistic, when the numbers are run it makes some sense: If the average worker makes $20 an hour, the CEO in even a 'low-paying' company can make $1,000,000. It only seems out of the question when the actual ratio in *Fortune 500* companies approaches 500:1.

Deliberation about the just ratio between the highest- and the lowest-paid person in an organization is a good way for corporate boards and executives to begin including ethical analysis in their compensation discussions. Alas, most large corporations use distributive compensation processes more reflective of their employees' relative power than of objective and ethical analyses of their relative contributions. And it is hard to do such a just and objective analysis. As Aristotle would be the first to recognize, employees must be paid market wages. However, markets do not determine the compensation of executives. In many cases, this particular market is rigged: The widespread use of compensation surveys allows executives to continually ratchet up their salaries.

At the other end of the salary scale, a company would price itself out of business if it paid its clerks as much as it pays managers, so boards tend to skip over the issue of relative justice for lower-level workers, leaving the market to determine that. But the market does not work in quite the same way for workers as it does for top managers and skilled professionals. Because jobs are offered to lower-level workers on a take-it-or-leave-it basis, their conditions of employment often amount to unethical 'exchanges of desperation.' In contrast, professionals and managers may have other employment opportunities and, as a result, some bargaining power.

Granted, that's the way of the world, and corporate executives and board members can't be expected to repeal the laws of economics. However, they are not without power to increase opportunities for even first-line employees to raise their own standards of living. For example, boards can distribute stock and stock options more broadly, and there are a number of well-tested methods for objectively and fairly linking rewards to relative contribution: profit-sharing, gain-sharing, ESOPs, and the like, all of which are consistent with the rules of the market.

Another Exam

Aristotle does not provide a single, clear principle for the just distribution of enterprise-created wealth, nor would it be possible for anyone to formulate such a monolithic rule. Nonetheless, here are some Aristotelian guidelines in the form of questions virtuous leaders need to ask of themselves:

- Am I taking more in my share of rewards than my contributions warrant?
- Does the distribution of goods in the organization preserve the happiness of the community, or does it harm morale and others' ability to achieve the good?
- Would everyone enter into employment under the current terms if they truly had other choices?

- Would we come to a different principle of allocation if all of the parties concerned were represented at the table?

Again, the only hard-and-fast principle of distributive justice is that fairness is most likely to arise out of a process of rational and moral deliberation. Prescriptively, all Aristotle says is that virtue and wisdom will certainly elude leaders who fail to engage in rigorous ethical analysis of their actions.

Coda: Why Ethics Matter

Unlike most of today's b-school professors, Aristotle was comfortable with the language of ethics: He spoke clearly about right and wrong, virtue and vice, should and shouldn't. He advocated the virtues of duty, responsibility, accountability, prudence, and magnanimous action. He saluted the character traits of moral courage and excellence. He required leaders to consider the interests of their followers and contribute to the welfare of their communities.

In recent times, those on the left have shied away from such language, and those on the right have claimed that questions of morality have no place in the pragmatic world of business (instead, markets should be the ultimate judge of our public actions). To both, one can only reply: Enron, WorldCom, Tyco, Global Crossing, and Arthur Andersen.

Aristotle understood what we in America conveniently chose to forget in the heady '90s: Free economies cannot function effectively without a strong ethical foundation. Ancient Athens was no welfare state. There was no social security, no public assistance, and no free schooling. But there were many poor and needy citizens. If an old person fell on hard times, and a poor but promising child needed schooling, it was expected they would be taken care of by 'friends.' Such friendship was not based on dependency or utility. It was predicated on the value of respect for others, and the concomitant virtue of generosity. Or so it should be, according to Aristotle. If the state did not provide for the needy, then it stood to reason the wealthy had to. Aristotle could not imagine a society with a market economy that did not also have an inherent commitment to social ethics and philanthropy.

Since the fall of Communism and the subsequent rise of market economies in formerly Stalinist and Maoist countries, the problems of corruption, cheating, stealing, price-gouging, and tax-evasion have become common, if not chronic. There is no enculturation to ethical norms of behavior. New laws have helped, but have not been sufficient. The conclusion to be drawn is that people have to be taught the professional, personal, and social merits of virtue. That's why new business schools in formerly Communist countries spend so much time dealing with ethics, a subject that had been foreign to the curriculum of Communist universities.

Curiously, in the 1990s, ethics and social responsibility disappeared from the agenda of many American corporations and business schools. Too many successful executives during that era came to understand freedom to mean they owed nothing to society. They called for drastic reductions in federal, state, and local taxes, and for cutting back government programs and regulations. What they then didn't do was to increase their support of charity and take responsibility for ethical and moral self-regulation of their economic enterprises.

Over two thousand years ago Aristotle argued that a strong ethical foundation was a requirement for an open society. In fact, history has shown that no advanced society can go outside of these two alternatives: private enterprise/ethics/philanthropy/individual responsibility, or, socialism/regulation/state welfare/social entitlements. The former leads to freedom, progress, and affluence, the later to tyranny, stagnation, and poverty.

Aristotle's teacher, Plato, had opted for a controlled society in which paternalistic guardians would make all the political and moral decisions for a dependent populace, who then could devote all their time to making and spending money. Aristotle advocated a free society, but he warned that such a society would function only for as long as, and to the extent that, its citizens engaged in moral deliberation, and then chose to pursue the path to virtue. The Athenians did not heed Aristotle's advice, and, as Edith Hamilton explains, the consequences were dire:

> They wanted a comfortable life and they lost it all—security, comfort and freedom. When the Athenians finally wanted not to give to society, but for society to give to them, when the freedom they wished for most was the freedom from responsibility, then Athenians ceased to be free (Hamilton, 1993).

We business professors ought not to let our students make the same mistake as the Athenians. If we incorporate the kinds of moral questions Aristotle raises in all our MBA classes—finance, marketing, accounting, management—we can begin to help tomorrow's executives to create ethical corporate cultures.

Bibliography

Bennis, Warren G., and O'Toole, James (May 2005), "How Business Schools Lost Their Way", *Harvard Business Review*.

Bragues, George (September 2006), "Seek the Good Life, Not Money: The Aristotelian Approach to Business Ethics", *Journal of Business Ethics* 67, pp. 341–57.

Hamilton, Edith (1993), *The Greek Way* (New York: W.W. Norton and Company, 1930; reprint, New York: W.W. Norton and Company).

Hartman, Edwin (March 2006), "Can We Teach Character? An Aristotelian Answer", *Academy of Management Learning and Education* 5, pp. 68–81.

Heilbroner, Robert (1999), *The Worldly Philosophers: The Lives, Times, and Ideas of the Great Economic Thinkers* (New York: Simon and Schuster).

Kraut, Richard (1989), *Aristotle on the Human Good* (Princeton, NJ: Princeton University Press).

Lawler, Edward E. (1986), *High-Involvement Management: Participative Strategies for Improving Organizational Performance* (San Francisco: Jossey-Bass).

Mintzberg, Henry 2004), *Managers Not M.B.A.s: A Hard Look at the Soft Practice of Managing and Management* (San Francisco: Berrett-Koehler).

O'Toole James, et al. (1973), *Work in America*, a report of a special task force to the U.S. Secretary of Health, Education, and Welfare (Cambridge, MA: M.I.T. Press).

O'Toole, James (2005), *Creating the Good Life: Applying Aristotle's Wisdom to Find Meaning and Happiness* (Emmaus, PA: Rodale).

O'Toole, James, and Lawler, Edward E. (2006), *The New American Workplace* (New York: Macmillan, Palgrave Macmillan).

Solomon, Robert (2006), "Aristotle, Ethics, and Business Organizations", *Organization Studies* 25, no. 6, pp. 1021–43.

Christopher Megone

Integrity, Virtue and the Financial Crisis

Let me begin with a quote from Alasdair Macintyre:

> [M]odernity partitions each human life into a variety of segments, each with its own norms and modes of behaviour. So work is divided from leisure, private life from public, the corporate from the personal. So both childhood and old age have been wrenched away from the rest of human life and made over into distinct realms. And all these separations have been achieved so that it is the distinctiveness of each, and not the unity of the life of the individual who passes through the parts, in terms of which we are taught to think and feel.[1]

Taking this quote as a starting point I shall suggest that, from an ethical viewpoint, one contributory strand affecting at least some of the choices and practices that contributed to the 2008 global financial crisis was the possibility of just such a kind of compartmentalisation and fragmentation in the lives of business people and financial professionals. In this paper, I will argue that when such compartmentalisation occurs, it reflects a lack of integrity, properly understood, and consequently a lack of virtue in business practice. (Of course, if Macintyre is right, then many of us will be suffering from the pressure to see our lives in this compartmentalised way, so the focus is only here on professionals and business people because business ethics is the theme of this volume.)

I will begin by outlining the kind of compartmentalisation of life that I have in mind. I shall then sketch some prominent features of the 2008t financial crisis, and indicate in a preliminary way how such

---

[1] Macintyre, 1981, p. 205. I was pointed towards this quote by work of John Cottingham on 'Integrity and Fragmentation', though the focus of that piece is rather different from mine here.

compartmentalisation might have had a bearing on that unfolding event. I shall then turn to the notion of integrity and defend a conception of it that is perhaps somewhat richer than many contemporary accounts. This will be developed within a virtue ethics perspective. I shall deny that integrity is itself a virtue, but argue that it is necessary for virtue, and thus for genuine happiness. In doing this, I will articulate the value of integrity in terms of its relation to two Aristotelian doctrines: first, the doctrine of the unity of the virtues; and, second, the claim that the evaluation of a person's happiness depends on the nature of their whole life, rather than that of passing moments or parts. I shall also suggest that this picture of integrated virtue and happiness is in turn underpinned by Aristotle's metaphysical conception of the unity of the person.

This discussion of integrity provides us with resources for an alternative conception of the importance of the unity of an individual's life, with which the tendency towards compartmentalisation can be contrasted. This pair of contrasting views can then be brought to bear on the financial crisis. In order to do this I will turn to an important account of the nature of business, and argue that this account leads to a conception of the relation between ethics and business which encourages compartmentalisation in the lives of those in business and finance. Thus I will indicate ways in which some of the practices leading to the 2008 financial crisis may also reflect a lack of the kind of personal integrity whose importance I have outlined.

Compartmentalisation

In the given quote, Macintyre suggests that it is characteristic of our modern age that individual human lives are segmented into a variety of distinct activities. Each of these activities has, as it were, its own distinct way of life. The norms by which I live, and the behaviour I display when at work can be (sharply) marked off from the norms and behavioural practices that characterise my leisure time. Similar comments, he claims, can be made about an individual's private and public lives, or corporate and personal lives. Such compartmentalisation of life encourages the development of different persona or personalities. This is very different from encouraging each of us to recognise the essential unity of our lives and to seek to integrate the distinctive elements into such a whole.[2]

---

[2] Of course in private life, for example, I will often engage with friends, whilst at work or in the public sphere I will usually be engaging with acquaintances, and

Some quite commonplace ways of talking about business life or working in finance seem to conform to this compartmentalisation view. How often have I heard it said, on announcing that I teach business ethics—"Oh, isn't business ethics an oxymoron?" Of course that can often be understood as merely a light-hearted remark, but equally common is the claim that when practical decisions are required in a corporate context we need to recognise that "business is business". There is a self-contained world, it is implied—the business world—and, as Macintyre indicates, it has its own norms and modes of behaviour.

A concrete example may illustrate the point. I recently heard a radio interview in which an entrepreneur was discussing his business. His company was making a cosmetic product whose purpose was to lighten the colour of people with darker skins. It was put to the entrepreneur that this was rather an objectionable product, which might encourage people of darker skins to feel alienated from themselves. The entrepreneur's response was to accept this unreservedly, acknowledging that this was a dreadful product. When asked why, given this view, he persisted in selling it, his answer was simply that he made a lot of money from it. Business is business.

The Financial Crisis

How then might such compartmentalisation of business life, or economic activity, have any bearing on the 2008 financial crisis affecting much of the world, and perhaps most notably the United States and Europe, at least so far as financial institutions are concerned? To approach this question, let me briefly review some of the salient features of the crisis. For ease of exposition I shall refer principally to events in the US and the UK.

One (perhaps folk-loreish) version of the crisis suggests that it emanated from problems in sub-prime mortgage lending, conducted particularly in the US housing market. Here a large amount of lending had been undertaken to house-buyers at rates, and in quantities, which those mortgagees were unable to sustain. This lending had in turn been underwritten by banks and building societies often far away from the initial lending. Those institutions frequently took on that debt in forms where the nature of it was unclear. Thus when the initial lending started to unravel at a great rate as mortgagees defaulted in large numbers and the US housing market rapidly declined, the impact was felt by banks and building societies

---

there will naturally be differences arising from that. But the warning is against being one kind of person in one environment, another kind in a second.

across the US and UK, and beyond. In addition the financial sector was already quite significantly extended having taken on huge quantities of personal debt in the US and UK. Both the US and the UK governments also had very heavy levels of borrowing even before the crisis in housing began to unfold. Thus credit markets froze and financial institutions either very rapidly collapsed (Lehman Brothers, Alliance and Leicester, Bradford and Bingley, Merrill Lynch) or required massive bailouts (Royal Bank of Scotland, Halifax Bank of Scotland, Fannie Mac and Freddie Mae, AIG).

As one recent writer has noted, a number of dubious practices had a significant impact on this crisis:

> (i) reckless and predatory lending by banks; (ii) the growth of highly leveraged investment banks; (iii) the selling of toxic financial products notably non-transparent packaged bundles of mortgages, including sub-prime mortgages; (iv) failure to avoid or adequately manage structural conflicts of interest, including ratings agencies assessing the non-transparent toxic financial products mentioned above as high quality because the investment banks that packaged them—and who fund the ratings agencies—allegedly had good risk assessment processes; (v) massive frauds (e.g. Bernard Madoff's ponzi scheme); (vi) excessive executive remuneration that in numerous cases effectively rewarded management failure, as in the case of failed investment banks and the giant insurer, AIG;[3] (vii) the unconstrained and unwarranted growth of the financial sector ("Wall Street") ultimately to the detriment of, rather than in the service of, the productive business sectors ("Main Street"[4]) (Miller, 2009, p. 1).

Let me say at the outset that the aim here is not to suggest that responsibility for this whole crisis is simply down to "the Banks" or "a small number of bankers", or just to "financial institutions" as a whole. Clearly there have been many institutions and agents within the financial services sector who may have played a significant role—high street bankers, investment bankers, lawyers, auditors, fund-managers, brokers, credit-rating professionals and so on.

---

[3] Incentivising risky behaviour which led to short-term profits but dramatically increased the risk to the business, and encouraged people in pursuit of bonuses, which rewarded such behaviour, to develop complex financial instruments such as collateralised debt obligations (CDOs).

[4] The growth of the financial sector was both encouraged by and itself encouraged financial deals such as leveraged buyouts and company acquisitions which lacked strategic rationale but depended instead on financial instruments to generate returns.

Equally clearly there have been many other actors, outside the financial institutions who have contributed. Some governments, for example, proclaimed an end to the cycles of boom and bust, and many agent choices will have been affected by that perceived economic environment. On "Main St", millions of people may have borrowed incautiously — perhaps more than they could afford. Journalists may have reported the crisis in terms that encouraged panicked responses. Governments, entering the crisis heavily borrowed, have been in a poor position to respond. Many companies with highly leveraged business models were poorly prepared for an economic downturn.

Nonetheless, as indicated above, it is possible to identify within the financial and business sector some of the undesirable practices previously discussed. How might those practices be taken to exemplify a lack of integrity? My basic claim is that some of them could at the very least be encouraged by allowing one's life and the aims governing it to be compartmentalised, or fragmented, rather than integrated. To explain this, I now turn to my account of integrity.

Despite the fact that integrity (or lack of it) is quite a commonly used concept in everyday ethical appraisal (as exhibited in its extensive use in discussions of UK parliamentarians' recent behaviour over expenses, as well as of the financial crisis), there is surprisingly little clarity on what the notion means. In the more theoretical literature in moral philosophy there is little agreement on this, with a variety of different accounts suggesting that it involves self-integration, identity, moral purpose and standing for something, respectively. This literature makes little attempt to link its discussions to the concept of integrity as it is applied in professional life and the workplace. In this context it is an ethical concept that is widely referred to in professional codes, several of which are relevant to the financial crisis (such as IFAC, ICAEW, ICAS). In the contemporary sense, however, as in the common usage noted above, it tends to have rather a thin content. It is often associated with honesty and trust (in the professional codes), but is generally suggestive of the idea of a minimum moral decency.

Here I want to suggest that a somewhat richer conception of integrity, but one which coheres with the ordinary ideas above, can be developed within the tradition of virtue ethics. However from that perspective it is noteworthy that integrity is not to be found on the traditional western lists of virtues in either the Greek or Judaeo-Christian tradition. Plato's list of core virtues in the republic —

wisdom, temperance, courage and justice—does not include it. Nor is it to be found in Aristotle's longer list in the *Nicomachean Ethics*. Nor is it amongst the theological virtues, faith, hope and charity, which are added by Aquinas. More generally, so far as the Judaeo-Christian tradition is concerned, it is not to be found as an acknowledged virtue in the Old or New Testament.

Its absence from the lists provided by the great Greek virtue ethicists is perhaps unsurprising since etymologically its roots lie in the Latin *integer*—wholeness. But once that connection between integrity and wholeness is recognised, then it can be argued that - although not a virtue itself—integrity is nonetheless a key idea in Aristotelian virtue ethics. This can be brought out by noting that the importance of living life as an integrated whole is developed in two distinctive claims that Aristotle made about virtue and happiness.

The first of these claims is usually termed the doctrine of the unity of the virtues. This doctrine is set out in book VI of the *Nicomachean Ethics*. As an initial clarification, it may be said that Aristotle is defending the claim that the virtues constitute a reciprocal unity. This is the view that in order to have any virtue one must have all the virtues, or that full possession of any virtue brings with it possession of all the virtues. This is because what is required for full possession of any virtue is practical wisdom (*phronesis*) and possession of *phronesis* brings with it possession of all the virtues.[5]

Aristotle makes the second claim that is relevant to integrity in book I of the *Nicomachean Ethics*. Having set out his preferred account of happiness as rational activity of the soul exhibiting excellence (or virtue),[6] he goes on to add that such happiness must be a feature of a complete life. "For one swallow does not make a summer, nor does one day; and so too one day, or a short time, does not make a man blessed or happy".[7] In some fairly brief further discussion, he indicates that one aspect of this relation between happiness and a complete life is the stability of the happy man's condition. "Nor, again, is he many-coloured and changeable; for neither will he be moved from his happy state easily…"[8]

Before saying more about each of these claims, it may be helpful to outline briefly their context. Aristotle may be seen as addressing two

---

[5] Aristotle, *Nicomachean Ethics*, VI,13, 1144b 15-35.
[6] Ibid., I,7, 1098a 1–18.
[7] Ibid., I,7, 1098a 20-22.
[8] Ibid., I,10 1101a 9-10.

principal questions in his *Nicomachean Ethics*. First, 'what is the ultimate human good?', which can be construed as his way of asking 'what kind of life should one live?' Second, 'what is the relationship between the virtuous life and happiness?' In very general terms, his answers to these two questions are: that the ultimate human good is generally agreed to be happiness, but there is disagreement as to what happiness consists in,[9] so that needs to be clarified; that the virtuous life is in fact constitutive of happiness;[10] and the reason for that is that the human good is achieved through actualising the human essential potential for rationality, and the life of virtue is the life that actualises that rational potential.

Inserting the two claims into this picture it follows that, for Aristotle, the *eudaimon* or genuinely happy life is one in which a human being manifests all of the virtues, since these virtues constitute a reciprocal unity. It further follows that for Aristotle the ultimate human good, or genuine happiness, is a feature of a whole integrated life, where the possession of the virtues as a reciprocal unity contributes significantly to that unity.

Let me now further explain these two claims.

The Unity of the Virtues and the Wholeness of Happiness

In recent times a number of those discussing the virtues have rejected the proposition that the virtues constitute a reciprocal unity, as Annas has noted (Annas, 2009, p. 1). Even Macintyre holds that commitment to the unity of the virtues would be 'a serious defect' in contemporary virtue ethics, despite his objections to the compartmentalisation of life. By contrast, in the ancient and mediaeval world "the thesis is generally taken to be true, and not particularly controversial" (Annas, 2009, p. 2). Whilst it is not possible to provide a full defence here, setting out the doctrine in a little more detail may indicate its plausibility as well as explaining more fully its connection to integrity as wholeness.

One key thought behind the doctrine is that the virtues are not compartmentalised from each other, each with its own self-contained sphere of authority (Annas, 2009, p. 3). Rather the circumstances of life have to be addressed by harmonious composites of virtues. This can be illuminated by considering a purported objection to the doctrine that I once heard as an undergraduate. The doctrine was held to be false since "it is clear that a burglar, who makes a brave getaway leap-

---

[9] *Ibid.*, I,4.
[10] *Ibid.*, I,7.

ing across roofs and overcoming other obstacles is courageous but unjust". In fact Aristotle holds that facing risks is not enough for courage — facing risks for unsuitable ends may be rash not courageous. This is very plausible as the following extreme example may illustrate. If a mouse is at risk of death trying to cross a motorway in a rush hour then, to put one's own life at risk trying to save the mouse in such circumstances, although it involves facing considerable danger, is foolishly rash and not courageous. This is because the goal is not one which warrants facing such risks. By the same token, although the burglar faces risks, because his goal is unjust he does so for an unworthy reason, so he too is rash and not courageous. Thus, genuine courage requires the possession of justice as well. In a similar way the virtue of truthfulness may sometimes not be displayed because one lacks courage. It will require courage to stand up for the truth in some circumstances (though, in some cases, to do so may just be rash). Likewise generosity may require justice — it is not generous to give away goods if those goods have been acquired unjustly in the first place, or if one simply gives the goods away in an unconsidered manner, without, for example, any attention to need (Annas, 2009, pp. 12–13).

What underlies the interconnectedness of the virtues is *phronesis*, or practical wisdom - the intellectual virtue which enables the practically wise agent to judge what is best to do, all things considered, on each occasion (Annas, 2009, pp. 2–3). What the above makes clear is that when virtuous action is in question practical wisdom enables the agent to consider the act from the point of view of all the virtues that are relevant to the case. Our examples have shown that the wisdom required for courage, for example, must bring with it the wisdom required for the other virtues. This is why practical wisdom is required for any virtue and brings with it all the other virtues.

It should now be clear that the practically wise person who possesses all the virtues is an unattainable ideal, a perfect human being. But it is not an unhelpful ideal (Annas, 2009, p. 5). One can be more or less wise, even if not perfectly wise. Thus it is possible for us, as imperfect human beings, to perform virtuous acts because we have enough practical wisdom to judge rightly in certain circumstances. In daily usage, we use the terms 'courageous', 'just' and so on for those who tend to be courageous or just in many situations, even though none of those we call brave or just will in fact be fully so. (In Aristotle's terms we are all in fact some combination of *encratic* and *acratic*.[11])

---

[11] *Ibid.*, VII,10 1152a 25–28.

As a final thought, consider what would be the case if the virtues did not form a unity. This would then seem to open the possibility that one virtue could tell in favour of one course of action whilst another virtue could require a conflicting course of action. The virtuous agent would be internally conflicted. This is unattractive perhaps to us all, and certainly if considered within the Aristotelian framework. Aristotle follows Plato in finding a harmonious unity in the psyche of the virtuous person, which is contrasted with the conflicted states of the weak-willed and the strong-willed. The virtuous person does the right actions for the right reasons and takes pleasure in doing so. This is in contrast with the strong-willed who does the right action for the right reasons, but only in the face of an internal struggle. This is because he faces conflicting motives. But if the virtuous were conflicted because of conflicts within the virtues he would seem little different from the conflicted strong-willed. In this commitment to the harmonious unity of the psyche of the virtuous, which is supported by the unity of the virtues, it is already possible to see a link to integrity as wholeness.

Consider now the claim that the human good—happiness—is a feature of a whole human life. Why should happiness depend on the shape of one's life as a whole? One reason Aristotle considers is the possible influence of luck, especially with respect to external factors. A life that has been happy up to a certain point can be blighted by misfortune like, for example, that which Priam suffered in his loss of Hector.[12] More important, for our purposes, is the claim that genuine happiness is not a many-coloured and changeable state. Hence the idea seems to be that genuine happiness is a feature of the whole of life because it is a settled state that will therefore be manifested in a settled way throughout life (Cottingham, 2009). What might the contrasting state be here? Consider an agent who has scattered goals. Someone with such goals may be lucky and lead a life in which it happens to be possible to achieve all these goals together. But without luck such an agent will face conflict. The different goals will prove not to be amenable to joint fulfilment and the energies put into pursuing at least one of them will be wasted. Such an agent will suffer internal struggles and, even if successful in some areas, is likely to feel regret where the work put into pursuing unfulfilled objectives seems wasted. On this view, then, happiness is a feature of the whole of life because happiness has a harmonious unitary shape, a shape

---

[12] *Ibid.*, I,9 1099b 35ff.

which is manifested over time and contrasted with the disunity of unhappiness.

Integrity, Happiness and Virtue

It is possible to see then how integrity as wholeness is a necessary condition of happiness if it is a feature of happiness that it is a harmonious unitary state. If the virtues, rather than being separate compartmentalised aspects of character, also constitute a harmonious unity, then it is possible to see how integrity as wholeness is also in just this sense (of harmony) a necessary condition for the unity of the virtues. This in turn is entirely consistent with the claim that the virtuous life is the genuinely happy life. Can any more be said about the relationship between integrity, virtue and happiness? Three further points might be suggested.

In discussing the unity of the virtues, Annas points out that although Aristotle defends the unity of the virtues this does not commit him to the idea that there is one simple blueprint for the virtuous life for every human. She suggests that this is because there is a distinction between the circumstances of a life and the living of a life. The circumstances of a life are those factors that are to a greater or lesser degree outside the agent's control – genetic make up, nationality, particular family, education and upbringing and so on. The living of a life "is the way you deal with the circumstances of your life". Here the virtues have a key role, as what is up to us is the way we deal with the circumstances of life "…intelligently and skilfully, so that the result is intelligent formation of the materials into a unified whole" (Annas, 2009, pp. 9–10). Annas uses this point about the variety of circumstances of life to point out that different virtues will therefore be relevant in shaping different circumstances. In some lives, courage and self-control may be to the fore, in others patience and truthfulness (though no virtue is excluded, of course, from any life). But the important point to notice is the role of the virtues in achieving a unified whole. It is not just that integrity is necessary for virtue because of the unity of the virtues. Here we note that circumstances of life, beyond our control, give our life no unity or shape - rather the exercise of the virtues is a key aspect of forging our life into a unified harmonious whole.

Second, one might wonder whether integrity as wholeness is sufficient for virtue and so for happiness. In response to this it might be claimed that integrity in this sense is necessary but not sufficient. This is because this kind of unitary wholeness might also be achieved without virtue. Faced with two conflicting aims the agent might simply seek to suppress one of them. Or, more radically, it might be pointed out that Aristotle's perfectly vicious person also seems to have a kind of unitary harmony. For the vicious person differs from the *acratic* in that he does the wrong thing for the wrong reasons and takes pleasure in so doing, whereas the *acratic* does the wrong thing for the wrong reasons but is conflicted, since he knows what the right thing to do is.[13] More may need to be said here since Aristotle seems to diverge rather surprisingly from Plato, who appears to hold that a harmonious psyche is characteristic of the just agent, while the unjust has a disharmonious psyche. But without going further into this matter, it might seem that integrity is indeed only necessary for virtue.

Third and finally, the Aristotelian position developed so far on the significance of integrity for human virtue and happiness may be further underpinned by attending briefly to his metaphysical views on the unity of persons. For Aristotle, individual humans have essential natures which make it the case that they are human. These essences are collections of essential powers (powers of nutrition, perception and rationality), which are instantiated in matter, each instantiation in particular matter giving rise to particular individuals. So one might wonder what gives that collection of essential powers its unity. One answer might be that when each of our essential human powers is actualised, then that part of the human plays its proper functional role—the role of the heart, or the eye, or the rational mind, say—and when those parts function well, they fit together into a characteristic lifelong existence for a human. The unity of the essential powers consists in the integrated shape of a whole human life when these powers are actualised. Thus integrity as wholeness is necessary for human virtue and human happiness because such integrity is part of the human essence (which is actualised if all goes well).

Integrity and Business Ethics

Having established a conception of integrity, which explains its relation to virtue and happiness, let us now consider its relation to business ethics.

I begin by noting that certain abstract relations might hold between the behaviour that is required of agents in a financial or business context and virtuous behaviour. On the one hand, it might

---

[13] *Ibid.,* VII, 8, 1150b 30–33.

be that business activity has one goal, and virtuous behaviour another goal (or other goals), and that these goals conflict – this leads to the 'oxymoron' view of business ethics. On the other hand, it might be held that good business has a goal and virtuous behaviour in business is simply pursuing that goal; or it might be held that business activity has a goal, and virtuous activity has another goal (or other goals), but these goals can cohere.

Clearly, on the first of these possibilities, compartmentalisation of virtue and business life would be required. I pass over it. I shall now outline proposed versions of each of the latter possibilities. These purport to show that business activity and virtue cohere. However I shall argue that the first view outlined in fact leads to compartmentalisation, and that only the second view remains able to show that business activity can be integrated in a life of virtue and happiness.

Two Views of Business Ethics

One prominent view of business holds that the purpose of business is the maximisation of long term shareholder value by selling goods and services (within the bounds of justice and decency) (Friedman, 1970; Sternberg, 2000). As well as having explicit defenders from an ethical point of view, this position has been influential in many business schools, as it is the view (or something like it) often proposed in the theory of the firm. Although Friedman, a prominent articulator of the view, does not spell out all its implications for virtuous behaviour in business, Sternberg, another thoughtful defender, has gone on to claim that virtuous behaviour in business must simply consist in doing those things that will maximise long term shareholder value. On the face of it, therefore, the life of virtue can be integrated with good business behaviour. I will not examine this view in detail here. However, I will argue that it does not in fact lead to the integration of business activity and virtuous behaviour, but must tend instead to encourage a compartmentalising attitude to business life, an attitude which may in turn have had an unfortunate impact in the financial crisis.

In order to develop this argument, it is helpful to consider a second view which agrees with the Friedman/Sternberg claim that in thinking about business ethics it is relevant to consider the purpose or goal of business. This second neo-Aristotelian view approaches this matter by noting that business is an art or skill, in Aristotle's terms a *techne*. Aristotle usefully provides materials for establishing the goal of a *techne* in books I and VI of *Nichomachean Ethics*. Without going into the details, Aristotle argues that all human activities must aim at some good, and that good must either be good in itself or must be valuable because it contributes in some way to the achievement of a further good which is good in itself. Thus tannery, carpentry, shipbuilding and so on each has a purpose which is a good, which ultimately contributes to the achievement of some further good that is good in itself.

As has already been noted in this paper, Aristotle holds that the ultimate human good is *eudaimonia*, or happiness, thus other activities must have goals that contribute to *eudaimonia*. Aristotle agrees in both *Nicomachean Ethics* I,1 and *Politics*, that the purpose of business is to produce wealth by selling goods and services. In *Nichomachean Ethics* I,5, however, he has noted that wealth is not a constituent of happiness, but merely a means to that end. It follows that, on this alternative Aristotelian account, the purpose of business activity would be to sell goods and services (which contribute to *eudaimonia*) in order to produce enough wealth. The notion of 'enough wealth' must here be glossed in terms of 'enough wealth for *eudaimonia*'. More could be said here, but for the present the key point is that the goal of producing 'enough wealth' is to be contrasted with the goal of maximising long-term owner value. The Aristotelian view rejects the idea that one should aim to maximise wealth. This is because wealth is not the ultimate end.

Even without fully developing this second view of the purpose of business, there is sufficient material here to bring out some significant concerns regarding the first view. Although that first view seeks to integrate good business and virtue, these concerns suggest that adopting its goal would in fact threaten both an individual's integrated unity and his capacity to be virtuous. This is for two reasons, each of which identifies a difficulty, from the point of view of integrity and virtue, with taking the maximisation of long-term owner value as the exclusive goal of business. The first difficulty is that adopting this objective requires the agent to maximise the production of something, wealth, which is only a means to *eudaimonia*, not an ultimate end in itself. But since wealth is a means, and not an ultimate end, it is only sensible to pursue enough wealth, namely what is needed for *eudaimonia*. Compare a shoemaker. It would be odd to suggest that the goal of a shoemaker is to maximise the number of shoes made. This is because shoes are a means, not an end in themselves. The shoemaker should aim to produce as many shoes as are needed for *eudaimonia*.

The second difficulty is the requirement to *maximise* the long-term owner value. This goal has no definite end, and thus is indefinitely demanding. It also demands pursuit of a competitive instrumental good, one whose achievement competes with the pursuit of other goods. For these reasons, setting this as the goal of business threatens the pursuit of other goods, the goods of virtue. This account of the goal of business therefore challenges the possibility of integrating business activity with the life of virtue and risks the development of a compartmentalised attitude in which business life has its own special norms and personal life its own separate norms of virtue.

Integrity, Virtue and the Financial Crisis

Thus far I have argued that one view of the purpose of business — that its purpose is to maximise long term owner value by selling goods and services — threatens integrity and virtue. The Aristotelian view by contrast in fact suggests two constraints on business activity: that it should aim at "enough" wealth (for *eudaimonia*) — and the "enough" can vary, depending on the person and their responsibilities — and that it should sell goods and services that contribute to *eudaimonia*.

I now want to indicate some aspects of the 2008 financial crisis which may, at least in some part, owe their occurrence to the pursuit of the maximisation of wealth, or long term owner value, at the expense of integrity (as understood here) and thus of virtue. Take first the selling of toxic financial products. One of the claims that has been made about these products, often used to bundle up debts, is that their novelty and complexity was such that many responsible agents within banks and building societies did not really understand what they were dealing with. It is not implausible that adopting the objective of maximising owner value by cornering a part of a novel market allowed people to overlook a basic requirement of any kind of virtuous agency which is that the agent has true beliefs about relevant features of his action.

Consider, second, the practice of selling mortgages worth 125 per cent of the value of the property mortgaged, often on relatively expensive properties and with limited deposits. Once again the motive of maximising long term owner value might have seemed to tell in favour of such behaviour in a competitive market where banks and building societies were struggling for market share. But it might be thought to conflict sharply with the Aristotelian virtue of friendliness, or wishing another well for his own sake, in encouraging customers to take on foolishly high risks. In a similar vein, the practice of selling 'sub-prime' mortgages to those who are already in indigent circumstances, and for that reason prepared to take foolish risks to obtain credit, might have seemed to be a way of maximising long term owner value by expanding into a new market. However it might also appear to be an unjust exploitation of the needy.

As a third example there is the practice of expansion undertaken by certain British banks. The most notable case here was the Royal Bank of Scotland which conducted a policy of aggressive expansion across the world, though Barclays and HBOS competed in a similar manner. Notoriously, the Royal Bank's strategy culminated in the purchase of ABN Amro at a disastrously high price in summer 2007. Once again one might wonder whether the objective of maximising long term owner value conflicted with the requirements of self control and a courageous rather than a rash attitude towards financial risk.

It is ironic that Lloyds TSB, previously recognised as having shown a virtue of benevolence towards its customers by developing a more cautious attitude to risk, was itself encouraged to undertake an extremely risky merger in October 2008 with very hasty due diligence. Its rationale was the long term owner value to be gained from securing thirty percent of the UK mortgage market. Again, however, it is arguable that this behaviour flouted a basic requirement of any kind of virtuous activity, namely having adequate knowledge of exactly what one is doing.

Of course the defender of the view that the purpose of business is to maximise long term owner value could argue that these decisions were bad decisions by that criterion. (Indeed they are probably also bad decisions in terms of making "enough" wealth too!) But my claim is that the aim of maximising long term owner value conflicts with the retention of integrity and virtue and that this leads to vicious decisions made by agents who have allowed their psyches to disintegrate and compartmentalise. Although the result may be bad from the point of view of maximising long term owner value, the reason for such a result is not a lack of skill in pursuing that goal, but the lack of an integrated virtuous character.

To conclude, this paper outlines a conception of integrity which relates it to the unity of the virtues and to happiness as a feature of a whole life. This generates a notion of an integrated virtuous happy life which can be contrasted with that of a disintegrated agent passing through the compartmentalised sections of life, each with its own norms. Given these resources, I have argued that one conception of the purpose of business that is designed to show that the life of virtue coheres with good business in fact tends to result in the compartmentalisation of business activity, separating it from virtuous personal life. I have tentatively suggested that this misconception of the relation of business to ethics may have played some part in some of the decisions that led to the 2008 financial crisis.[14]

Bibliography

Annas, Julia (June 2009), "The Unity of the Virtues", presented at the Society for Applied Philosophy Annual Conference, Leeds.

Cottingham, John (June 2009), 'Integrity and Fragmentation' presented at the Society for Applied Philosophy Annual Conference, Leeds.

Friedman, M. (13 September 1970), "The Social Responsibility of Business is to Increase its Profits", *The New York Times Magazine*.

Macintyre, Alasdair (1981), *After Virtue* (London: Duckworth).

Miller, Seamus (June 2009), "Financial services providers, reputation and the virtuous triangle", presented at the Society for Applied Philosophy Annual Conference, Leeds.

Sternberg, E. (2000), *Just Business*, 2nd edition (Oxford: Oxford University Press).

---

[14] In preparing this paper I have benefited from discussion of unpublished papers presented by Julia Annas, John Cottingham and Seamus Miller at the Society for Applied Philosophy Annual conference held in Leeds in June 2009. I am grateful to all these authors.

Samuel Gregg

Failure and Reform
Business Schools and the 2008 Financial Crisis

Introduction

In the wake of the financial meltdown of late 2008 and 2009 of the economies of United States and Europe, a range of occupations and practices associated with private enterprise and more particularly the financial sector were subject to harsh criticism. The economics profession also experienced substantial criticism, first on the basis of the failure of most econometric models to either predict the crisis which unfolded and, secondly, because of a sense that much of the financial modeling employed over the previous 15 years may well have encouraged significant numbers of banks and financial institutions to act in an imprudent manner.

One of the side-effects of the financial crisis was an increased enrollment at business schools throughout the world as many retrenched business executives sought to use the period of the recession to 'retool' and acquire additional qualifications to help their employment chances whenever the global economy began to cease shrinking and returned to growth. The question, however, is whether most business schools were indeed adequately positioned to equip present and future business leaders with some of the skills that they will need to navigate economic crises of the type that afflicted the world economy in the last quarter of 2008. As one professor at the University of North Carolina's Kenan-Flagler Business School, Michael Jacobs, put it in a *Wall St Journal* editorial:

> As we try to understand why our economy is so troubled, fingers are increasingly being pointed at the academic institutions that educated those who got us into this mess. What have business

schools failed to teach our business leaders and policy makers? (Jacobs, 2009).

Jacobs goes on to explain how serious problems concerning board oversight, management compensation, and agency costs that contributed to the 2008 financial crisis were not being addressed by almost all business schools. Indeed, he argued:

> By failing to teach the principles of corporate governance, our business schools have failed our students. And by not internalizing sound principles of governance and accountability, B-school graduates have matured into executives and investment bankers who have failed American workers and retirees who have witnessed their jobs and savings vanish. Most B-schools paper over the topic by requiring first-year students to take a compulsory ethics class, which is necessary, but not sufficient. Would Bernie Madoff have acted differently if he had aced his ethics final? (*Ibid.*)

The causes of the 2008 financial meltdown were many and complicated. Individuals, private businesses, government sponsored enterprises such as Fannie Mae and Freddie Mac, central banks, and governments all share large parts of the overall responsibility. But there are also other institutions less directly involved who have, in different ways, contributed to the climate and culture of financial irresponsibility and excessive risk-taking that led to the most serious economic recession since the Great Depression. In this essay, we outline some of the indirect ways in which the education imparted in business schools may have contributed to the 2008 financial crisis before outlining some possible ways in which reforms to business school education might help to avert similar future calamities.

Inadequacies in Ethical Formation and Economic Instruction

Jacobs' article underlines the existence of business ethics classes as an indication that some business schools understand that they need to give their students some level of ethical instruction. In one sense, this reflects the fact that many business schools are aware that they cannot assume that formation in such knowledge and habits is occurring in an adequate manner in the institutions where basic moral education should occur, such as families, churches, and synagogues. It is to their credit that some business schools recognize that, whether they like it or not, they have been left with the responsibility of redressing these inadequacies in their students or, if the student has been given some ethical formation, showing their students how to apply sound moral reasoning in the context of the world of business.

Unfortunately, it is not even clear that the ethics of business are being adequately addressed at even the most basic level by most business schools' compulsory first year business ethics class. One reason for this is that far too many business schools and business ethics courses refuse to seriously engage questions of right and wrong. Often the business ethics course amounts to an introduction to various schools of moral reasoning, and how they might address a particular difficult ethical dilemma in business. Rarely, however, will a business ethics professor suggest that there is in fact a serious moral good at stake, or that some ethical theories — such as act or rule utilitarianism — are essentially incoherent and therefore ought to be dispensed with. Like all other institutions, business schools have not remained immune to the general climate of moral relativism that increasingly pervades public discourse and private and public behavior. A 'safe' way therefore to engage in reflection upon the demands of morality upon business leaders is to advocate 'corporate social responsibility'. This more often than not translates into a soft obligation to support and promote whatever are the politically-correct agendas (which often embody subtle and not-so-subtle negative views of business) being promoted by the *zeitgeist* at a particular point in time. Another way to respond is simply to subtly inculcate the mindset of 'if it is not illegal, then it is permissible' among students.

Neither of these stances is adequate for business if working for profit in the private sector is to assume the characteristics of a genuine vocation. Enron, for example, had an extensive corporate social responsibility program. Few, however, would suggest that this made up for the gross negligence and immoral choices that contributed to the corporation's collapse in late 2001. Nor is it wise or reasonable for anyone to assume that the absence of laws prohibiting certain forms of behavior means that it is prudent or morally acceptable to engage in or promote such behaviors. These stances also encourage the development of technocratic mindsets among business school professors and students. This results in business schools becoming focused on imbuing individuals with technical and management skills that, theoretically, can be employed in any form of business. Of course, training in skills such as marketing, strategic planning, and financial management are important and are among the indispensible contributions made by business schools to the modern market economy's unparalleled ability to create wealth and pull more people out of poverty at a faster rate than any other time in history. Business, however, is about more than practical skills and management. It also involves stewardship in the sense that managers have moral and fiduciary responsibilities to their clients and investors.

Nor is it clear that some business schools are giving future business leaders an adequate formation in another area of knowledge that is crucial for their ability to be sound stewards of the human and material resources entrusted to them. A good example of this is the tendency of a good number of business schools to neglect a subject as fundamental to modern economic life such as entrepreneurship — an indispensible element of the actual creation of wealth which itself is surely a core feature of the activity of private business. It comes as a shock to many business leaders, especially those who have started their own enterprises, to discover that the study of entrepreneurship is often an optional subject in many business schools today instead of being a central part of the curriculum. Even in those instances where it is studied, it is entirely possible to learn about entrepreneurship in many business schools today without any reference being made to the role played by factors such as rule of law, property-rights, and low-taxes in stimulating wealth-creating entrepreneurship. In short, successful private sector entrepreneurship requires a certain moral, institutional and economic setting. If taxes are high, property-rights unprotected, and corruption the norm, then the economic environment embodies major deterrents to wealth-generating entrepreneurship. Why would people risk being entrepreneurial when they cannot assume that their ideas will not be stolen or their profits arbitrarily confiscated by other private actors or governments that have lost all sense of financial responsibility? Business schools should also be willing to ask what happens when incentives to entrepreneurship become misaligned and are instead found in politics rather than the economy. In these cases entrepreneurship is no longer about creating ideas or products that others value. Instead people become 'entrepreneurial' in identifying and exploiting political contacts and bureaucratic opportunities to amass power and/or transfer wealth to themselves and their clients and supporters. More than one observer would suggest that the collusion between government sponsored enterprises such as Freddie Mac and Fannie Mae, prominent American Congressmen and Senators, and a range of activist groups which contributed so much to the mortgage imposition that helped precipitate the 2008 financial crisis, is a prime example of the consequences of 'political entrepreneurship'.

This in turn underlines another problem for many contemporary business schools. It is by no means clear that a good number of business school professors are convinced of the basic morality and efficacy of economic systems based on free enterprise, a clear but limited role for government, the upholding of rule of law, and relatively strong property rights. In many instances, this ambivalence cannot help but be communicated to business school students, which they may well take with them to the marketplace. It is very difficult for business schools to teach a good number of the habits—especially the moral habits—associated with successful business when a good number of business school professors regard business itself as, at best, merely a useful but morally neutral (even ethically questionable) phenomena, and believe that the business-orientated economy might well create wealth but generally does so in ways that no morally serious person could in their heart of hearts endorse. It is one thing to express dismay, even outrage at the behavior of individual business leaders, especially in cases of proven corruption and criminality. There is no shortage of such individuals to identify, and they are rightly pilloried, just as we should rightly pillory a doctor, lawyer, soldier, engineer, government bureaucrat, teacher, or university professor found guilty of equally culpable behavior. But it is quite another matter to communicate, subtly or otherwise, the idea that business is not a morally serious exercise, or that participation in the business economy is bound to facilitate some form of slow disintegration of one's moral character or involvement in more and more moral compromises.

Incorporating Moral and Economic Reflection into Business School Instruction

If, then, one of the problems revealed by the financial crisis has been problems in the moral formation and economic education that occurs in business schools in Europe and North America, then the question becomes how they might rectify these difficulties. One alternative would be to expand business ethics courses beyond the usual first year compulsory subject and simply boost the number of courses given in this area, perhaps with a certain degree of specialization, depending upon what field students chose to focus on. This has its advantages, but it may also encourage students to regard ethics in business as an important but somewhat abstract dimension of their studies. Another, more challenging alternative would be to move away from corralling ethical and economic reflection upon life in business into one or more specific classes, and instead try to incorporate reflection upon the demands of morality and the lessons of economics into *all* subjects. Obviously this would be easier to achieve in some classes than others. It would also require major pedagogical changes in the style and content of instruction in some business schools. These, however, are not insurmountable obstacles.

As an example of this, let us consider a subject that was thrown into sharp relief by the 2008 financial crisis: the institution and practice of credit itself. Virtually all the elements leading to the 2008 financial meltdown were affected in some way by particular lending practices as well as reliance on financial modeling that not only failed to realize their purported objectives but led to enormous financial problems, ranging from merchant banks overleveraging themselves at rates of 30:1, to individual householders taking out loans whose rationale depended on a housing-market boom that could not possibly be sustained. In the United States and Britain, this resulted in considerable anger was directed against those who specialize in the credit business, as well as the financial industry as a whole. On the level of policy, it resulted in legislation being passed in a number of jurisdictions to change the manner in which the financial industry and credit in general is regulated.

At the level of business school instruction, however, these events have created an opportunity for a revisiting of how subjects such as risk and finance are taught so that an attention to the ethics and economics of credit can be more thoroughly incorporated into the teaching of this subject. A revealing feature of the analyses of the borrowing and lending habits contributing to aspects of the 2008 financial crisis is that they indirectly underline the extent to which many moral philosophers and economists have forgotten that the extension and seeking of credit was a subject of considerable and often heated discussion for centuries. The very morality of charging interest on loans has been intensely debated by religious and secular thinkers for over two thousand years. Many contemporary practitioners of finance may be surprised to know that Adam Smith actually favoured usury laws (Smith [1776] 1981).[1] As John T. Noonan illustrates in his classic study of the Roman Catholic Church's teaching

---

[1] Sections of this part of the text draw upon the author's chapters inPhilip Booth (ed.) (2009), *Verdict on the Crash* (London: IEA). The editors thank the IEA for permission to republish those parts.

on usury, Christianity's internal debate about this subject lead to major clarifications of money's nature, the development of the first 'embryonic theory of economics', and 'the first attempt at a science of economics known to the West' (Noonan, 1957, p. 2). It helped, for example, to establish in theoretical terms when money transcended its character as a means of exchange and assumed the qualities of what we today call 'capital'.

One does not need to probe very far to grasp that a proper understanding of the nature of credit—something that business schools are uniquely positioned to teach—requires instruction in the moral and economic assumptions underlying the extension and acceptance of credit. In practical terms, credit is about lending others the financial means—the capital—that most people need at some point of their lives. Whether it is starting a business or buying a house, most people need capital. To acquire capital, people have three options. One is to steal it. Another alternative is simply to save enough capital to begin the enterprise. A third alternative is to borrow it. Given that the capital needed to start a business, finance a new venture from an existing business, or purchase a house might take years, even decades to save, most people choose the third of these options. This means someone else such as a bank or a private lender has to be willing to take a risk. They, like the borrower of the capital, do stand to profit if the mortgage is paid off or the business succeeds. But they also lose if a house is foreclosed or a business goes bankrupt.

In this context, the charging of interest serves several functions. In economic terms, it reflects the borrower's willingness to pay for acquiring capital *now* rather than waiting to save the same amount over a long period of time. A second economic function is that charging interest allows the lenders to maintain the value of their loans and make a profit, the margins of which are much narrower than most people realize. If all goes well, the sum-total of capital available in a given society is increased over time. Lastly interest permits both borrowers and lenders to calibrate the risk that they are willing to assume: the higher the risk, the higher the interest-rate in order to compensate for the greater possibility of loss.

But at a deeper level, we also forget that while credit is about capital, it is ultimately about something more intangible but nonetheless real. The word 'credit' is derived from *credere*—the Latin verb for 'to believe' but also 'to trust'. Thus, whether it is a matter of giving someone a credit-card for the first time, or extending a small business the capital that it needs to grow into a great enterprise, providing people with credit means that you trust and believe in them enough to take a risk on their insight, reliability, honesty, prudence, thrift, courage and enterprise: in short, the moral habits without which wealth-creation cannot occur.

Much more could be said about credit, but a business school that was willing to go beyond educating students in the technicalities of various models of financing and explore the deeper moral and economic meaning and assumptions of credit would surely serve to remind business school graduates just how much the essentially market-based economies—in which most of them will work and in which credit, despite the 2008 financial crisis, will continue to play an important role—relies deeply upon a web of moral qualities and non-material relationships. As the 2008 credit crunch taught us, once these relationships are corrupted, whether by basic dishonesty, excessive regulation, or political manipulation, the wheels of wealth-creation splutter and eventually grind to a halt. Likewise, once the practice of credit is separated from a clear understanding of its economic functions and limits, then we should not be surprised that, eventually, credit will cease to be extended, no matter how compelling the particular mathematical model that might underlie any number of financial leveraging schemes.

The same formation in the ethics and economics of credit might also alert business school students to the limits of what can be achieved by regulation, not to mention the unintended consequences that can follow from well-intentioned regulatory frameworks. If, for example, interest-rate ceilings were imposed by government fiat, presumably in an effort to limit predatory lending, this would mean that lenders would effectively be prohibited from charging interest-rates commensurate to the risks involved. Two things would follow. First, banks and financial houses would be unlikely to lend capital to entrepreneurs and businesses pursuing high-risk endeavors. Many risky but wealth-creating and employment-generating activities would thus simply never occur. Secondly, legislated interest-rate ceilings would mean that some people with few material means would never have the chance to acquire the capital they might need, for example, to go to university, start a business, or even begin developing a credit-record. This would mean that some strong potential barriers would be placed in the way of large numbers of entire categories of people such as recent immigrants and the urban poor improving their economic situation. In short, those whom such regulation was meant to protect might actually be significantly harmed by the same often well-intentioned legislation. It would also mean that the extension of credit would be increasingly limited to established businesses, many of which have no incentive to be entrepreneurial and are indeed anxious to prevent the emergence of new competitors in "their" market. The role of government is, of course, to promote the common good of a given society — the common good being understood here as the conditions that allow each and every member of a given society to choose to pursue human flourishing in ways commensurate to their particular vocations. But the example outlined above illustrates how easily government regulations enacted in the name of the common good and applied to the realm of credit and finance regulation can actually impede not just wealth-creation but also the human flourishing that occurs as a prudently-financed business grows, creates employment, and facilitates opportunities for people to pursue their vocations in particular careers in the world of business.

Moral Hazard and the Business School

Beyond incorporating this and similar forms of ethical and economic analysis into the treatment of subjects as apparently technical as credit and finance, there are a number of areas in which business schools may wish to focus specific attention if they want to help prepare their graduates to avoid some of the specific problems associated with the 2008 financial crisis. One such area is the issue of moral hazard.

Moral hazard is a term commonly used to describe those situations when a person or institution is effectively insulated from the possible negative consequences of their choices. This makes them more likely to take risks that they would not otherwise take, most notably with assets and capital entrusted to them by others: the higher the extent of the guarantee, the greater is the risk of moral hazard. The American mortgage lenders Fannie Mae and Freddie Mac are prominent examples of this problem. Implicit to their lending policies was the assumption that, as government-sponsored enterprises with lower capital requirements than private institutions, they could always look to the Federal government for assistance if an unusually high number of their clients defaulted. In a 2007 *Wall Street Journal* article, the Nobel Prize-winning economist Vernon Smith noted that both Fannie Mae and Freddie Mac were always understood as 'implicitly taxpayer-backed agencies' (Smith,

2007). Hence they continued what are now recognized as their politically-driven lending policies until both suffered the ignominy of being placed in Federal conservatorship in September 2008.

Similar points could be made about the legal protection of limited liability. On one level, the unquestioned economic benefit is that it encourages managers and investors to take full advantage of the massive wealth-creating potential often associated with high-risk endeavors. But there is a downside. Limited liability does tend to shelter these individuals from a major incentive not to take excessive risk: the prospect of personal bankruptcy. To this extent, limited liability regulation creates incentives for businesses to do things that they might not do if they were subject to the provisions of unlimited liability.

At the level of government policy, a prominent instance of moral hazard was what some call the 'Greenspan doctrine' of 2002. This involved the U.S. Federal Reserve stating that, while it was powerless to prevent the emergence of asset bubbles (such as the dot-com and housing booms), the Federal Reserve would do everything that it could to soften the effects of an imploding bubble. This included providing investors with the option of selling their depreciated assets to the Federal Reserve at a time of crisis. Not surprisingly, the result was a surge in excessive risk-taking by investors confident that, if everything did not proceed as planned, they could recoup their losses at someone else's expense. In his 2008 book, *Fixing Global Finance*, the financial journalist Martin Wolf underlined the distortions introduced by government guarantees to risk-taking. These, he argued, create an overwhelming incentive to privatize gains and socialize losses.

In many respects, the American car industry is an example of what sometimes happens to specific businesses when the danger of moral hazard is underplayed. When the Carter Administration chose to rescue Chrysler in 1980, this action conveyed a message to the three Detroit-based car manufacturers: they could take the risk of producing cars that fewer and fewer consumers apparently wanted to buy; they could also risk refraining from confronting the serious inefficiencies introduced into their companies' operations by years of automobile executives acquiescing in outlandish demands from the United Automobile Workers union. Why? Because if the car companies subsequently found themselves facing economic Armageddon, they had high expectations — based on an established policy-precedent — that the Federal government would bail them out. Thus no one should have been surprised to find that the chief executive officers of the three American owned car companies accompanied by a legion of lobbyists and the ever-present United Automobile Workers Union appeared before the United States Congress in late 2008, again requesting assistance in order to avert bankruptcy. Such is the logic of disdaining moral hazard.

While there is a great deal of literature on the economics of moral hazard, the same material contains curiously little reflection on why the adjective 'moral' is attached to the word 'hazard'. Indeed, when economists started studying the subject of moral hazard in the 1960s, their analysis rarely included an explicitly ethical dimension. For the most part, this remains true today. So why do we not simply describe these situations as instances of 'risk hazard'?

It may be that the word 'moral' reflects some innate, albeit largely unexpressed, awareness that there is something ethically questionable about creating situations in which people are severely tempted to make imprudent choices. To employ a loose analogy from the realm of moral theology, the one who creates 'an occasion of sin' bears some indirect responsibility for the choices of the person tempted by this situation to do something very imprudent or just plain wrong. If governments and businesses took moral hazard seriously, they would make an effort to identify those state and non-state structures, policies, and practices that create incentives for people to take excessive risks with their own and other peoples' assets. They would then do what they could to minimize these instances of moral hazard. The economic price might be fewer booms. But economic growth over time would likely be steadier. The chances of mild or severe recessions would also be reduced.

In a 2007 *Financial Times* column, a prominent member of the former Clinton and now Obama Administration's economic team, Larry Summers, argued that we should beware of what he called 'moral hazard fundamentalism' (Summers, 2007). This was, he said, 'as dangerous as moral hazard itself'. By this, Summers meant that ruling out significant government economic intervention on the grounds that it might encourage moral hazard would itself be irresponsible. The problem is that the Keynesian-interventionist outlook associated with widespread government intervention involves, by necessity, a degree of systematic denial of the reality of moral hazard. In an attempt to maintain full employment in perpetuity, Keynesian policies embrace measures ranging from keeping interest-rates artificially low, partially nationalizing industries, to engineering large public works programs. An unfortunate effect is that many businesses as well as ordinary consumers become somewhat insulated from many of the negative consequences of poor decisions and bad investments. As a result, some will become complacent, which is the road to economic stagnation. Others, however, are likely to take risks that become increasingly irresponsible over time until we find ourselves in situations similar to the world economy of 2008.

Of course, as long as human beings are fallible creatures, many will take excessive risks at different points in their lives. For some people, it will be with their marriage. Others will behave in an excessively risky manner with their own and others' financial resources. As a consequence, some people will suffer losses. In a society where right reason and the ethic of loving one's neighbor reigns, individuals and communities should be ready to help those in genuine need. Law also has a potentially important role to play. As the legal philosopher John Finnis observes in *Natural Law and Natural Rights* (1980), a sound bankruptcy law can meet all the demands of justice—legal, commutative, and distributive—while respecting the dignity of all those effected, especially the dispossessed, but also those at fault. But we do not do anyone any favors by creating circumstances or incentives that encourage people to behave imprudently and recklessly in the worlds of finance and business.

Any business school that wishes to contribute to addressing some of the major causes of the 2008 financial crisis would do well to incorporate serious reflection upon the specifics of moral hazard into their curricula. Not all business school graduates end up working in the private sector. Many find employment in government positions, often as policy-advisors, while others are often formally and informally consulted in their capacity as business leaders by politicians and civil servants who have the responsibility of crafting economic policy as well regulatory frameworks which, as we have seen, have the potential to create significant moral hazard problems. Business schools that gave their students a thorough grounding in both the ethics and economics of moral hazard might well make over time a significant contribution to reducing irresponsible behavior on the part of business leaders as well as reducing the potential for the emergence of poorly conceived regulatory frameworks that contribute so significantly to this problem. To the extent that business schools incorporate and encourage research agendas, it would seem that they are in an ideal position to pursue extensive research into the nature and effects of moral hazard, not to mention the perverse incentives that sometimes give rise to it in the first place.

Conclusion

There is little question that the 2008 financial crisis will continue to effect business schools in the near and long-term. For one thing, it is safe to assume that large numbers of business school graduates were among the thousands who unexpectedly found themselves without employment in the fall of 2008. Many no doubt were left wondering whether the significant investment of time, energy and money that many of them had made in their business school education had come to naught. Those returning to business school were likely to have many moral and economics questions arising from their experience of the 2008 financial crisis, and many business schools might have difficulty in answering such questions from within their pre-2008 framework of educating students. One might hope that business schools would recognize that, after 2008, small, medium and large-sized businesses across the world face a very different environment. This means that business schools are faced squarely with a choice. One is not to change, to pay lip-service to the problems revealed by the 2008 financial crisis in business and government, and to continue with educational methods and priorities that will do little to contribute to averting similar crises in the future. The second, more difficult approach is to engage in a root-and-branch review of *what* is taught in business schools and how knowledge is imparted to business school students, along the lines suggested in this chapter. Part of the genius of successful business is constant and prudent innovation and adaption to new circumstances. Those institutions that educate so many business leaders and executives should surely be capable of no less.

Bibliography

Campbell, R.H., and Skinner, A.S. (eds.) (1981), *The Glasgow Edition of the Works and Correspondence of Adam Smith* (Indianapolis IN: Liberty Fund).

Finnis, John (1980), *Natural Law and Natural Rights* (Oxford: Clarendon Press).

Jacobs, Michael (24 April 2009), "How Business Schools Have Failed Business: Why not more education on the responsibility of boards?", *Wall St Journal*.

Noonan, J.T (1957), *The Scholastic Analysis of Usury* (Harvard: Harvard University Press).

Smith, Adam (1776), *An Inquiry into the Nature and Causes of the Wealth of Nations*, reprinted in Campbell & Skinner (1981).

Smith, Vernon L. (18 December 2007), 'The Clinton Housing Bubble', *Wall Street Journal*.

Summers, Lawrence (23 September 2007), 'Beware Moral Hazard Fundamentalism', *Financial Times*.

Philip Booth

Learning from the Crash, and Teaching after it

Introduction[1]

Should Business Teaching be Refocused?

Strong criticisms have been made of practitioners in financial markets in the wake of the 2008 financial crash. It is often suggested that the crash was brought about by the greed and arrogance of bankers and other participants in financial markets. In this context, one article in the *New York Times*[2] strongly criticised the focus of business school teaching on shareholder value and profit implying that this was partly responsible for the crash. However, though it can be argued that there has been a lack of prudence and a lack of virtue in financial markets, it is difficult to argue that the actions of banks has led to greater profitability or shareholder value. Indeed, shareholders of many banks have had their capital more or less wiped out as a result of their failure. This suggests either that banks have been extremely unlucky (perhaps being hit by some kind of external shock) or that there are some kind of structural failings that have caused financial markets to malfunction so that the apparent pursuit of shareholder value has led to shareholder value being destroyed. Surely, the business school response to this should be to address that

---

[1] Parts of this chapter rely heavily on the author's two chapters in *Verdict on the Crash*, edited by Philip Booth and published by the Institute of Economic Affairs, available from www.iea.org.uk . The editors thank the IEA for permission to republish these parts.

[2] http://www.nytimes.com/2009/03/15/business/15school.html?_r=2&em=&pagewanted=all

malfunction (that is the right goal not being achieved) rather than to treat the problem as a dysfunction (that is the wrong goal being pursued).

It is certainly appropriate for business schools to develop their courses to discuss wider issues but to suggest that the focus on shareholder value in business school courses should be reduced is misguided. After all, there is a straightforward principal-agent issue for business managers: the managers have both a legal and moral obligation to use the assets of the business for the purposes for which their owners intend them to be used. There may be important contextual issues within which this obligation needs to be understood, but it is a serious mistake to suggest that business managers are at liberty to use their discretion in deciding to what ends they direct business assets (see the chapter by Booth in Harper and Gregg, 2008, and Sternberg, 2004).

It could be argued in response that banks pursued 'short-term profits at the expense of the long-term'. As Tony Blair said in a speech on 8 January 2009: 'To have trust, the system as a whole needs to be inbred with values other than those of short-term profit maximisation'.[3] But, shareholder value maximisation, properly understood, is not the same as short-term profit maximisation in any case. The value of a corporation's shares at any one time will ultimately depend on the present value of the income stream that shareholders believe the corporation will generate in the long-term. Shareholder value depends critically on the long-term sustainability of the business.

This is not to say that business managers in the banking sector might not have pursued short-term profits at the expense of the long-term value of the business. But this would be not normally be the approach to management that a business school would teach as being appropriate. An important aim of business school teaching should be to ensure that managers understand how to use the assets of a business to maximise business value and to ensure that directors know how to hold management to account to ensure that the business achieves that objective.

Market Malfunction: Searching for Underlying Causes

It is still quite possible, of course, that something became disordered in the financial system that led to banks' managers pursuing

---

[3] see: http://tonyblairoffice.org/2009/01/speech-by-tony-blair-at-the-ne.html

short-term cash flows (or profits) *at the expense of* the value of the business. Or it could be the case that managers and owners *believed* that they were adding to the value of the business when, in fact, they were destroying it. In a market system we normally expect prudent behaviour to be associated with profitable business outcomes and to be compatible with the pursuit of self interest. In diligently pursuing my own objectives in business, I can only generally succeed if I help others achieve theirs. Even the pursuit of greed may not be incompatible with increased material welfare in a market economy. It is not normal that one can become rich in a market economy without satisfying the economic and material needs of others.

It is therefore not sufficient to argue that greed and the pursuit of shareholder value led to the financial market crash. But deeper underlying problems could have created a situation whereby the pursuit of self interest led to the destruction of shareholder value. It is important, therefore, to seek the underlying causes of major events such as the financial market crash of 2008, not merely to interpret what may seem like the obvious causes.

Business Education and Economics Teaching

If business schools are going to be of assistance in contributing to reducing the possibility of a crisis such as the crash of 2008 being repeated, then business school educators need to have an accurate understanding of what actually went wrong and also be willing to question the popular consensus about what went wrong and what are the best solutions. An aspect of this involves teaching risk management techniques more effectively. A further aspect, however, involves communicating an understanding of the wider economic issues.

In this respect, neither the press nor the political class are especially good at either taking the long-term view or engaging in a serious impartial analysis. But it is surely the job of educational institutions such as business schools to do both of these. This means that they need to take seriously the insights of economists into these matters.

Economics does not always feature heavily in business school curricula. Perhaps the financial meltdown indicates that business schools need to engage in this subject more systematically if business school graduates are going to be prepared for life in the marketplace. Economics is far from being an uncontroversial social science but maybe one of the lessons of the financial crisis for business schools is that they need to engage these matters at some level. This will produce debate and disagreement, but educational institutions such as business schools provide environments in which one should be able to discuss these matters with some detachment. Given that most business people have an entrepreneurial aspect to their jobs—even if they are employed—it is also important that those schools of economics that emphasise and explain the process of entrepreneurial discovery are at the heart of teaching. This will be discussed in more detail below, but, first, three of the underlying causes of the financial market crash will be discussed in greater detail.

Underlying Causes of the Financial Market Crash

Monetary Policy

It is now widely accepted that the boom and bust, culminating in the Great Depression of the 1930s, arose as a result of catastrophically mismanaged monetary policy. The same is true of the Japanese boom, bust and malaise of the late twentieth century. It would seem that mismanaged monetary policy was also at least partly responsible for the crash of 2008.

Monetary policy was far too loose in the USA over an extended period of time, and in the UK over a shorter period of time and this was a considerable contributor to the financial bubble. In the USA, the Federal Reserve held interest rates at very low levels throughout much of the early twenty-first century.[4] In the UK, things started to go wrong in 2005 when the Monetary Policy Committee of the Bank of England agreed at their August meeting decided to cut interest rates from 4.75% to 4.5%. This led to a sustained acceleration of money supply growth and, despite this, interest rates were not raised again until August 2006.

This episode of loose monetary policy had several effects. It contributed to the growth of bank and non-bank financial sector balance sheets—including the growth of the innovative financial products that led to so much difficulty in the crash. In addition, low interest rates led to expanding monetary aggregates and this fed an asset-price boom and encouraged low saving and increased consumption and investment. These, in turn, led to a substantial misallocation of resources. Higher asset prices raised the value of

---

[4] The article by Anna Schwartz at http://online.wsj.com/article/SB122428279231046053.html is interesting regarding the US experience.

collateral against secured loans and thus encouraged more lending and higher leverage whilst reducing the apparent risk faced by lenders and borrowers. Consumer price inflation remained subdued, to a degree, as the relative price of tradable goods fell. However, loose monetary policy will always have an impact on the economic system and the particular manifestation of loose monetary policy in the early twenty-first century was an asset-price and credit boom—with credit often being secured against higher asset values.

Whilst other factors must have conspired to bring down the banking system, there can be little doubt that loose monetary policy played a part in bringing about the financial conditions that led to serious structural problems. It is important that these issues are understood by people working in business finance because monetary policy can create market disequilibria that can seriously distort business decisions.

Regulation

Though many commentators suggest that the crash was caused by 'under-regulation', it does not seem that a lack of regulation was an important factor in the crash. Government regulation actually encouraged US institutions to lend to bad risks (see Woods, 2009). The US government was also strongly supporting the process of securitisation of mortgages through its corporatist, nominally private, institutions Fannie Mae and Freddie Mac. Indeed, central banks, governments and regulators across the world seemed supportive of the process of securitisation that created many of the instruments that led to later trouble. Paul Tucker, recently promoted to Deputy Governor of the Bank of England, said in a speech as late as April 2007: 'So it would seem that there is a good deal to welcome in the greater dispersion of risk made possible by modern instruments, markets and institutions.'[5] There are two lessons from this. The first is that intervention by government in financial markets played a part in the events that led up to the crash—in other words government failure should be the object of serious attention. The second is that, even if one does not accept that government action was a considerable contributory factor in the boom and following crash, it is quite clear that government agencies did not spot the crash coming before market participants did. We should not, then, assume that government agencies can 'correct' market failure. In other words, if

---

[5] See http://www.bankofengland.co.uk/publications/quarterlybulletin/qb070211.pdf. This remark was qualified later in the speech.

the conditions are lacking that ensure markets themselves avoid serious error, it should not be assumed that governments can create these conditions and make markets work better. More generally, just as some have argued that there were distorted incentives within banks caused, for example, by high bonuses and limited liability there are also distorted incentives structurally embedded within regulators which prevent them from regulating for the greater good.

In general, regulators have an incentive to regulate to reduce risk to too great a degree because they do not want problems to arise on their watch for which they will be held responsible. Paradoxically, once a problem arises in a particular firm, regulators have an incentive to delay action so as not to draw attention to it. Firstly, they may hope that an improvement in the markets will lead to the problem rectifying itself. Secondly, many regulators seek jobs with institutions that they have previously regulated and they may well not wish to treat such institutions too harshly. We shall discuss the implications of this, in terms of our approach to business teaching, below.

There is, indeed, the likelihood that financial market regulation made matters worse and not better in other respects. Though it may be overstating the point to argue that the crash was caused by government failure it certainly appears that there is nothing that governments and regulators have done that made the crash less likely or made its consequences less dire. International banking regulation has encouraged the creation of opaque financial instruments.[6] The increased focus on regulation at an international and European Union level necessarily means that regulation has to be more complex as it has had to deal with a greater variety of industry structures and practices. Because gearing and capital are regulated, banks find more and more opaque ways to obtain the effect of gearing without doing the things that regulators penalise. This leads to the creation of complex financial instruments and structures that few within, never mind outside, the industry understand. Risk taking is therefore harder for shareholders to monitor and penalise. Furthermore, regulators encouraged all financial institutions to use similar quantitative risk models for setting their capital and assessing risks. It is quite possible that these models were flawed. Certainly they seemed unable to assess extreme risks effectively.

Financial regulation also caused market participants to create a fundamentally disordered set of processes. Instead of releasing

---

[6] See in particular the chapters by Alexander and Dowd in Booth, 2009.

information to the market and shareholders, the most important relationships amongst the senior management of financial institutions were with regulators.

Failures of Corporate Governance

This all leads to the question of whether actors within financial markets were at all culpable. Was the crash simply a symptom of government failure, whilst participants in financial markets behaved like angels? Of course, this was not the case.

Arguably, banks made big mistakes by departing from the traditional model of banking. They have lost, of course, huge amounts of money as a result (between 90% and 100% of the equity value in many cases) as well as imposing wider economic losses on society at large. But, it is dangerous to assume that regulatory responses to such so-called market failures can lead to better results than a liberal market. As has been noted above, regulators were behind the curve during the development of the credit boom and it is, indeed, banks' owners who have the strongest incentive to learn from their mistakes having made such large losses.

It could certainly be argued that there was a failure of corporate governance in that shareholders failed to hold management properly to account for their actions. As well as a failure of diligence in this respect, trust and prudence have perhaps broken down more generally amongst both borrowers and lenders. It is clear, for example, that borrowers lied on mortgage proposal forms, possibly on a large scale in the US. Again, this observation of what some would call market failure, does not provide us with normative lessons for the role of regulation. It could be argued that compliance has displaced trust and that no amount of additional regulation in financial markets in the last twenty years has done anything to increase the level of trust. And perhaps a reliance on regulation has also crowded out the processes whereby institutions take responsibility for the risks that they underwrite and has discouraged them from undertaking due diligence checks in their relationships with other market participants.

Lessons for Business Education

This brief consideration of some of the background to the crash helps to provide some indicators of lessons for economics teaching within business education, as well as lessons for the teaching of business ethics. It can be strongly argued that certain non-traditional[7] strands of economics ought to be at the forefront of business economics teaching.

Neo-Classical Economics versus Austrian Economics

Neo-classical economics can be helpful for understanding particular economic problems. The closed form solutions to many modern finance problems, such as the pricing of derivatives, derive their method from the neo-classical way of thinking. However, in many respects, neo-classical economics omits the most important aspects of dynamic market processes and it is a consideration of these aspects which is essential for people receiving business education.

For example, in the field of monetary economics, an Austrian analysis[8] focuses on the misallocation of resources that can arise when interest rates are held too low. Neo-classical economics, with its focus on equilibrium, ignores the possibility that mismanaged monetary policy can manufacture serious disequilibrium. When interest rates are held low and the money supply expands, this will cause a misallocation of economic resources, lower saving, increased investment, speculation, high security prices and house prices, and so on. This disequilibrium will be unsustainable and, one way or another, will eventually be reversed. Thus, when the monetary bubble stops inflating, a recession is inevitable in the Austrian view as resources have become misallocated in the previous boom. An important difference between traditional monetarist and Austrian thinkers is that the former—though they do discuss the channels through which monetary policy takes effect—tend to emphasise much less the distortion between different types of economic activity that expansionary and contractionary monetary policies can generate.

It is important for practitioners in business—especially in finance but not just in finance—to be aware that they may be working in environments in which price signals may be distorted by mismanaged monetary policy so that they do not get caught up in the frenzy of speculation and asset price booms that can accompany periods of loose monetary policy. Business educators should teach about the market processes and signals that can become distorted so that the

---

[7] At least non-traditional as far as business school teaching is concerned, many would argue that the approach suggested below actually returns economics to its traditional roots.

[8] A good summary of all aspects of Austrian economics can be found in de Soto, 2008.

naïve neo-classical belief that market values are objective indicators of the long-term worth of an asset is treated with scepticism.

A second danger of a naïve application of neo-classical economics is the belief that economic and financial market equilibria can be described by mathematical models and equations. Whilst such models may hold at particular times, for example when financial markets are relatively stable, they do not hold, perhaps, at times when financial risks are at their most acute. The use of highly quantitative linear models fits in with the widely taught 'efficient markets hypothesis' whereby market prices are assumed to reflect all information at any time. This implies that any changes to market prices will only arise as a result of the discovery of new information which tends to affect prices randomly and non-systematically. The whole point of markets, in the Austrian view, is to uncover new information about how economic resources can be used and allocated. The concept of a financial market that is efficient and reflects all information is therefore of doubtful practical use as it essentially ignores the entrepreneurial process by which information is uncovered.

The neo-classical justifications for a free-market were absorbed not just into business practice but also into a socialist system of financial regulation which used market mechanisms of risk management and measurement and market information as its main pillars. Thus stewardship accounting, based on professional judgement and disclosure, were replaced by compulsory accounting standards based on market values; highly quantitative models based on past statistical patterns were certified by regulators to measure risk and determine capital requirements; market-based credit ratings were important in capital setting by bank regulators; and so on. This was described by some as the 'triumph of the free market'. In fact, it was the triumph of the socialist belief that planners and regulators could use prevailing market prices as if they were static entities that reflected all information and base extensive regulatory systems on those so-called market mechanisms.

In the process, market participants were lulled into a false sense of security. There was little competition in approaches to risk management and capital setting (indeed competition was discouraged). And, those institutional mechanisms that can be used to control or reduce risk, that arise because people are aware of their ignorance (for example, keeping financial institutions simple), were crowded out or regarded as unnecessary. Furthermore, the uniform ways of measuring risk based on market information themselves affected behaviour in ways which made the statistical models invalid. If all institutions measure and manage risk in a similar way, they will develop similar portfolios and all respond in similar ways to changes in financial information, thus potentially turning a small crisis into a catastrophe as banks first buy and then dump illiquid assets onto the market.

A third aspect of economic method relevant to business teaching also has links to the disputes between the Austrian and neo-classical school. There is a tendency in modern economics to ignore variables that do not fit neatly into econometric models. But, even if we accept that modelling for the purposes of prediction has its part to play in finance and business economics, there may be many economic variables and processes that are not amenable to measurement or to modelling but that have important information content.[9] By focusing on what can be measured and modelled the most important variables may be completely ignored.

One example of this is the role of money in creating inflation. Too rapid an expansion of the money supply will lead to inflation (possibly preceded by the kind of asset-price boom that we saw in the early twenty-first century). It may be difficult for central banks (or financial market forecasters) to precisely model the impact of money supply on inflation as relationships have become less predictable over time. This does not mean, however, that monetary aggregates are not a very important (indeed, possibly the most important) variable in determining inflation. It simply means that to understand the processes we have to interpret the data and we may have to accept that any predictions we make are simply predictions of tendencies rather than of precise magnitudes (see Hayek, 1988; de Soto, 2008).

This need to focus on variables that are important rather than just on variables that are precisely measurable is more generally true in financial management. When considering risk there has been a tendency to use ever-more complex financial models (see also above). This has some benefits, but it can also give rise to problems. Firms believe that they can take more complex risks because their models can quantify those risks. Conceptual thinking about risk is then discouraged (or becomes impossible) and it becomes difficult or impossible for the board to hold management to account. Those who should have been monitoring banks (such as shareholders) were reassured that risk was being kept in bounds, even though the extent

---

[9] This issue was, to a large extent, at the heart of F.A. Hayek's Nobel Laureate lecture, *The Pretence of Knowledge,* reprinted in Hayek, 1978.

of the risks they were taking could not be understood at a conceptual level. In short, knowledge replaced understanding.

Future generations of directors should be more sceptical of management's ability to boil down risk management to a few numbers or pictorial representations of probability distributions. It may be the case that the models used include all the measurable variables that have stable relationships but exclude the most important variables! More conceptual thinking about financial risks should be encouraged. If the risks are too complex to consider conceptually then a variety of approaches should be taken to communicate the underlying nature of the risks.[10]

Other Insights from Austrian Economics

Austrian economics discusses how the continual process of competition leads to welfare enhancement through the discovery of new entrepreneurial opportunities.[11] These entrepreneurial discoveries do not simply involve the development of new products or more efficient ways of producing products but the development of new institutional approaches to overcome the obstacles to efficiency that neo-classical economists often suggest are permanent features of financial markets. Thus stock exchanges, professional standards, industry codes of conduct and rating agencies all exist to help, in their different ways, overcome problems caused by information asymmetries and the incentives to reckless behaviour that limited liability can provide. Furthermore, in a competitive market, financial services companies can promote trust as a commercial virtue and also promote particular corporate structures where it is felt that these signal to consumers a greater degree of security.

Credit rating agencies provide one example of a market institution designed to overcome problems caused by information asymmetries.[12] The chapter by Morrison in Booth (2009) explains how the incentives of rating agencies were distorted by regulation in the

---

[10] This can include processes such as stress testing where, instead of complex statistical models being used, the balance sheet of a financial institution is tested against the implications of particular economic or financial events that are subjectively chosen.
[11] See, for example, de Soto, 2008 and Kirzner, 1992, 1997.
[12] Information asymmetries are a well-defined problem in financial markets — see the seminal paper by Akerlof, 1970. Stiglitz was one of the three joint winners of the Nobel Prize, with Akerlof, for work in this field.

crash.[13] More generally, market signalling mechanisms can also be crowded out by regulation and government guarantees: does it matter if a bank is trustworthy or has a high level of capital if the regulator is regarded as being responsible for such things and the government will provide guarantees if things go wrong? The study of how market mechanisms can provide effective codes of regulation should be a vital part of understanding the institutional framework of financial markets (see also Morrison, 2007).

Regulation: Public Choice or Public Interest?

The crash has led to much comment on the need for changes in the way we regulate financial institutions. Unsurprisingly, economists such as Joseph Stiglitz have called for greater regulation of both financial products and financial market participants.[14] Will Hutton, in an open letter to David Cameron, apparently oblivious to the generally accepted economic history of the Great Depression, commented:

> I fear that, like Tony Blair, you shrink from the truth of the matter; that free and lightly regulated financial markets, upon which so much of our business elite's prosperity is dependent, have delinquent propensities for speculation and short-termism that profoundly damage the real economy. The crash of 2008–09, like 1929, is because once again we did not keep finance on a tight rein.[15]

The EU, at its summit meeting on 22 February 2009, agreed to bring in a new charter to increase EU-wide regulation across all financial markets, including those hitherto largely unaffected by state regulation. This charter, if implemented, would lead to the regulation of all financial activities around the world, including those of credit-rating agencies. There was no questioning of whether increased regulation was the appropriate instrument to achieve the

---

[13] There are two aspects to this argument. Firstly, US regulators licensed rating agencies thus entrenching a monopoly in a field where competition is vital. Secondly, a good credit rating on a particular set of bonds would allow a bank to reduce the capital they held against those bonds. Rating agencies therefore had an incentive to provide bonds with a good rating as that would artificially raise their value (because of the bonds' regulatory treatment) and they therefore cared less about their reputation for giving an accurate rating.

[14] See for example, http://www.guardian.co.uk/commentisfree/cifamerica/2008/oct/22/economy-financial-crisis-regulation (accessed 19th February 2009).

[15] See: http://www.guardian.co.uk/politics/2009/feb/01/will-hutton-david-cameron-debate (accessed 19 February 2009).

desired goals or of whether regulation could lead to other undesirable consequences.

However, the extensive system of banking regulation coming from domestic, EU and international sources did not stop the crash of 2008 from happening. Indeed, regulators did not use the powers that they had to stop banks building up risky positions in securitised instruments and credit derivatives. Central bankers and regulators, as well as organisations such as the International Monetary Fund, were sanguine about the growth in complex financial products that occurred in the early part of the twenty-first century. To understand why and to understand the implications for considering public policy in the field of regulation, there needs to be some consideration of public choice economics.

Public Choice Economics

It seems that many of the facts relating to the crash fit into the way of thinking of the public choice school of economics (see, for example, Tullock, 2006). In both the US and the UK, financial regulators have simultaneously bound up the financial sector up in detailed regulation and yet, when it comes to action to deal with an institution that is building up risks, regulators have been very lethargic. Public choice theory predicts that this is a likely outcome of giving regulators wide powers that are not well defined. Regulators will wish to build the size and power of their bureaus, which they can do by drafting handbooks of detailed regulation.[16] Regulators will also be risk averse and not wish to see a failure on their 'watch'. This may well lead to them regulating firms to avoid risks building up but, crucially and perhaps paradoxically, not intervening when risks materialise. The regulator faces incentives not to intervene when a financial company is facing trouble as the regulator may hope that

---

[16] It is not easy to navigate the FSA's handbooks. However, the full handbook contains ten sections. We can drill down to get relevant information as in the following example. The section entitled 'Prudential Standards' is divided into 11 sub-sections. The sub-section 'Prudential Sourcebook for Banks, Building Societies and Investment Firms' is made up of 14 sub-sub-sections. The sub-sub section 'Market Risk' is divided into 11 sub-sub-sub sections. The sub-sub-sub-section on 'Interest Rate PRR' has 66 paragraphs. This is known as 'principles-based regulation' by the FSA. As far as I could see, based on this example there could be over 1,100,000 paragraphs: it is not feasible to count all the paragraphs and nor is it possible to download the whole book. Remarkably, I could find nothing on liquidity risk, the main failing of Northern Rock, though I am sure it must be addressed somewhere. See http://fsahandbook.info/FSA/html/handbook/BIPRU/7/2 (downloaded 19 February 2009).

the firm can trade its way back to solvency if investment markets move in its favour. If the firm does so successfully, those to whom regulators are accountable will be unaware that they have allowed a failure to happen. This means that when there are problems, and they fail to go away, they are likely to build up and possibly pose systemic risks.

The use of detailed but misdirected regulation is predicted by another aspect of public choice theory. This suggests that regulators can become captured by the regulated industry — this is particularly true if there is a substantial amount of employment traffic between the industry and the regulator. Detailed regulation suits the industry because it raises costs to potential rivals and competitor small firms. The lack of prompt action also suits the industry. As noted, delaying intervention allows a company to try to trade out of its difficulties, to the obvious advantage of shareholders (who have limited liability) and management (who may retain their jobs) but at a cost to the other creditors of the business, including depositors.

One might ask why do the monitors of regulators not address these problems? Unfortunately, the monitors of regulators have no incentive to be well informed. Electors vote on a range of issues and have an infinitesimal chance of influencing an election. Politicians, in turn, respond to the incentives facing electors and also have little incentive to become well informed. It is ironic that regulators often talk about the need for regulation to overcome information asymmetries that exist within the financial system when there are such chronic incentives for such information asymmetries to exist within the regulatory system.

Finally, public choice economics, together with Austrian economics, points out that regulators cannot systematically correct market failures, even if there are times when regulation can theoretically improve on market outcomes. Regulators do not have the knowledge to create the conditions of a perfect market where those conditions do not exist in practice.

Public choice economics should, in the first place, lead us to have some humilty about what regulation can achieve. Secondly, it suggests that a narrow and specific regulatory remit will be more effective than a general remit to achieve widely-defined objectives.

In the wake of the financial crash, we can respond to the difficulties in the regulatory system by giving broad general powers of regulatory oversight to a government bureau to try to improve on market outcomes. Unfortunately, public choice economics gives us little confidence that this will be effective. Alternatively, we can use thoughtful economic analysis to identify specific problems in financial markets and resolve those with a simple and targeted legislative framework. This tended to be the response to very serious financial crises that developed in the UK in the nineteenth century—and it was a very effective response. It is not the purpose of this chapter to go into possible changes in the legal framework for banks in detail. However, the basic principle should be that changes in regulation should enhance the incentives of the market to monitor and discipline banks. As part of this it is also important that banks are wound up when they fail and an orderly legal process is necessary to facilitate this. Such specific legislation would not try to fulfil the impossible objective of perfecting the market and preventing so-called market failure (an obsession of much modern economics) but it could enable market discipline to work more effectively.

Ethics in Business

As far as business school teaching is concerned, it is also important to emphasise the necessity for ethical behaviour in business. However, a lot of modern teaching of corporate social responsbility (CSR) tends to focus not on ethical behaviour as such but on making the aims of a business corporation more disparate. The agents within a corporation (management) should pursue the objectives of the principals (shareholders). If those aims are shareholder value maximisation then it would be an abrogation of responsibility for management to pursue different aims, such as improving the reading skills of people living in inner-cities.[17] Of course, the owners of a business may well wish to use their capital in ways that meet the general approval of a community and helps support the social infrastructure in which businesses operate, but they should not feel under any moral obligation to do so. Furthermore, it is certainly not for management to seek to achieve their own objectives in this way. It is notable, in fact, that many of the banks that have performed most poorly—where managers have destroyed shareholder value—had very active CSR programmes.

---

[17] There are many businesses that are not corporations and many corporations that are not businesses. The shareholders of a business corporation will generally want their management to maximise shareholder value. There will be other corporations (charities, foundations, universities and so on that will have different aims). There is no reason why businesses should be expected to meet wider social objectives that we associate with non-business corporations and organisations.

However, people in business should behave ethically. In particular they should not engage in conduct that violates natural law. They should not cheat, lie, deliberately advise that their clients buy unsuitable products, undermine property rights that are, perhaps, not properly protected by government and so on. There has been interesting and mature comment on this from some senior clergy. Archbishop Vincent Nichols of Westminster (then at Birmingham), for example, commented:

> We have neglected the development of shared ethical values and principles to guide and shape our behaviour, believing that to be an unattainable goal and we have substituted raft after raft of regulation.[18]

In short, there needs to be a reorientation of business ethics teaching towards ethics. These issues are discussed further in relation to the recent financial crisis in the chapter by Gregg in Booth (2009).

Conclusion

There are many ways in which business school teaching can be adapted to take into account the problems caused by the financial crash. The main areas I would identify are as follows:

- The importance of managers of a business focusing on shareholder value needs to be re-emphasised and communicated more effectively and more rigorously.
- It is important to search for the underlying causes of events and not merely focus blame on those who are closest to the scene of a 'crime' at the time at which it is committed. If this is done we find that the banking crisis arose as a result of the failure of the regulatory system, of monetary policy makers and those responsible for corporate governance. These lessons should be reflected in business school teaching.
- Business schools need to teach rigorous economics and discuss the issues raised by economics. The curriculum should include Austrian economics and public choice economics. Austrian economics is particularly relevant to real-life business practice because it takes proper account of disequilibrium in markets and distortions in financial markets caused by mismanaged monetary policy. Public choice economics helps students better understand the likely failings in regulatory systems.

---

[18] http://www.birminghamdiocese.org.uk/assets/pdf/CIVIC%20MASS%202008.pdf (accessed 24th February).

- Business ethics should replace the teaching of corporate social responsibility. Business ethics should relate to the shared framework of ethical principles defined by natural law. Business ethics are not simply what owners or managers might regard as rules of behaviour that are socially acceptable at a particular time.

Such an evolution of business school teaching would leave the next generation of managers better able to understand economic processes and the incentives that face business owners, managers and regulators.

References

Akerlof, G.A. (1970) "The Market for Lemons: Quality Uncertainty and the Market Mechanism", *Quarterly Journal of Economics*, 84(3), 488–500.

Booth, P.M. ed. (2009), *Verdict on the Crash: Causes and Policy Implications*, Hobart Paperback 37 (London: Institute of Economic Affairs).

de Soto, J.H. (2008), *The Austrian School: Market Order and Entrepreneurial Creativity* (Cheltenham: Edward Elgar).

Harper, I.R. and Gregg, S. ed. (2008), *Christian Theology and Market Economics* (Cheltenham: Edward Elgar).

Hayek, F.A. (1988), *The Fatal Conceit: The Errors of Socialism* (Chicago: University of Chicago Press).

Hayek, F.A. (1978), *New Studies in Philosophy, Politics, Economics and the History of Ideas* (London: Routledge).

Kirzner, I.M., (1997), *How Markets Work: Disequilibrium, Entrepreneurship and Discovery*, IEA Hobart Paper 133 (London: Institute of Economic Affairs).

Kirzner, I., (1992), *The Meaning of the Market Process: Essays in the Development Of Modern Austrian Economics* (London: Routledge).

Morrison, A.D. (2007), *Investment Banking: Institutions, Politics and Law* (Oxford: Oxford University Press).

Sternberg, E. (2004), *Corporate Governance: Accountability in the Marketplace*, Hobart Paper 147 (London: Institute of Economic Affairs).

Tullock, G. (2006), *The Vote Motive*, Hobart Paperback 33 (London: Institute of Economic Affairs).

Woods, T.E. Jr. (2009), *Meltdown* (Washington DC: Regnery).

Edward Skidelsky

Capitalism and the Good Life

Does the accumulation of wealth under capitalism have any ultimate end? For John Maynard Keynes, writing in 1930, the answer was clear. In a hundred years, he predicted, living standards will have risen at least fourfold, leading to a qualitative transformation of life. We might still work three hours a day or so, 'to satisfy the old Adam in us', but for the rest we will devote ourselves to living itself.

> We shall once more value ends above means and prefer the good to the useful. We shall honour those who can teach us how to pluck the hour and the day virtuously and well, the delightful people who are capable of taking direct enjoyment in things, the lilies of the field who toil not, neither do they spin (Keynes, 1963, p. 372).

Close to a hundred years have past since Keynes wrote those words and per capita income has more than quadrupled, as he foretold. Yet the promised denouement is nowhere in sight. British working hours have fallen only slightly, and are now on the rise again (see Bunting, 2005, p. 9). Economic growth remains the touchstone of national prestige. The arts of living have decayed. Leisure has come to signify a mere interruption of the work cycle, an interlude of consumption or dissipation; in some circles, it has merged with work entirely. Parties are an opportunity to 'network', holidays to 'refuel'. Our lives are more purposive than ever, yet without ultimate purpose.

Why has Keynes' vision failed to materialise? My answer, to anticipate briefly the conclusion of this essay, is that we have lost the conception of a way of life as good in itself and of wealth as a means thereto. This conception—the 'good life' as I will call it—came naturally to Keynes, steeped as he was in the Platonism of G.E. Moore and the aestheticism of Bloomsbury. He took it for granted that with rising incomes it would come to permeate society as a whole; he did not anticipate that the mechanism of wealth creation and its attendant attitudes might eventually undermine the very ideal they were intended to serve. Yet that is what has happened. The social and intellectual upheavals of the twentieth century have unsettled all wonted ways of life, all fixed objects of ambition and desire, leaving only the shifting fortunes of 'the Joneses' to guide us. Our condition is that which Hobbes attributed (falsely) to mankind in general: 'a perpetual and restless desire of power after power, that ceaseth only in death.'

Two Economic Explanations

There are two standard economic explanations of why Keynes' vision has failed to materialise, both of which contain elements of truth yet fail to get at the intellectual and ethical heart of the matter.

The first explanation is Marxist in inspiration, and focuses on the structure of production under capitalism. Rising productivity offers firms the choice of either expanding output or reducing working hours, yet the pressure of competition biases them consistently towards the former. Workers who would prefer the extra leisure are left unsatisfied—a market failure that the old mechanism of collective action no longer remedies. In any case, capitalism strongly inclines us to prefer money over leisure. Its hidden and not-so-hidden persuaders devote vast resources to filling us with new and spurious 'needs' which we must work ever harder to satisfy. (There is, conversely, no market in free time.) Thus arises a classic Marxist contradiction: capitalism's productive *forces* hold out the historic promise of liberation from toil, yet its productive *relations* ensure that this promise remains forever unfulfilled.[1]

This picture certainly captures many aspects of our situation, yet it leaves untouched the deeper question of why consumers have proved so malleable in the hands of producers. Appeals to advertising, mass media, the 'culture industry' and so forth are beside the point; it is our susceptibility to these monsters that is the mystery. The most sophisticated marketing would be wasted on us if we could only say, 'I don't need it, I have enough'. It is the fact that we cannot say this that gives it its hold. And we cannot say this, to

---

[1] This composite picture is drawn from a number of sources, including Marcuse, 2002; Cohen, 1977; and Schor, 1992. Not all these authors would accept all parts of the picture, but there is enough overlap to warrant putting them together.

repeat, because we lack a conception of the good life relative to which terms such as 'need' and 'enough' might be given determinate meaning. It is this ethical void, rather than any narrowly material force, that keeps the wheels of production in motion.

The failure of Keynes' prediction poses an even greater problem for neoclassical economics. If each additional unit of wealth yields less utility than the last, as marginalist theory suggests it should, why has the value of income relative to leisure not started to decline? One influential answer draws on Fred Hirsch's concept of 'positional goods' — goods such as unspoilt holiday destinations, leadership jobs and scenic estates (see Hirsch, 1977). Like top places in a queue, positional goods are inherently limited in number. As incomes rise, competition for them intensifies, driving prices higher and higher. (To enjoy the pristine ski slopes once offered by Val-d'Isère, I must now travel to Verbier.) Here is one powerful explanation for why the love of money has shown no tendency to dwindle with affluence.

Several economists following Hirsch have developed his insight further, arguing that many non-positional goods also have positional features. The Jaguar is an intrinsically fine car, but my pleasure in owning one is heightened by the knowledge that it puts me in a small and privileged minority. If everyone had a Jaguar, I would need a still more expensive car to achieve the same effect. This generalisation of Hirsch's theory entails a break with the orthodox economic assumption that wants are independent — a break justified by appeal to psychology. Robert Frank and others have drawn on experimental data to argue that evaluation, like perception, is relational in structure. The same brain mechanism that makes a spot appear light or dark depending on its background also makes a Jaguar appear smart or shabby depending on the other cars on the road. This mechanism has nothing to do with envy or vanity, insists Frank. It is a natural adaptation, forged in the struggle for existence, which only now, in conditions of mass affluence, gives rise to the unfortunate side-effects described by Hirsch (see Frank, 1999, p. 122–45; Layard, 2005, pp. 41–8).

This is all deeply muddled. Evaluation is not governed by the same instinctual mechanisms that govern perception, but by distinct *norms* — norms which can be drawn either from the contemporary milieu, as in the case of the Jaguar, or else from some more permanent source. Consider, for example, the room in which Virginia Woolf wrote her novels, the original 'room of one's own'. It was a small room, far smaller than those she would have known in Garsington or Sissinghurst, yet *it was not too small to write novels in*. It perfectly fulfilled its role in Virginia Woolf's life, which was (all things considered) a good life. She had no reason to be dissatisfied with it. This mode of evaluation—taking its cue from the requirements of a good life, not from what other people happen to have—has long been encouraged by the dominant religious and philosophical traditions of the West. The Bible prohibits covetousness; the pagan classics elaborate ideals of simplicity and self-sufficiency. It is the collapse of these traditions, not any psychological mechanism of the sort postulated by Frank, that explains the intensity of positional competition in our society.[2]

Both Marxist and neoclassical explanations fail, then, and for similar reasons. The former postulates an iron law of capitalist production, the latter an iron law of consumer demand. Both overlook the role of ideals, in particular the ideal I have called the 'good life'. Let us now turn to that ideal.

The Good Life and its Eclipse

Conceptions of the good life have varied hugely, both within and between cultures. Some give pride of place to contemplation, others to action; some to friendship, others to solitude; some to pleasure, others to self-denial. Yet all share certain general features belonging to the good life as such, including most importantly a certain attitude to money. These features were spelt out with unique clarity by Aristotle.

The good life, for Aristotle, is an end in itself, not a means to some further end. The ascetic with eyes turned heavenwards; the miser and his hoard; the faithful servant of the revolution—none of these are living the good life in Aristotle's sense. Nor is Kant's hero of the will, grimly sacrificing inclination to duty. The good life is one of *eudaimonia*, of happiness or flourishing. It is desirable, meaning that it satisfies the essential desires of our species, not that it is always actually desired. We can fail to desire what is in fact desirable

---

[2] Positional goods in Hirsch's original, strict sense ought to be unaffected by such normative shifts, for it not *demand* for them, but only their *supply*, that is conditional on the behaviour of others. On closer analysis, though, this distinction breaks down. A leadership job might be desirable in itself, but it only counts as 'a leadership job' because not everyone has one. And why exactly is a crowded beach so undesirable? The sun, sea and sand are just what they are in an empty beach. Isn't it rather a secret sense of shame, of being one of the *hoi polloi*, that spoils our pleasure?

because we are ill-born or ill-breed. Desire is corrigible; it can miss its mark. Here is a crucial point of difference between Aristotle and most modern thinkers, to which I shall return later.

If the good life is an end in itself, it cannot consist of work, for work is only ever a means to an end. (The idea that it might be an end in itself had to wait for Calvin.) The good life is one of leisure, meaning not relaxation or self-indulgence but activity over and above what is needed to live. The highest forms of leisure are politics — participation in the life of the *polis* — and philosophy. Both require wealth, 'since we cannot ... do fine actions if we lack the resources' (Aristotle, 1985, p. 21). Aristotle's conception is, then, a frankly worldly one. The good life is not compatible with great poverty or suffering, as Plato had taught, and it certainly does not *require* these things, as certain Christian writers were later to assert.

Wealth for Aristotle consists of possessions, primarily land and slaves. These are valuable insofar as they fulfil some concrete need. Yet they also possess a different kind of value, which lies in their aptness to be *exchanged*. Exchange causes Aristotle much headache, for it seems to him both to violate the proper use of things and to impose a unified quantitative form on qualitatively distinct substances. Still, he is prepared to tolerate it so long as it is limited to acquiring the necessities of life. Exchange-value, to borrow Marx's terminology, is strictly subordinated to use-value.[3]

This natural relationship between use and exchange is threatened by money. Originally just a means for facilitating exchange, once established money can become an end in itself, with possessions degraded to means. Instead of selling possessions for money with a view to buying more possessions, we can spend money on possessions with a view to making more money. (Once again, and not coincidentally, Marx's formulae C-M-C and M-C-M spring to mind.) These two forms of exchange overlap in practice, but they are conceptually quite distinct. The pursuit of possessions has a controlling end — the good life — whereas the desire for money is insatiable. 'All getters of wealth increase their hoard of coin without limit.' This insatiability repels Aristotle, the disciple of the mean, for whom all natural desires have their proper *telos*. Worst of all is usury, 'which makes a gain out of money itself, and not from the natural object of it' (Aristotle, 1988, pp. 14, 15).

---

[3] My interpretation of Aristotle here and in the next paragraph is indebted to Meikle, 1995.

Aristotle's theory of the good life is in many ways rooted in its time and place. Its exclusive emphasis on politics and philosophy will charm few today. There is no room in it for family happiness or for the enjoyment of art and nature. And of course, the good life is reserved for male citizens; women and slaves are excluded. Nonetheless, the basic structure of Aristotle's theory was sufficiently flexible to enter into combination with ethical ideals very different from his own. That a certain way of life is good in itself; that money is at best a means thereto; that the love of money is unnatural and usury detestable — these were all doctrines acceptable, for instance, to Thomas Aquinas. Keynes himself was thoroughly Aristotelian on all these points, though very unAristotelian in his vision of the human good.

Keynes, however, was an anomaly. The most influential currents of modern thought have been resolutely hostile to Aristotelianism in all its varieties. For empiricism and its various social scientific offshoots, desire has no proper end, no mark to hit or miss. It is a bare psychological fact, guiltless and inerrant. All ways of life, insofar as they are freely chosen and do not violate the rights or interests of others, are on a par. There is no such thing as *the* good life, only a range of *desirable lifestyles*.

Once this keystone of Aristotle's economic system is removed, the other blocks fall rapidly to the ground. First to go is the concept of need. For the modern economist, 'need' has meaning, if at all, only in relation to the body; beyond that, there are simply wants of varying degrees of urgency.[4] Next in line is the distinction between use- and exchange-value. If value is rooted in subjective utility, it cannot come in a multitude of incommensurable forms. Money and goods are interchangeable expressions of the same basic stock of value, not metaphysically distinct objects of desire. The decision as to which to pursue is purely pragmatic.[5] Finally, it goes without saying that the condemnation of interest as 'unnatural' is an arbitrary moral judgement lying outside the scope of economics as a positive science.

---

[4] Price-inelasticity of demand is sometimes presented as a surrogate for need, but quite misleadingly. The demand for heroin is highly price-inelastic, but addicts do not *need* heroin.

[5] Carl Menger, one of the pioneers of the modern theory of utility, employs the terms use- and exchange-value, but only to indicate the capacity of goods to satisfy wants either directly or through exchange. This is a far cry from the metaphysical gulf postulated by Aristotle and Marx. See Menger, 1950), pp. 226–35.

This new set of ideas did not triumph instantly. More ancient conceptions lurk in the background of much classical economics and are explicit in Marx and Keynes. It wasn't until Paul Samuelson formulated the concept of revealed preference in 1938 that the ghost of Aristotle was finally laid to rest.[6] Today, economists routinely condemn all talk of the ends of life or of what people 'really need' as metaphysical and paternalistic. In this they are in agreement with established opinion more generally. Few members of our intellectual elite, on either left or right, would reject the proposition that whatever x freely chooses is good for x.[7] Disagreement between them centres on the secondary issue of how this choice is best expressed.

But surely, it might reasonably be protested, the good life's demise cannot be blamed solely on a few philosophers or economists. The good life is not just a *theory* to be accepted or rejected but a *practice* to be acquired or lost. Its primary home is not in the brains of individual thinkers but in groups of people sharing similar tastes and ideals. My idea of the good life may be to sit in the town square playing chess with my friends, but if my friends don't play chess, or if there is no town square, it will come to nothing. (Even the unsociable St. Simeon Stylites required a wider community to make sense of his feat. Today he would be sectioned.) It is *institutions* that are responsible for giving concrete social form to abstract ethical ideas. Of course, institutions usually end up travestying the very ideas they represent, but without them those ideas would remain entirely subjective and theoretical—'too excellent to have actuality', as Hegel ironically puts it, 'or too impotent to procure it for themselves' (Hegel, 1892, p. 11).

If ideas and institutions are interwoven in this way, we should expect the intellectual story sketched above to be underwritten by a *sociological* story tracing the decline of institutional authority. And that is just what we find. At the centre of this story lies the oft-noted tendency of capitalism and the bureaucratic state (the emphasis varies from writer to writer) to dissolve all permanent institutions and fixed ties. 'All that is solid melts into air', as Marx famously put it, 'all that is holy is profaned.' This solutive tendency was for a long while

---

[6] Roughly, the idea that a consumer's preferences are fully revealed in his consumption behaviour. See Samuelson, 1938.

[7] One striking exception to this general rule are choices affecting health and safety, but then these lie under the jurisdiction of another supposedly positive science: medicine.

held in check by the power of the landed aristocracy and gentry, as well as by an 'intellectual aristocracy' of clergymen, lawyers and dons. Meanwhile, in industrial towns, shared patterns of work gave rise to ways of life which, if not exactly 'good' in Aristotle's sense, were at least more than purely maximising. All this is now gone. The aristocracy, deprived of its political role, has merged into the idle rich; the intellectual aristocracy has become a small and uninfluential coterie; the working class is scattered and powerless. This is the social fact of which neoclassical economics, in its atomism and value-neutralism, is the theoretical reflection and justification.

In this situation, an individual can of course select some particular way of life as 'good' and work no harder than he needs to sustain it. He can 'downshift', to use the current term. But this will be a purely personal choice, a subjective preference, with no general authority. He is unlikely to find others to share his way of life, or if he does, this will be no more than a makeshift, a temporary alliance of interests. He will not receive from others the *recognition* necessary to validate his preferred way of life—the recognition that the Church gave St. Simeon. The downshifter is thus liable to fall victim to self-doubt and resentment. He may try to justify his decision with arguments to do with social justice or the environment, but as these are not generally accepted or even understood, and in any case do not confirm his way of life as *good* in Aristotle's sense, as the fulfilment of some essential human need, they are likely to be taken as mere rationalisations of failure. They will not carry the suasive force once carried by 'I am devoted to the Church' or 'I have enough to live as a gentleman.'

Let me draw together the strands. I have suggested a shift—on one level theoretical, on another sociological—from a world in which certain ways of life are intrinsically desirable to one in which they are desirable only insofar as they are actually desired. In the former world, material ambition has a fixed goal: the maintenance of a good life. To continue striving for wealth after that goal has been achieved is irrational. But where there is no good life, there can be no fixed goal, only the relative one of 'as much as' or 'more than' the others— a goal which, since it is shared by those others, must recede forever into the distance. Here is that endless scramble for positional advantage described by Frank and others. Note, however, that the cause of this scramble is not any innate psychological mechanism but a transformation of worldview. The scramble is endless because we no longer know what could constitute its *end*.

Imagine, by way of illustration, a group of mountaineers climbing a cliff. Their aim is to reach the top, where they will rest. But at some point during the assent, it dawns on them that the cliff has no top, that it is endless. Nonetheless, they carry on climbing, now with the sole aim of staying ahead of their fellow mountaineers. Here is an image of our situation. The disappearance of all intrinsic ends leaves the social stage as flat, featureless and infinite as our hypothetical cliff face. We are presented with only two options: to be ahead or to be behind. Positional struggle is our fate. If there is no right place to be, it is best to be ahead.

What is amiss with this situation? It is not that our mountaineers are unhappy — they may or may not be — but rather that they are absurd. A perpetual mountaineer can explain any single one of his steps ('it was necessary to get ahead of so-and-so'), but he cannot explain *why he is climbing the cliff at all*. His life as a whole is opaque to him, even if each particular part makes sense. He has become incomprehensible to himself. Real life presents many examples of the same absurdity. A body building fanatic might be able to justify each step of his career ('I needed to win this competition', 'I wanted to get the best abs in my gym') but not its final, hideous outcome. Academics always need to read just another article, 'to keep abreast of the field', yet the cumulative effect of such a diet is just as disfiguring in its way as pumping too much iron. Wherever pursuit of intrinsic ends gives way to positional competition one sees the same odd combination of intense purposiveness in matters of detail and overall futility. The familiar metaphors of the treadmill and the squirrel cage capture this incongruity.

We can now see why Keynes got it so wrong. He believed that the values and institutions of capitalism could be utilised in the service of wealth creation and then thrown away. 'Avarice and usury and precaution must be our gods for a little longer still. For only they can lead us out of the tunnel of economic necessity into daylight' (Keynes, 1963, p. 372). After that, the lilies of the field can bloom unhindered. But capitalism was never going to allow itself to be used as the instrument of a quasi-aristocratic, quasi-religious ideal. Its inner tendency is to level all ideals, to reduce them to mere tastes. This is a contradiction Keynes never fully faced. Here as elsewhere, he took for granted traditional, class-based attitudes that his own economic prescriptions would help to undermine.

Conclusion

I have argued that the modern economic system, in both its theoretical and practical dimensions, is hostile to any notion of the good life. But isn't this too fatalistic? Am I not working up into an impersonal monster vices that belong to each of us severally? The problem is not capitalism, the empiricist worldview or whatever; it is that we are *greedy*. We need a change of heart. This is a refrain we have heard a lot over the past year, especially from the bishops.

There is a sense in which this is true: evil's springs are ever the same. But as Alasdair MacIntyre has often pointed out, the weakness of the 'change of heart' approach is that it draws on a moral vocabulary whose meaning has long since been lost or distorted. The term 'greed' is a case in point. In its primary, physical sense, it means 'wanting more than enough food' — an unproblematic expression, since we know roughly how much food the human frame requires. But in its secondary, economic sense, greed means something like 'wanting more than enough money' — a vacuous phrase, since without a notion of the good life we have no idea how much money constitutes enough. In these conditions, accusations of greed have a purely incantatory force and fall, rightly, under suspicion of *ressentiment*. A change of heart is insufficient. Our first task is not to become less greedy, but to create a society in which the word 'greedy' has determinate meaning.

Another line of criticism might question my identification of the good life with the life of leisure. Didn't Calvin and his fellow reformers teach us that work can be a source of meaning and satisfaction in its own right, not just a means to an end? Don't modern management gurus repeat the same message in ever more fervent tones, urging 'total commitment' to the company 'brand'? In his essay in this volume, Roger Scruton claims that successful firms do not regard profit as their main goal but as a by-product of some more integral purpose (Scruton, 2009). If this is true, then long working hours are nothing to puzzle or alarm us; they are simply evidence that for most people today, the working life *is* the good life.

I am unconvinced. There are no doubt a few people — artists, writers, small artisan producers — for whom work is an intrinsic good, in the sense that they would persist with it even if they had some other source of income. But for the vast majority, the ancient axiom holds true: work is the sphere of necessity, a means to an end external to itself. True, modern management techniques have helped a few confused souls find deeper meaning in essentially mercenary activities, but that is hardly cause for celebration.[8] And when large corporations claim to be concerned primarily with 'virtue' or 'community', and only incidentally with making money, one discerns the hand of public relations. Oddest of all is the attempt of Edwin M. Hartman in this volume to enlist Aristotle, that severe critic of the money motive, in the service of business ethics (Hartman, 2009).

What are the prospects for the revival of a *genuine* Aristotelian social ethic? Not good, I fear. For such a revival presupposes a social and intellectual infrastructure which, as I have suggested, no longer exists. The following passage by Monsignor John A. Ryan, an influential early twentieth-century American moral theologian, nicely illustrates the difficulty:

> One of the most baneful assumptions of our materialistic industrial civilisation is that all men should spend at least one-third of the twenty four hour day in some productive occupation. … If men still have leisure, new luxuries must be invented to keep them busy and new wants must be stimulated. … Of course, the true and rational doctrine is that when men have produced sufficient necessaries and reasonable comforts and conveniences to supply all the population, they should spend what time is left in the cultivation of their intellects and wills, in the pursuit of the higher life (quoted in Schor, 1992, p. 121).

That is eloquently put, and in general terms unobjectionable. The problem is working out what it could mean in practice. What exactly constitutes a *reasonable* comfort and convenience? An indoor lavatory? A television? A second home? Perhaps Monsignor Ryan possessed an answer to these questions, but the regnant liberal secularism offers no such answer, and hence no warrant for a general limitation of production.

Where liberal secularism has failed, though, the environmental movement may yet succeed. If every purchase has a measurable impact on the environment, a 'carbon footprint', then we might indeed distinguish those that are 'reasonable' from those that are not. Environmentalism promises to restore concrete meaning to the language of Christian social ethics, to establish a scientific measure of greed, avarice and luxury. It has been less successful in connecting

---

[8] For an illustration, see the interview with the head of human resources at Orange in Bunting, 2005, p. 109: 'I'm proud of what Orange stands for in the marketplace. I'm passionate about the business, and I care about the people and what we do. I get frustrated when I see us behaving in a way that isn't Orange. … I don't hold my self up to being a saint, but I try to incorporate the brand values into everything I do.'

the public good of the environment to the private good of the individual. Its ideal remains unappealingly sacrificial; it does not amount to a *good* life in Aristotle's sense. Perhaps the Epicurean doctrine that pleasure is best achieved through the limitation of wants can help here. But this is all speculation. The fact is that we have no idea what form the new good life will take, or how it will be realised.

Bibliography

Aristotle (1985), *Nicomachean Ethics*, ed. Terence Irwin (Indianapolis: Hackett).

Aristotle (1988), *The Politics*, ed. Stephen Everson (Cambridge: Cambridge University Press).

Bunting, Madeline (2005), *Willing Slaves: How the Overwork Culture is Ruling our Lives* (London: HarperCollins).

Cohen, Gerald A. (1977), "Labor, Leisure, and a Distinctive Contradiction of Advanced Capitalism", in Gerald Dworkin, Gordon Bermant and Peter G. Brown (ed.), *Markets and Morals* (Washington D.C.: Hemisphere).

Frank, Robert H. (1999), *Luxury Fever: Money and Happiness in an Era of Excess* (Princeton: Princeton University Press).

Hartman, Edwin M. (2009), "Teaching Business Ethics with Aristotle", *Profit, Prudence and Virtue: Essays in Ethics, Business & Management*, ed. Samuel Gregg and James Stoner (Exeter: Imprint Academic).

Hegel (1892), *Logic*, trans. William Wallace (Oxford: Clarendon).

Hirsch, Fred (1977), *Social Limits to Growth* (London: Routledge).

Keynes, John Maynard (1963), "Economic Possibilities for our Grandchildren", in *Essays in Persuasion* (New York: Norton).

Layard, Richard (2005), *Happiness: Lessons from a New Science* (London: Penguin).

Marcuse, Herbert (2002), *One-Dimensional Man: Studies in the Ideology of Advanced Industrial Society* (London: Routledge).

Meikle, Scott (1995), *Aristotle's Economic Thought* (Oxford: Clarendon).

Menger, Carl (1950), *Principles of Economics*, trans. James Dingwall and Bert. F. Hoselitz (Glencoe, Illinois: The Free Press).

Samuelson, Paul (1938), "A Note on the Pure Theory of Consumer's Behaviour", *Economica* 5, no. 17, pp. 61–71.

Schor, Juliet B. (1992), *The Overworked American: the Unexpected Decline of Leisure* (New York: BasicBooks).

Scruton, Roger (2009), "Virtue and Profit: A Critique of Managerial Reasoning", *Profit, Prudence and Virtue: Essays in Ethics, Business & Management*, ed. Samuel Gregg and James Stoner (Exeter: Imprint Academic).

Index

AACSB. *See* American Assembly of Collegiate Schools of Business
ABB, Ltd., 149
ABN Amro, 209
The Academic Revolution (Riesman and Jencks), 80
Academic Strategy: The Management Revolution in Higher Education (Keller), 83–84, 86, 88, 90
academy. *See* business education; education; universities
The Academy of Management Review, 109
Adidas, 148
advertising, 140–41
African-Americans, 62–63
agency theory, 18, 21, 166–67
AIAG. *See* Rheinfelden aluminum works
AIG, 198
Alliance and Leicester, 198
American Assembly of Collegiate Schools of Business (AACSB), 108, 128, 135
American Revolution, 12
Amish communities, 60
Anders, George, 57
Anderson, Ray, 147
Annas, Julia, 201, 204–5
Ann Taylor, 15
anthropology, philosophical, 1, 2
Aquinas, St. Thomas, 4, 9, 16, 30, 38, 200, 247
Arendt, Hannah, 122
Aristotle, 16, 40; business and, 10–11; business education and, 6, 155–72, 174–93; business ethics and, 206–7; character and interests and, 158–62; common sense and, 164–67; complete good and, 179; dialectic and, 158; distribution of goods and, 6; ethical perception and, 167–69; ethics and, 6, 9, 156–58, 192–93; good life and, 163, 176, 181, 245–50; happiness and, 4–5, 31–32, 178–79, 181–83, 201–4, 204–5, 207; justice and, 6, 34; leadership and, 188–89; means and ends and, 4; microeconomics and, 176–77; money, role of and, 179–80; moral philosophy of, 175–76; practical wisdom (*phronesis*) and, 183–84; profit and virtue and, 30–33, 36, 252; rationality and psychic harmony and, 163–64; social contract and, 184–85; trade and, 10; virtue and, 6, 160, 199–204; work and leisure and, 6; workplace of, 185–88
Arthur Andersen, 168, 192
Asia, 143
Athens, 192, 193
Austrian economics, 24, 232–35, 235–36, 240

"Bad Management Theories Are Destroying Good Management Practices" (Ghoshal), 115
Ballmer, Steve, 177

banking: business as human enterprise and, 117; ethical foundations of, xii–xiii, xiii; financial crisis (2008) and, xiii, 226, 229–31, 237, 240; monetary policy and, 229; regulation and, 230, 237, 240
Bank of England, 228, 229
Barclays, 149, 209
Baring's, 21, 40
Barzun, Jacques, 83
BCG, 110
Belgium, 14
Berger, Peter, 25
Berlin, Isaiah, 48
Bible, 245
biomedical ethics, 44
Black, Eli, 15
Blair, Tony, 226, 236
Böhm-Bawerk, Eugen von, 24
Bonham, Wallace, 17
Booth, Philip, vii, 7, 235, 240
Bradford and Bingley, 198
Brazil, 112
Britain, 14; consultancy in, 75; health care system in, 5, 67–72; limited-liability joint-stock corporations and, 14; public service in, 5, 67–78
British East India Company, 12
British Petroleum, 15, 21
British Royal Dutch Shell, 15
Brown, Jerry, 178
Built to Last (Collins and Porras), 26
Burker King, 146
Burnham, James, 73
business: cooperative character of, 99–100; family and, 5, 57–65; human dignity and, 64; as human enterprise, 117–23; humanities and, 123–24; integration thesis and, 6; natural law and, 45–46; origins of, 4, 9–23; pillars of decency and, 58–65; profit and, 24–41, 94, 97–99; purpose of, 97–99, 206–8; regulation of, 11–15, 19–21; separation fallacy and, 6; service and, 57; social life and, 42; social responsibility and, 3; society and, 2, 57–58; trust and, 113; values and, 2; as vocation, 57. *See also* business education; business ethics
Business as a Calling (Novak), 25
business curriculum. *See* business education
business education: business as human enterprise and, 117–23; compartmentalization and, 141; context, redefining and, 143–50; culture of, 109–10; disciplinary matrix of, 124–25; disciplines, reconstituting and, 140–43; economic instruction and, 212–15; economics teaching and, 227–28; entrepreneurship and, 7, 214–15; ethical crisis in, 1, 9–10, 57, 211–12; ethical formation and, 212–15; financial crisis (2008) and, 1, 6–7, 211–24, 225–40; goals of, 3, 135–40; history of, 107–13; law and, 139–40; moral hazard and, 219–23; moral reflection and, 7, 215–19; nature of, 3; origins of, 4, 9–23; pluralism and, 143–45, 146–47; profit and, 2, 129, 225–26; purpose of, 10; recent critiques of, 114–17; regulation and, 17; reputational capital and, 129, 150; reputational sanctions and, 145–48; rescuing, 120–23; research and, 110–12; science and, 109–10; society and, 3; teaching methods and, 3, 125–26
business ethics: business, purpose of and, 94, 97–99; cities, origins of and, 94–96; compliance and, 97, 100; corporate social responsibility and, 14–15, 37,

39–40, 93, 130, 213, 239, 240; culture, changing and, 93, 103–4; financial crisis (2008) and, 239–40; integrity and, 205–6; natural law and, 38; as oxymoron, 96, 130, 159, 197, 206; profit and, 94, 97–99; reputation and, 96–97; workplace safety and, 102–4. *See also* ethics
business leaders. *See* leadership
business management. *See* management

California, University of, Berkeley, 90
Calvin, John, 246, 251
Calvinism, 25, 35
Cameron, David, 236
capital: cultural, 72; financial crisis (2008) and, 217; reputational, 129–34, 148–50; social, 27–28
capitalism, 49; business schools and, 1; dynamism and, 1; good life and, 7, 242–53; leisure and, 243; managerial, 19; money and, 243; moral basis of, 27; planning and, 31; Protestant ethic and, 25
Carnegie Institute of Technology, 17
Carnegie Report, 109
Carter Administration, 220
Catholic Church, Catholicism: social justice and, 35; usury and, 216–17
Caux Round Table, 148
Cavallé, Carlos, xii, xiii
CEO. *See* chief executive officer
character, 4; business and, 16; business schools and, 16; consistency of desires and, 163–64; ethics and, 38; family and, 59; identity and, 156; organizational culture and, 161–62; virtues and, 6
Charles V, Emperor, 13
Chick fil-A, 26

chief executive officer (CEO), 141, 166
chief reputation adviser (CRA), 141
chief reputation officer (CRO), 141–42
China, 112, 113, 148
Christianity, 216–17
Christian social thought, 35, 252
Chrysler, 15, 220
cities, origins of, 94–96
citizenship, 19–20
Clinton, Bill, 113
Clinton Administration, 149, 221
CNN, 145
Collins, Jim, 26, 39, 170
Columbia University, 5, 83, 90
commerce. *See* business
common good, 3, 33, 55, 59, 219
common law, 11
common sense, 158, 164–67
communism, 1, 35, 49, 113, 192
community, 32, 157–58, 160
company policy, 6
comparative advantage, 85, 89, 90
compartmentalization: business education and, 141; financial crisis (2008) and, 195–97, 197–201; integrity and, 7, 199–201, 210; modernity and, 7; virtues, unity of and, 201–4
competition, 31
Competitive Strategy (Porter), 110
compliance, 4, 93, 97, 100, 138
Condorcet, Marquis de, 29–30
conscience, 51–52
consultancy, consultants, 37, 75, 117
consumer culture, 14–15
contemplation, 178–79, 181–82
corporate responsibility, 18, 19, 22, 113
corporate social responsibility (CSR), 14–15, 37, 39–40, 93, 130, 213, 239, 240

corporations: citizenship of, 19–20; culture of, 19, 22, 175; financial crisis (2008) and, 231; governance of, 231; hierarchy of, 21; identity of, 135; image of, 14–15, 97, 135; law and, 14, 50; legal personhood in, 4; limited-liability joint-stock, 13–14, 220; modern notion of, 11; personality of, 14–15, 135; scandals and, 1, 18, 22, 103, 113; soul of, 38–40; trust and, 19; vision of, 93
courage, 30–31, 32, 33, 156–57, 171
CRA. *See* chief reputation adviser
credit rating agencies, 235–36
crime, organized, 99
CRO. *See* chief reputation officer
Csikszentmihalyi, Mihaly, 26–27
CSR. *See* Corporate Social Responsibility
Cubberly, E.B., 108
cultural capital, 72
culture: business, 13; changing, 93, 103–4; consumer, 14–15; corporate, 19, 22, 175; counter-, 55; elite intellectual, 65; global market and, 3; organizational, 168–69; political, 46–48, 51
curricula. *See* business education
Czechoslovakia, 39

Dacor, 26
Daedulus, 81
Damon, William, 26–27
Daniels, Anthony (A.M.), vii, 5
Danone Group, 150
Darfur, Sudan, 149, 150
Darwin, Charles, 116
decision-making, 2, 185
democracy, 25, 184
Dewey, John, 124
dialectic, 158, 165–66, 169
Disney, 190
distribution of goods, 6
distribution of rewards, 177, 189–91

division of labor, 81–82, 176–77
dotcom companies, 112
Dreiser, Theodore, 14
Drucker, Peter, 118
Dunfee, Thomas, 144
DuPont, 110
duties: natural law and, 5, 52–55; political culture and, 52–55
dynamism: of capitalism, 1; economic, 63; of modern economy, 5; pillars of decency and, 60–61; social institutions, 61

eBay, 112
economic crisis (2008). *See* financial crisis (2008)
economics: Austrian, 24, 232–35, 235–36, 240; business education and, 227–28; embryonic theory of, 217; ethics and, 128–51; law and, 11–12; neo-classical, 18, 31, 232–35; post-classical, 1; public choice, 237–39, 240; science and, 217
Economist, 10
education: French, 76; liberal arts, 84; moral, 108–9. *See also* business education
Education Department, U.S., 79, 85
Ehrenreich, Barbara, 90
Einstein, Albert, 178
Eisner, Michael, 190
Elon University, 89–90
empiricism, 29, 247, 251
England. *See* Britain
Enlightenment, 9, 10, 11, 16
Enron, 18, 37, 113, 168, 192, 213
entrepreneurship, 7, 25, 214–15
environment, 113, 147–48, 252–53
Epicureanism, 253
Esso/Exxon, 15
ethics: Aristotle and, 156–58; basic terms of, 42–44; biomedical, 44; character and, 38; character and interests and, 158–62; classical view of, 3; common sense and,

164–67; economics and, 128–51; good life and, 159; happiness and, 159–60; importance of, 192–93; integration thesis and, 6; integrity and, 196; in management, 5; moral formation and, 4; natural law and, 38; perception and, 167–69; political culture and, 46–48; principles and, 156–57; rationality and, 158; society and, 6; strategy and, 169–72; workplace, 5. *See also* business ethics

EU. *See* European Union

European Union (EU), 236–37

executive: American universities, management of and, 86–87; compensation for, 6; distribution of goods and, 6; energy in, 80–82; thievery of, 46–48, 51

executives: corporate culture and, 175; distribution of rewards and, 189–91; short-term thinking and, 175

Exxon Valdez, 21, 39

Fama, Eugene, 18

family: business and, 5, 57–65; character and, 59; pillars of decency and, 5, 59, 62–64; threatening forces and, 62–64; virtue and, 59

fanaticism, 58

Fannie Mae, 198, 212, 214, 219, 229

Federal Reserve, U.S., 220, 228

Festinger, Leon, 163

Fidelity, 149–50

financial crisis (2008), xiii, 3; business education and, 211–24, 225–40; business ethics and, 239–40; business schools and, 1, 6–7; causes of, 222, 226–27, 228–40; compartmentalization and, 195–97, 197–201; corporate governance and, 231; credit and, 216–19; economics, Austrian and, 232–35, 235–36; economics, neo-classical and, 232–35; integrity and, 7, 195–210; lending and, 216–19; market malfunction and, 226–27; monetary policy and, 228–29; moral hazard and, 219–23; public choice economics and, 237–39; regulation and, 4, 229–31, 235–36, 236–37; virtue and, 208–10

Financial Times, 221

The Financier and the Titan (Dreiser), 14

Finnis, John, 222

Fiorina, Carla, 15

Fixing Global Finance (Wolf), 220

Fong, Christina, 114, 116

Ford Foundation, 109

Fordham University, 6

foreclosure, xiii

Fortune 500, 190

Foucault, Michel, 67

France, 14, 37, 76, 143

Frank, Robert, 244, 245, 249

Frankfurt, Harry G., 156

Freddie Mac, 198, 212, 214, 219, 229

freedom: economic, 61; negative, 48; of speech, 61; subsidiarity and, 35; of will, 58

Freeman, Anthony, xiii

Freeman, R. Edward, vii, 6, 130

French East India Company, 12

French Revolution, 12, 13

Freud, Sigmund, 116

Friedman, Milton, 119, 129

friendship, 4, 28–30, 49

From Higher Aims to Hired Hands (Khurana), 17

Fugger, Jakob, 13

Fukuyama, Francis, 27

Gap, The, 148

Gardner, Howard, 26–27

Gates, Bill, 177

GE. *See* General Electric
General Electric (GE), 15, 16, 110
General Motors, 20
George, Robert P., viii, 5
Germany, 37, 143
Ghoshal, Sumantra, 115–16, 117, 123, 126
Glaucon, 94–95, 99, 100
Global and Northern Trust, 149
Global Compact for Business, 148
Global Crossing, 192
global economy, 3–4
globalization, 22, 40, 122, 128
global market, 1, 3
God, 25, 26, 42, 54, 58
Gogol, Nikolai, 67
good life, 176; capitalism and, 7, 242–53; community and, 160; definition of, 181; as end, 245; ethics and, 159; happiness and, 245; leisure and, 246; liberalism and, 7; means and ends and, 7; politics and, 246; wealth and, 7
Google, 112
Gordon, R.A., 109
government: bailouts and, 220–21; common good and, 219; limited, 63–64; pillars of decency and, 59–60; profit and, 5. *See also* regulation
Great Depression, 17, 118, 212, 228, 236
greed, 17, 24, 175, 251, 252–53
Greeks, 33–34, 119, 200
Greenspan doctrine (2002), 220
Gregg, Samuel, viii, xii, xiii, 7, 240
Grove, Andy, 171

Haey, 27–28
Halifax Bank of Scotland, 198
Hamilton, Edith, 193
happiness, 30; acting well and, 4–5; community and, 32, 160; contemplation and, 178–79, 181–82; ethics and, 159–60; good life and, 245; integrity and, 196, 204–5, 209–10; interests of others and, 159; money, role of and, 179–80; pursuit of, 178–83; rationality and, 159, 163, 200; virtue and, 31–32, 196, 204–5; wholeness of, 201–4
Hartman, Edwin, viii, 6, 252
Harvard Business School (HBS), 9, 16, 17, 90
Harvard University, 149
Hayek, F. A., 24, 115
H.B. Fuller Company, 145
HBOS, 209
HBS. *See* Harvard Business School
health care, 5, 67–72
Hector, 203
Henderson, Bruce, 110
Hewlett-Packard (HP), 15, 26
higher education. *See* business education; education; universities
Higher Education and the New Society (Keller), 83
The Higher Learning in America (Veblin), 81
Hirsch, Fred, 244
History of Education (Cubberly), 108
Hobbes, Thomas, 95, 243
home, work and, 11
Homo Economicus, 182
honesty, trust and, 11
Horwitz, Morton, 11–12
Howell, J.E., 109
HP. *See* Hewlett-Packard
Huber, Max, 20
human beings: dignity of, 54–55, 58, 59, 64; personhood of, 54; respect for, 5; as social, 2; unity of, 196
humanities, business and, 123–24
human nature, 45, 54–55, 122–23
human rights, 58, 146, 148–50
Hume, David, 9, 10, 163
Hungary, 77–78
Hutton, Will, 236

Iacocca, Lee, 15, 89
IESE business school, 10

India, 112, 113
individualism, 17
industrialism, 60
Industrial Revolution, 14, 19
industrial safety, 102–4
information technology (IT), 19, 21, 97
initial public offerings (IPOs), 112
In Search of Excellence (Waterman), 111
institutional pride, 5, 72
integration thesis, 6, 119, 120
integrity: business ethics and, 205–6; compartmentalization and, 7, 199–201, 210; ethics and, 196; financial crisis (2008) and, 7, 195–210; happiness and, 196, 204–5, 209–10; reputational capital and, 150; reputation and, 96–97; virtue and, 196, 204–5, 209–10; as wholeness, 204–5
Intel, 133–34
Interface Carpets, 147–48
International Monetary Fund, 237
Internet, 112–13, 145
invisible hand, 24, 26, 29
IPOs. *See* initial public offerings
Iran, 43
IT. *See* information technology

Jackson, Kevin T., viii–ix, 6
Jacobs, Michael, 211–12
James, Harold, ix, 2, 4
Japan, 228
Jencks, Christopher, 80
Jensen, Michael, 18, 166
Jesus, 40
Jews, 54
job choice, 6, 162
justice, 5, 25, 32, 58; ancient conception of, 34; Aristotle and, 6; cities, origins of and, 94–96; commutative, 34; consequentialist view of, 37; contracts and, 36; distributive, 34, 35, 189–92; natural, 12; pillars of decency and, 60; profit and, 33–35; social, 34–35, 35–36, 37; society and, 5, 34; virtue and, 5

Kafka, Franz, 67
Kant, Immanuel, 160, 165, 245
Keller, George: American universities, management of and, 5, 82–91
Kelsey, Sean, ix, 5
Kenan-Flagler Business School (University of North Carolina), 211
Keynes, John Maynard, 7, 24, 221, 242, 243–44, 247, 248, 250
Khurana, Rakesh, 17–19, 57, 65
Knights of Malta, 12
Koran, 40
Krause, Thomas, ix–x, 5
Kraut, Richard, 188
Kuyper, Abraham, 35

laissez-faire, 63
La Rochefoucauld, François de, 29
law, 93; business and, 5; cities and, 94; common, 11; corporations and, 14, 50; economics and, 11–12; personhood and, 4; pillars of decency and, 59–60; rule of, 5, 25; state and, 4; trust and, 11, 50
Law, John, 14
leadership, 138; culture, changing and, 93; development of, 188–89; ethical formation and, 7; moral reflection and, 7; organizational, 175; political, 184; practical wisdom (*phronesis*) and, 183–84; problems of, 120–23
Lee, Robert E., 107
Leeson, Nick, 21
legislation. *See* regulation
Lehman Brothers, 198
leisure, 6, 180, 242, 243, 246
lending, 197–98, 208–9, 216
LendingTree, 112

Index

Leviathan (Hobbes), 95
Levi Strauss and Co., 148
Lewis, Michael, 171
Liar's Poker (Lewis), 171
liberalism: good life and, 7; human dignity and, 58
libertarianism, libertarians, 63
limited-liability joint-stock corporations, 13-14, 220
Lloyds TSB, 209
The Lonely Crowd (Riesman), 80

MacIntyre, Alasdair, 195, 196, 197, 201, 251
Madoff, Bernie, 198, 212
management: in American universities, 5, 79-91; in British public service, 5, 67-78; business schools and, 2, 16-17; of capitalism, 1; development of, 188-89; division of labor and, 81-82; as elites, 16-17; ethical crisis in, 1; ethics in, 5; problems of, 120-23; professionalization of, 16-19; profit and, 2, 129; reputational capital and, 129; scientific view of, 117-18; stewardship and, 214; of workplace safety, 5
managerialism, 11; British public service and, 67-72, 74; corporations, personalization of and, 15; public service and, 67-78
The Managerial Revolution (Burnham), 73
Managers Not MBAs (Mintzberg), 114
Mandeville, Bernard, 26
Maoism, Maoists, 192
Marai, Sandor, 77-78
marriage, 62-64
Marshall, L.C., 107
Marx, Karl, 246, 248
Marxism, Marxists, 34, 61, 243, 245
materialism, 25, 180

MBA programs. *See* business education
McClay, Wilfred M., x, 5
McKinsey and Company, 111
Meckling, William, 18
Megone, Chris, x
Megone, Christopher, 7
meritocracy, 175, 177
Merrill Lynch, 198
Messier, Jean-Marie, 15
Microsoft, 177
Milgram, Stanley, 122
Milgram experiment, 168-69, 171
Mintzberg, Henry, 114-15, 126
Mises, Ludwig von, 24
monetary policy, 228-29
Monetary Policy Committee (Bank of England), 228
money: capitalism and, 243; happiness and, 179-80; inflation and, 234; monetary policy and, 228-29
Moore, G.E., 242
moral imagination, 27, 140-41, 167-68, 170
morality: marketplace, 144; meaning of, 4; neutral, 2; virtues and, 4
moral relativism, 2, 155, 213
Morrison, A.D., 235
Moynihan, Daniel Patrick, 62-63
Mulligan, Thomas, 109
Murray, Charles, 28

National Health Service (NHS), 68, 70, 71, 72
natural law: business and, 45-46; business ethics and, 38; duties and, 52-55; ethics and, 38, 45-46; human nature and, 45; modern economy and, 5; political culture and, 46-48, 51, 52-55; property rights and, 48-50; rights and, 45, 52-55; trust and, 50-51; universal rights and duties and, 5; virtue and, 38

Natural Law and Natural Rights (Finnis), 222
Nazism, Nazis, 43, 165
Newkirk, David L., x, 6
New Testament, 200
New York Times, 225
New York University, 6
NGOs. See non-governmental organizations
NHS. See National Health Service
Nicholls, Vincent, 240
Nicomachean Ethics (Aristotle), 165, 175, 200–201, 206, 207
Nietzsche, Friedrich, 122
Nigeria, 148
non-governmental organizations (NGOs), 12, 20, 37, 112, 125
Noonan, John T., 216
North Carolina, University of, 211
Novak, David, x–xi, 5
Novak, Michael, 25

Obama Administration, 221
Old Testament, 40, 200
Old World, 11
Open Question Argument, 118–19, 120
organized crime, 99
Orwell, George, 5
O'Toole, James, xi, 6
Oxford University, 109

Paul, St., 40, 160
Pennsylvania, University of, 83, 107–8
Pericles, 183
personality, corporate, 14–15
personhood, 4, 5, 54, 59
Peters, Tom, 111, 170
PetroChina, 149
Pfeffer, Jeffrey, 114, 116
pillars of decency, 58–65
planning, 31, 86–90, 90–91
Planning (journal), 83
Plato, 34, 94–96, 164, 184, 193, 198–99, 203, 205, 246
Platonism, 242

pleasure, 43, 44, 178, 253
Plundering the Public Sector (Craig), 75
pluralism, 143–45, 146–47
Poland, 39–40
political culture: conscience and, 51–52; ethics and, 46–48; natural law and, 46–48, 51, 52–55; rights and duties and, 52–55; self-interest and, 51
Politics (Aristotle), 175, 207
Popper, Karl, 116
popular sovereignty, 11, 13
Porras, Jerry, 26, 170
Porter, Michael, 110–11
positivism, 117
practical wisdom (*phronesis*), 32, 33–34; leadership and, 183–84; virtue and, 159, 200, 202
pragmatism, 2
Priam, 203
Princeton conference (2007), xii, xiii, 2
Princeton University, xii, 2
Proctor and Gamble, 150
profit: business and, 94, 97–99; business education and, 2, 129, 225–26; as by-product, 25–27, 40–41; corporations and, 4–5; government and, 5; intrinsic goods and, 28–31; justice, problem of and, 33–35; planning and, 31–32; reputation and, 133; self-interest and, 25–26; shareholder theory and, 130; social capital and, 27–28; social justice and, 35–36; soul of the firm and, 38–40; virtue and, 24–41
profit motive. See profit
property rights, 12, 48–50
Protestant ethic, 25
The Protestant Ethic and the Spirit of Capitalism (Weber), 25
prudence. See practical wisdom (*phronesis*)

psychology, 1, 141, 168
public choice theory, 237–39, 240
public service, 76; attack on, 73–74; British health care system and, 67–72; ethic of, 5; managerialism and, 67–78; social revolution in, 73–75
Puritanism, 16
Putnam, Robert, 28
Pyramids of Sacrifice (Berger), 25

Radio Corporation of America, 16
Rainforest Action Network, 146
rationality: ethics and, 158; happiness and, 159, 163, 200; psychic harmony and, 163–64; virtue and, 176
Rawls, John, 4, 35, 165
regulation: banking and, 230, 237, 240; of business, 11–15, 19–21; business schools and, 17; credit rating agencies and, 235–36; financial crisis (2008) and, 4, 229–31, 235–36, 236–37
relativism, moral, 2, 155, 213
religious fanaticism, 58
Republic (Plato), 34, 94–96
reputational capital: business education and, 129, 150; human rights and, 148–50; integrity and, 150; management and, 129; motivation and, 133–34; profit and, 133; shareholder theory and, 129–31; stakeholder theory and, 6, 129–31; trust and, 134–35; value of, 96–97; value of intangibles and, 132–33
reputational liability, 145, 148–49
reputational sanctions, 145–48
research, 110–12, 125
research and learning institutions, 5, 61
responsibility principle, 119–20
Responsibility Thesis, 120
"Rethinking Business Management" conference (2007), xii, xiii, 2

Rethinking Business Management: Examining the Foundations of Business Education (ed. Gregg and Stoner), xii, xiii
Rheinfelden aluminum works (AIAG), 20
Riesman, David, 80, 85
rights: human, 58, 146, 148–50; natural law and, 5, 45, 48–50, 52–55; political culture and, 52–55; property, 12
risk hazard, 221–22
robber barons, 49
Roman Law, 34, 51
Röpke, Wilhelm, 35
Rorty, Richard, 171
Rosenzweig, Phil, 170–71
Royal Bank of Scotland, 198, 209
Rubin, Bob, 171
rule of law, 5, 25
Ruml, Francis, 107–8
Russia, 112
Ryan, John A., 252

Samuelson, Paul, 248
Sarbanes-Oxley Act of 2002, 136
Sartre, Jean-Paul, 119
scandals, corporate, 1, 18, 22, 103, 113, 189
Schon, Donald, 115
scientism, 109–10, 117
Scotland, 71–72
Scruton, Roger, xi, 4–5, 251
self-interest, 10, 24, 48, 55; foreign policy and, 13; political culture and, 51; profit and, 25–26, 31; public service and, 73; social life and, 5; trust and, 50
separation fallacy, 6, 118–19, 120, 130
service. *See* public service
shareholder theory, 129–31
shareholder value, 6, 57, 115, 225–26, 240
Shaw, George Bernard, 73
Shell, 148
Siemens, 149

Simeon Stylites, St., 248, 249
Sinopec, 149
Skidelskly, Edward, xi, 7
Sloan, Alfred, 20
Smith, Adam, 14, 24–25, 26, 31, 176, 182, 216
Smith, Vernon, 219
social capital, 39
social contract, 184–85
socialism, 24, 34–35, 113; justice and, 34–35, 35–36
social responsibility. *See* corporate social responsibility (CSR)
Social Trends Institute, xii
society: academic institutions and, 5; business and, 2, 5, 57–58; business education and, 3; corporatist, 76–78; ethics and, 6; family and, 5; justice and, 5, 34; pillars of decency and, 5, 58–65
Socrates, 95–96
Solomon, 133
SOS Children's Villages Network, 150
South Africa, 150
Souther Agrarianism, Southern Agrarians, 60
Southern California, University of, 6
South Sea Company, 14
Soviet Union, 43, 61, 68
Spellings Report, 79
SRC Holdings, 188
Stack, Jack, 188
stakeholderism, 3
stakeholder theory, 93; business as human enterprise and, 106, 120; reputational capital and, 6, 129–31; soul of the corporation and, 38–40
Stalinism, Stalinist, 192
Stanford University, 149
Starbucks, 143
state: business, regulation of by, 11–15, 19–21; business education, origins of and, 4; justice and, 37; law and, 4; popular sovereignty and, 11, 13; profit and virtue and, 37
Sternberg, E., 206
stewardship, 57, 65, 214
Stewart, Martha, 15
Stiglitz, Joseph, 236
Stoner, James R., Jr., xi, xii
strategy, ethics and, 169–72
sub-prime mortgage lending, 197–98, 208–9
Sudan, 149
Summers, Larry, 221

Talisman Energy, 149
Talmud, 42, 47
technology, 19, 20–21
Tellez, Luis, xii, xiii
Teutonic Knights, 12
Texas Instruments, 26
A Theory of Justice (Rawls), 35
The Theory of Moral Sentiments (Smith), 31
Thomas Aquinas, St., 4, 9, 16, 30, 38, 200, 247
Thomas Pink, 15
totalitarianism, 58
Tower of Babel, 54
trade, 10
Transforming a College (Keller), 89
Trilling, Lionel, 83
Trollope, Anthony, 14
trust, 10, 19, 47, 155–56; business and, 113; corporations and, 19; honesty and, 11; institutional innovation and, 11; law and, 11, 50; natural law and, 50–51; religious beliefs and, 25; reputational capital and, 134–35; self-interest and, 50; social capital and, 27; values and, 22
Tucker, Paul, 229
Tyco, 192

Ulpian, 34
UN. *See* United Nations

UNICEF, 150
United Automobile Workers, 220–21
United Fruit Company, 15
United Nations (UN), 148
United Parcel Service (UPS), 39
United States: housing market in, 197–98; management of universities in, 5; scandals in, 1; universities in, 5, 79–91
universities: diversity of, 85; executive and, 80–82, 86–87; management in, 5, 79–91; strategic planning and, 86–90, 90–91. *See also* business education; education
University Business, 83
UPS. *See* United Parcel Service
usury, 216–17, 246
utilitarianism, 9, 49, 158–59, 165, 166–67

values: business and, 2, 22; capitalism and, 14, 120, 250; culture and, 46, 47, 103; economic, 26; ethical, 97, 99, 100; family, 22; intrinsic, 30, 99; market, 86, 233, 234; materialistic, 25; pragmatic, 2, 96; trust and, 22
Virginia, University of, 6
virtue: cardinal, 32, 33; character and, 6; community and, 32, 157–58; corporate social responsibility and, 93; costs of, 160–61; family and, 59; financial crisis (2008) and, 208–10; happiness and, 31–32, 196, 204–5; integrity and, 196, 204–5; morality and, 4; natural law and, 38; practical wisdom (*phronesis*) and, 159, 200; profit and, 24–41; pursuit of, 32–33; rationality and psychic harmony and, 176; stakeholder theory and, 93; unity of, 33, 196, 200–204, 209

Vivendi, 15

Wall Street Journal, 57, 211, 219
Wal-Mart, 26, 143
Walzer, Michael, 124
Washington and Lee University, 107
Waterman, Robert, 111, 170
The Way We Live Now (Trollope), 14
wealth creation, 7, 25, 27
Wealth of Nations (Smith), 14
Weber, Max, 25
*Web*MD, 112
Weick, Karl, 116
Welch, Jack, 15
Wharton, Joseph, 107–8, 108–9, 126
Wharton School (University of Pennsylvania), 107–8, 108–9
Whitehead, Alfred North, 108
Williamson, Oliver, 18
Wilson, James Q., 28
Witherspoon Institute, xii, 2
Wolf, Martin, 220
women, 11, 62, 144
Woolf, Virginia, 244–45
work: home and, 11; leisure and, 6, 180
workplace: Aristotle and, 185–88; safety in, 5, 102–4
WorldCom, 18, 192
World War II, 110, 119

YAHOO!, 112
Yale University, 109, 149
Young, John, 26
Young, Owen D., 16

zero-sum vision, 30, 34
Zimbardo, Philip, 122